Bring One Home

A Memoir of Boyhood, Basketball, and Hometown Spirit

Thomas L. Pelissero

DEDICATION

This is for you, Dad.

CONTENTS

Author's Note

I grew up in the early 1960s in a small mining town in the Upper Peninsula of Michigan. My friends and I created our own fun and followed with great interest the highs and lows of our high school basketball team, the Bessemer Speedboys.

I spent nearly eight years interviewing over 50 people to reminisce about life in Bessemer back in the day. They were open, honest and forthcoming with their recollections. The more folks I interviewed, the more an intriguing basketball story emerged. The struggles of the Bessemer Speedboys at times mirrored those of the town itself.

I have tried sincerely to capture the voices of the community in these pages and to tell their story and mine in a creative way. Often the dialogue in this book is not actual, but rather what I remember as typical conversation in the locker room, in local businesses, and at school. Many times, it's the actual words of those I interviewed as they reflected back on this story. In some places, I use fictionalized scenes that compress time to allow me to tell multiple true stories at once in a familiar setting. Some of my personal stories of growing up are woven into the Bessemer basketball narrative, and others are offset in chapters of their own, beginning in Chapter 4. I witnessed many of the Bessemer basketball games as a child, then later researched them as an adult; in these scenes, I often shift the point of view accordingly. Thus, others' stories and my own memories are blended into a narrative to create *Bring One Home*.

At its core, this book is about life in small-town America in the 1960s. There was fun and laughter. There was sadness and tension. There was good old-fashioned competition between neighboring towns. There were wonderful characters. And at times, there was deep disappointment. But more than anything else, there was a hometown spirit that rang so loud I still can hear it.

PROLOGUE

Bessemer Speedboys Day, 1947

The school bus was quiet except for the pinging of the engine as it approached its destination on the trip from Marquette. The team was tired from celebrating all night at the Northland Hotel, with Room 322 as central headquarters. The boys could not muster a good morning grunt to each other.

Helge Pukema, the first-year head coach for the Speedboys, the Bessemer High School basketball team, stood up in the front of the bus to address his twelve sleepy cagers. He wore a tweed suit that was one size too small. There was a tear in the right shoulder of the coat that could no longer hold back Pukema's muscular arms. His pants were cuffed three inches above his scuffed black shoes, exposing his white socks. The knot on his diamond patterned tie hung loose, his thick neck preventing the top button on his shirt from closing.

"Pojat, kuuntelevat," Pukema shouted in Finnish. "Boys, listen."

The coach spoke with a heavy accent that at times was hard to understand. Ray Kangas, known as "Windy," spoke Finnish, so he was the interpreter by default.

"Listen up, guys!" Kangas shouted. "Coach has got something to say."

Johnny Pelissero poked his row mate Paul Pozega to wake him. Robert Barron did the same to Donald Skwor. Royal Smith, who had been promoted to the varsity team after the District Tournament, was wide awake in the second row right behind his coach. Soon all twelve players and team manager Robert Vogeler were seated at attention.

"What you accomplished last night has never been done before in our high school," Pukema stated. "This is the first basketball championship our school has ever won. You are the Upper Peninsula Class B High School Basketball Champions."

The boys applauded. Dave Webber got out of his seat and moved up three rows to sit with Allan Syrjala so he could hear the coach better.

"There are no more games to play," Pukema continued. "No more games to win to advance. You won your final game. How many teams can say that? You need to savor this moment, boys, as this may be the biggest one in your life."

There were cheers, pats on the back and handshakes. The realization of their accomplishment was beginning to sink in. They were winners.

Pukema knew something about winning. He was a star athlete at Duluth Central High School, excelling in football and track & field. He was a stand-out for the University of Minnesota Golden Gophers in the 1940s, playing alongside Heisman Trophy winner Bruce Smith. Now, at age 29, he had led his team to a basketball championship, a game he knew little about. Bessemer was known as a football town, not a basketball town. If a man wanted to coach football in the county seat, he also had to take the helm as basketball coach. Yet for Pukema, basketball was not his thing. He was more of a basketball manager than a coach. Running practices. Making a line-up. Offering encouragement. Then he'd let the boys' pure talent take over. The coach learned the game as the season progressed.

Football was the game he knew best, and as the Speedboys football coach he led the team to a 5-3 record in the fall of 1946. It was good for second place in the Michigan-Wisconsin Conference. Yet somehow in the game in which he was a novice, basketball, Pukema led his Speedboys all the way to the top. The very top. That brought a big smile to the round face of this young Finlander.

"Next basketball season," Pukema continued, "I understand they'll let us U.P. teams go downstate to continue the journey and play the Class B schools there. But that's next year."

Pukema held up a copy of *The Detroit Free Press*. "This newspaper referred to the Alma Panthers in the Lower Peninsula as the Class B State Champs today. Well, they never played us. So, boys, for the last time, there will be two state champions in Class B in Michigan, the Alma Panthers and the Bessemer Speedboys."

The bus erupted with raucous cheers. The boys were now wide awake and ready to see their friends and family. They would soon find that the town of Bessemer was ready to see them, too.

By the time the school bus passed the coal elevators on Lead Street, the boys were kneeling on their seats, looking out the windows to see the throng of supporters. They lowered the windows and waved to their friends and neighbors. The townsfolk lined the street on this unseasonably warm Sunday in March, their winter jackets unzipped and gloves in their pockets. After a long winter, the 48-degree day felt like a summer morning. Some were standing on top of melting snowbanks waving to the hometown team and yelling, "Welcome home, Champs!"

The 11:00 Mass had just ended at St. Sebastian Church. Father Charles Swoboda, wearing a black biretta on the top of his head and a large crucifix around his neck, hurried as fast as his 74-year-old legs could carry him along Case Street. He had two altar boys in tow to meet the bus. The acolytes, still dressed in their black cassocks and white surplices, had rushed with the priest from the old brick church. They splashed through the puddles, spraying the bottom of their robes, but they didn't mind.

One altar boy carried a silver holy water sprinkler, an aspergillum, while the other boy held the bucket of holy water. The bus was full of many Catholic boys who had missed Sunday Mass and needed absolution to remove a mortal sin from their souls, or so the priest thought.

The bus driver stopped the vehicle in front of the Bessemer Creamery to allow Father Swoboda to bless the champs. The aging priest dipped the sprinkler head into the bucket of holy water, and with a strong flick of his wrist, he snapped off five shakes of the sprinkler along the side of the bus.

"In nomine Patris et Filii et Spiritus Sancti," Father Swoboda recited.

The boys, Catholic or not, made the sign of the cross as the holy water brushed by their windows. This blessing was a rite of purification in the Catholic Church, a way to remove uncleanliness. After last night's celebration in Room 322, featuring a few bottles of homemade wine that had been smuggled from Johnny Pelissero's home, some boys needed the blessing more than others.

What a sight! Fans had lined the main street of Bessemer like it was the 4th of July. American flags hung from the light poles. Locals were shaking pom poms and holding up homemade signs. The high school marching band, forty-five musicians strong, under the direction of Calvin Bennetts, stepped out from the old firehall and led the bus up Main Street. Just beyond the band were the varsity cheerleaders leading a variety of cheers and singing the school fight song as the band played on. Some young boys ran from the Dandee Bakery just for a chance to touch the slow-moving bus, as if reaching for greatness.

The whistle at the new fire hall blew as the bus swung up and around the Veterans Memorial Building. The team thought for a moment it was for them, but it was noon, the hour that the whistle always blew to signal to the residents that another shift change was about to occur at the local iron ore mines. A few of the boys' fathers were deep underground, breathing the dust and chipping away at a new ore vein.

The Speedboys yelled out the bus window to everyone they knew. Johnny Pelissero spotted his stepbrother Art Stancher and his cousin Ray Barbacovi standing at the corner of Sellar and Sophie. Art and Ray were a couple of young entrepreneurs who had just purchased the Bessemer Food Shop from Joe Gastino. Right next to them stood Johnny's 16-year-old brother Bruno who had lent Johnny the money for his hotel room in Marquette.

The bus was moving slowly down the main drag. High school kids rushed from the drug store and Arco's Tip Top Ice Cream and Coffee Shop to jog alongside the bus while singing their 1947 Bessemer school song.

"Fling high the Bessemer banner,
Don't let the standard fall.
Three cheers for Bessemer,
For good old Bessemer,

The school we love the best of all. U rah rah!

Bring on the ball, boys, and blow the whistle.

Fair play will win this fight,

For Bessemer's honor must be defended.

Hail the Gold and White!"

Dave Webber hung his gold jersey, number 15, out the window and shook it in the light winter breeze. The girls ran towards the bus and tried to snatch it from his grip. He pulled it back repeatedly and laughed.

"Hey, Webb, you better not lose that," the team manager, Robert Vogeler, yelled at him. "I'm gonna be in trouble with Mr. Oas when I come up short on uniforms."

"Relax, Vogeler," Webber said. "It's just good fun." He pulled the jersey back inside, placed it in his duffel bag and zipped it shut.

"See you at the gym!" Webber yelled to the adoring fans.

The crowd jostled their way into the A.D. Johnston gymnasium to find a seat in the bleachers. The team arrived at the locker room to turn in their uniforms for the season. For seniors Dave Rampanelli, Paul Pozega and Johnny Pelissero, this was the last time they would wear the school colors of blue, gold and white. But they were going out on top and were bursting with pride.

"Boys, turn in your uniforms, except your blue warmup," Pukema said. "I want the fans to see you wearing Bessemer proudly across your chests."

At the same time the crowd was finding their seats and the band had moved into their position on the floor, a senior ROTC cadet was hidden beneath the south bleachers, behind a heavy metal door, preparing for a rifle team competition. He was oblivious to the celebration outside. He lay prone with a bolt-action, single-shot .22 rifle in his hand, safely locked behind the door in the range.

Pop! Pop! Pop! went the rifle, as he fired at the practice target.

He could not hear the crowd assembling above him. He continued to load, aim, and squeeze off more rounds. Shell casings were scattered across the floor.

Master Sergeant Godlaf Bucholtz, a World War II veteran and now one of the leaders of the ROTC program, was sitting in the stands. His trained ear picked up the muted sounds of gunfire.

"What the hell," he mumbled.

He walked straight across center court to the metal door on the south side of the gym. It was locked. He pounded, but no one answered. Bucholtz used his key. When he opened the door, he saw Eddie Savitski, a First Lieutenant in the Junior ROTC program, kneeling in shooting position with the rifle to his shoulder, eye peering down the metal site at the target.

"Savitski!" shouted the Sergeant.

The young man flinched upon hearing his name, causing him to fire off a round and miss the target.

"What the hell are you doing?" Sgt. Bucholtz asked his cadet.

"Sorry, Sarge," Savitski responded. He stood immediately. "I'm practicing for our rifle match against Calumet on Monday."

"How the hell did you get in here?" the Sergeant asked.

"I'm captain of the rifle team. I have a key."

Bucholtz seemed confused, but that reply seemed to ring true.

"Well, you can't be shooting in here now," Buckholtz replied. "Didn't you look out there? We've got one hell of a celebration going on for the Speedboys."

Savitski peered out the door. His eyes widened in surprise. "Oh, did they win yesterday?"

"Yes! That's why these people are here. Now, pick up the casings and get out there to help with crowd control," Buckholtz commanded.

"I'll get right on it, Sergeant," Savitski replied, holding back a smile.

Sgt. Bucholtz returned to his seat next to Major Martin Grigg, his commander. Bucholtz whispered in Grigg's ear about the rifle range activity. The Major just chuckled. He knew Savitski was a good cadet, and a leader in the ROTC program.

Meanwhile, the pep band had struck their positions and played the school song on the band director's cue. All one thousand fans in attendance got to their feet and began singing the school song in unison. As the chorus rang out, the Speedboys came walking through the

tunnel and onto the hardwood floor. The crowd waved and cheered as
the boys walked onto a makeshift stage erected on the gym floor. It was
draped in school colors. When the school song ended, the twelve players, manager, and coach were treated to a one-minute standing ovation.

A microphone had been set up at the front of the stage, so it
was clear there would be speeches by anyone who was somebody in
this town. The first to speak would be Superintendent E. J. Oas. He
buttoned his double-breasted suit as he walked to the microphone,
adjusted his rimless glasses, and cleared his throat.

Oas looked at the crowd and then began to speak.

"I want to offer my appreciation to the band, the cheerleaders,
the student body, and to the fans for all the support you have given
to our Speedboys during this historic basketball season," Oas said.
"I also want to thank our Junior ROTC for managing the crowd of
over 2,000 people at last week's District Tournament here in our high
school gym."

Lt. Eddie Savitski smiled as he stood near the tunnel that led to
the gym floor, his eyes locking on Sergeant Bucholtz. Bucholtz nodded back with his approval.

"Now, I would like to have our Bessemer City Clerk Frank
Drazkowski, who represents all the citizens of Bessemer, say a few
words."

Drazkowski stepped to microphone with a scroll in his hand
and unfurled it.

"Boys," Drazkowski said. "On behalf of the City of Bessemer, in
recognition of your tremendous accomplishment, you have brought
honor and pride to our fine city. In so much as a U.P. High School
Championship has never been accomplished in basketball at A.D.
Johnston High School, with the power vested in me, I hereby declare
this day, March 23, 1947, to be *Bessemer Speedboys Day*."

Everyone, including the new heroes, stood and applauded the
declaration.

Superintendent Oas returned to the microphone and thanked
the many Bessemer fans that made the long drive to Marquette for
the games. "Next, I want to take this moment to thank our great first-
year coach, Helge Pukema."

The crowd applauded, whistled and cheered. The drummer pounded the bass drum and then hit the cymbal in crescendo. Some students in the crowd started chanting "Helge! Helge! Helge!" but the chant didn't catch on. Oas stepped back from the microphone, a bit perturbed, and coughed into his fist. Arnold Vispi, a mechanical drawing teacher, leaped to his feet, walked over to area where the chanting lads sat, and motioned with his two fingers that the instigators should zip their lips. He turned and nodded towards Mr. Oas to continue his speech.

"Well, then," said Oas, again clearing his throat. "Without further ado, let me introduce our head coach, Helge Pukema."

The shy Finlander walked to the microphone. He didn't like to speak in public. He had always been self-conscious of his accent. Windy Kangas, team interpreter, yelled to his coach in Finnish: "Hymyile valmentaja!"

It meant: "Smile, coach." The coach smirked, then laughed. A deep belly roll laugh.

"Hei. Hello," Pukema said. "As you know, this was my first year as a teacher and basketball coach in Bessemer. I came here to coach football because I heard that this was a football town. But guess what? Last night, we just became a basketball town."

The crowd stood and erupted with thunderous applause. Coach Pukema picked up the trophy and held it high for all to see. When the cheering died down, he placed the trophy on the stage floor beside the microphone and then spoke from the heart.

"Athletics is like life," Pukema said. "The more closely a team works together for the good of the cause, the greater is the efficiency."

He turned to his team and motioned for them to stand.

"Let me introduce these guys to you. Please hold your applause until I'm done. My sophomores are Donald Skwor and Royal Smith. Juniors are Dave Webber, Ray Fournier, Ray Kangas, Allan Syrjala, Robert Barron, Eddy Balasz and John Backman. Our team manager is Robert Vogeler."

On Pukema's cue, the crowd applauded again.

"Lastly, let me introduce my three seniors. They are Paul Pozega, Dave Rampanelli and John Pelissero. I've asked them to say a few words."

The three seniors looked and pointed at each other to try to determine who would go first. Pozega and Pelissero pointed to their buddy Ramp to lead things off. Rampanelli stood and walked to the microphone.

He was short and stocky, captain of the football team and a unanimous first team all-conference football selection. In basketball, he was one of the first players off the bench in every game.

"This was a great week for our team and our town," Rampanelli said. "I'm proud of my teammates and what we accomplished." Then his tone turned serious. "My only regret is that I didn't get to play in the championship game."

There was a noticeable murmur making its way through the crowd. Most had assumed that Rampanelli had played in the title game.

"I wasn't feeling well, and for some reason the doctors thought I needed to be isolated from the team," Rampanelli said with annoyance in his voice. "Although I lost out on being there to play, it doesn't take anything away from this great victory."

The 17 year old looked down from the microphone and took a moment to gather himself. He looked at his teammates, then said, "Even though I'm graduating, and we'll no longer be Speedboys together, these guys will remain my best friends. I'm sure we'll rehash this victory together for a long time. Thank you."

Paul "Doc" Pozega was up off his seat before Rampanelli was done speaking, ready to address the fans. He was a natural leader, and the only senior to start every game. An unselfish player who understood his role was to get the ball to the scorers: Kangas, Webber, and Skwor. He was well aware of his own capabilities, yet he always put the team ahead of his own desire to take a shot.

"When we were kids, we used to walk out to this abandoned barn north of town on the way to the Black River," Doc began. "We would climb into the empty hay loft, rig a hoop out of something, and play basketball. We imagined then, that one day, with seconds to go, one of us would make the winning shot, like Eddy Balasz did last night."

Doc turned around and pointed to Balasz.

"Thanks, Eddy. But, geez, I got to tell you, when you missed that first free throw at the end of the game, I got worried. But you were your cool self on the second shot. And dropped it in like a raindrop to win it."

The crowd cheered for Balasz. He acknowledged them with a shy wave.

"We dreamed back then what it would be like to win a championship," Doc continued. "Last night, that dream came true. It took a while this year for us to gel as a team. Our coach was new, too. Once we got rolling, we were unstoppable."

Doc paused and looked over the crowd. "The one thing that made this a talented team was togetherness. This group didn't care if you were on the end of the bench or a top starter. Everybody was for everybody else. It didn't matter how many points you scored or if you played. You were there pushing the others on this team. What impresses me even more is that we have togetherness off the court, too. We're true friends. It was an honor to be part of this team."

The crowd applauded.

"Johnny Pel," as everyone called him, stood next to say a few words. He was naturally graceful, not just on the basketball court but on the dance floor too, and the girls of Bessemer took notice. As he walked to the microphone he winked at the red-headed cheerleader that he was currently dating. He looked up into the crowd before he began to speak. He saw the faces of the fathers of his teammates, one after another, proudly sitting in the stands. Yet, the face of his own father was not to be found. Johnny's father, Pietro, had died the previous May from *pneumoconiosis*, commonly known as miner's lung disease. The Italian immigrant had worked for years for 45 cents a day, gathering as much iron ore as possible so his family could enjoy life. Day after day, he breathed the silicate dust into his lungs, and it killed him at age 49.

Johnny Pel was proud of his Pa and the sacrifices he had made for his family. He would have loved to have shared this moment with his father. He adjusted the microphone and gathered his thoughts.

"When all of you attended the pep fest last Thursday to honor us on winning our first District Championship and then sent us off to the U.P. Tournament, you heard our coach speak about our chances. Coach told you we were all healthy, in ship-shape, and playing our best basketball at the right time of the season. Coach told you if we lost, we would have no excuses. No alibis. As a team, we understood that, too."

Johnny reached down and picked up the championship trophy. He looked at the brass plate on the front of the trophy and then turned back to the crowd.

"Our school had never won a U.P. Championship in basketball," Johnny continued. "When we left for Marquette, we had one goal and only one goal in mind."

He raised the large trophy above his head.

"To bring one home!"

With that, the crowd leaped to its feet once again and showered applause onto their hometown heroes. In that moment, all of Bessemer believed a tradition of winning had just begun. It felt like the town and the team would always be on top of the world, a proud, thriving community where teamwork, town pride, and undying loyalty to each other would serve as cornerstones for decades to come. They had scaled the tallest mountain and were the envy of Michigan's Upper Peninsula for the very first time, and they savored the feeling. But with their heads so high above the clouds, they could not foresee the storm brewing below.

1947 Upper Peninsula of Michigan Class B Basketball Champions

L-R: John Pelissero, Ed Balasz, Dave Rampanelli, Paul Pozega, John Backman,
Royal Smith, Ray Fournier, Allan Syrjala, Don Skwor, Ray Kangas,
Dave Webber, Robert Barron

First Quarter
1963-1964

CHAPTER 1

Superintendent Carlo Heikkinen addressed the Bessemer Board of Education in early 1962.

"Our revenue has been declining since 1959," Heikkinen said. "And our expenses have continued to increase. This is no longer sustainable. It's time to make some difficult program cuts and curtail services."

The Board of Education stared at their copy of the financial statement, and then began the task of approving, reducing or eliminating requests. Tennis and skiing were the first programs to be eliminated. Transportation for the summer recreational program, gone. The Athletic Honors Banquet, dropped. Grade school basketball revival, DOA.

A request from John Backman, the athletic director and football coach, for new varsity football equipment was approved, but new uniforms for the band were declined. A plan was approved to have the janitor turn off all lights after school hours except in the room he was cleaning.

"Where else can we cut?" asked Principal Walter "Butch" Newman.

"Well, Butch, you'll be the Superintendent next school year," Heikkinen responded. "What do you want to do?"

Newman voiced his concerns. He explained that the cost of coal and oil to heat the schools had continued to climb, and the old windows at each school failed to hold the heat in and electricity bills had skyrocketed.

"The mines are closing," Newman said. "Fewer students are attending our schools. There is less revenue per child from the state. We need money in our capital improvement account to replace drafty windows with glass blocks. I'm sorry to say we need to tighten our belts. We need to lock everything down. The spending. The programs. The buildings."

The board approved the changes.

Jim had circled each Saturday morning on the family calendar since the late 1950's to join his pals at the high school for an open gym led by John Backman and Michael Destasio. Boys as young as six could come to the gymnasium and learn basic basketball skills, like dribbling, passing and shooting. But with boys as old as 13 also playing, the youngest and smallest of the bunch were often left standing on the sidelines watching the big kids. When the little kids got bored, they chased each other through the school, adding one more reason for the administration to eliminate the open gym program during these hard economic times.

Thus, on this freezing cold Saturday morning, Jim and his buddy David decided to get creative and find an indoor court where they could play. They set eyes on the Washington School gym. They knew the St. Sebastian Knights practiced there on Saturday mornings, so they figured mid-afternoon would be a good time to sneak in. Maybe the Knights left a door open.

Washington School opened in 1922 and welcomed children from kindergarten through the ninth grade. It was quite a marvel at the time, featuring 24 classrooms, a swimming pool with violet ray filters, a well-equipped shop, a large stage, and a state-of-the-art coal-fired heating system. It boasted the largest gymnasium in the area in the early '20s, and this is where the Bessemer Speedboys played their basketball games until 1932, when a new gymnasium was added to the high school.

The boys tried both entrances at the front of Washington School. Both were chained and padlocked. They peered through the windows, but did not see any movement from a janitor. They tried the door on the east side of the building. Locked. The shop garage door was latched. The only thing moving was the sawdust being blown around lightly near the heat registers.

"Did you try the windows?" Jim asked.

"The ones I could reach," said David. "All locked or frozen shut."

The boys trudged through the snow in the parking lot to try their final option: the gym door at the back of the building. Jim carried his basketball, a *Wilson Jet*, which had started to peel and show its age. Jim pulled on the gym door. It didn't give an inch. Locked up tighter than Bessemer National Bank at 3:00 p.m.

"Hey, I think we can get in this way," David said.

"The coal bin?" Jim asked.

"Look, I'll go through the chute and then through that door in there," David said.

He held the coal chute lid open so his buddy could stick his head in and see the path forward.

"Once I'm in, I'll open this door to the gym," he said pointing to the back door.

Jim liked the plan. He held the coal bin hatch open as David crawled feet first through the chute. He eased himself down to the floor. Jim heard the coal crunching under David's boots as his buddy walked through the bin.

Less than a minute later, David opened the back gymnasium door. He looked like a chimney sweeper, covered head to toe in black dust.

Jim looked at his buddy and asked, "What took you so long?"

Both boys laughed and hurried inside.

David reported that no one else was in sight when he came out of the coal bin. That was music to Jim's ears. It was time to get to work on his game. Jim took off his winter jacket and rubber boots and tossed each to the side. No gloves. No hat. No cold. Just 55 degrees of coal-fired heat and a basketball in his hands. He loved the squeak of sneakers on the hardwood floor and the echo of the basketball bouncing around the gym.

The boys took turns driving in for layups and getting in the right position on set-shots. Pretty soon they had worked up quite a sweat.

Jim had learned to shoot layups in grade school. Ronnie Carlson, one of the big kids at the Saturday morning open gym, had taught him footwork and mechanics. Jim never forgot that good deed and worked at being flawless with his layup. He took a dribble and sprung up in the air for a jump shot. He felt as light as a feather inside the confines of the Washington School gym. But before he could fire off the shot, the gym door sprang open and banged off the wall.

It was the janitor on duty.

"What are you boys doing in here?" he shouted.

Jim and David froze. The janitor walked straight at them.

"We just wanted to play basketball," Jim responded. "Can't we shoot around?"

"You can't be in here," the janitor scolded.

"But, sir, we're only playing basketball," Jim said. "We're not running in the classrooms. We're not trying to steal anything."

"How did you boys get in here?" The janitor looked David up and down. "Oh, come on, not the coal bin," he said. "Oh, my goodness you did." The janitor was exasperated. He pointed the boys to the back door. "Get out now before I get in trouble."

"Sir, we'll clean up if that's what you're worried about," Jim said. "Just show us where the broom is and we'll sweep the entire gym floor."

"Boys, I'm under strict direction to keep the lights off, the heat down and not to allow any unauthorized use of the gym outside of school hours," the janitor said. "It's Saturday. You have to leave now, or Arnold Vispi will have my head."

Vispi was the school principal.

Dejected, the boys gathered their things and walked towards the exit, David leaving black coal prints as he walked.

The janitor yelled to Jim. "Hey kid, what's your name? Just in case I decide to report this."

"It's Jim," he replied. "Jim Milakovich."

CHAPTER 2

John and Alice Bonk drove east on Highway 2 towards their new home in Bessemer, Michigan. John, just 22 years old, had just accepted his first teaching and coaching position in the Bessemer School District. The couple was returning from their honeymoon trip, a drive around Lake Superior. It was a route many residents in the Upper Peninsula of Michigan, Northern Wisconsin and Minnesota had on their bucket list. The circle tour, as it was called. Unfortunately for the Bonks, it rained every day. Bonk prayed it was not an omen for this next chapter in his life, where they soon would make Bessemer their new home.

Bessemer is a small city in the Upper Peninsula of Michigan, "the U.P." as it is known to most folks. The city is nestled between tree-covered bluffs to the north and iron ore mines to the south. U.S. Highway 2 runs through the heart of the town. Trainloads of immigrants started coming to the area in the late 1880s from Italy, Croatia, Austria, Russia, Finland, Poland, Ireland and England. They came to work in the mines, the logging camps, and the railroads. They built roads. They built their churches. They opened retail shops and dozens of drinking establishments. But mostly, they labored in the iron ore mines, the biggest employer in the U.P. The first mine established was the Colby Mine in Bessemer, around 1884. The immigrants were hardworking folks, and the mines were fortunate to have such a dedicated group of men who sought a better life than what they left behind in their home country.

Bessemer's A.D. Johnston High School offered four major sports, each with its own season: football in the fall, basketball in the winter, track & field in the spring and baseball in summer. The teams were called the Speedboys, a nickname given to the school back in the 1920s by H.O "Sonny" Sonnesyn, a local columnist at the *Ironwood Times Newspaper* and the *Ironwood Daily Globe*.

In Sonny's April 3, 1929, column, *It's All In The Slant*, he wrote:

"We think Bessemer ought to set about adopting an **official** *nickname (for all sports). For a time, the county seat football teams were known as the 'Speed Boys'. Ironwood athletic teams are known throughout the Upper Peninsula as the Red Devils, Wakefield has adopted the name of Cardinals and Hurley squads bear the title of Midgets. Why not make it official Bessemer?"*

The nickname stuck. Though it was always written in newspaper articles as two words, *Speed Boys*, the school adopted it as one word, *Speedboys*.

Bessemer High School won its first Gogebic Range football championship in 1919. In 1930, Bessemer beat Iron River 6-0 to become the first school on the Gogebic Range to ever claim as high an honor as Upper Peninsula Champions. That 1930 football team was coached by James Halama and John "Turk" Sartoris.

On July 3, 1963, the school board announced that John Bonk had been hired to coach the 1963-64 Speedboys basketball team. Bonk had been a standout player at nearby Drummond High School in northwest Wisconsin. He was the all-time leading scorer at Drummond and received all-conference honors in both his junior and senior years. In college, he was captain, leading scorer, and four-year letterman at Wisconsin State College-Superior.

The Bessemer School Board of Education was impressed with Bonk's resume. All agreed that he knew something about winning basketball games. The Bonk hire was the first time that the School Board had gone out and hired a pure basketball guy. It marked a new era in this town.

Bonk's 1957 Chevy labored to crest the hill on the western outskirts of Bessemer. Once at the top, the city came into view.

"Look, Alice," John said to his wife, "you can see the school's cupola from here."

The enormity of leaving everything behind to come here for John's job hit Alice at that moment. She said, "This has just become real. Our new home. What do you know about this town, John?"

"Not a thing," John said with a chuckle. "All I know is that they were hiring teachers and a basketball coach, and I needed a job."

The Bonks arrived at the high school where John would meet his new boss, Principal John Sartoris. They were right on time. John left his new bride in the car and made his way to the second floor of the 55-year-old school building.

Sartoris's office was tucked behind a tall school counter. There was no secretary on duty on this summer day, so Bonk knocked on the open door of the principal's office.

Without lifting his eyes to see who was at his door, Sartoris said, "Yes, what do you need?"

"Sir, I'm John Bonk, your new teacher and coach."

Sartoris looked up to see a tall young man with greased-back hair and black-framed glasses standing in the doorway. Sartoris rose to his feet to shake the big man's hand. "Oh, oh," he said. "Welcome, welcome."

Although Sartoris was six feet tall and over 200 pounds, it was the 6'6" coach with square shoulders that cast the big shadow on this day.

"John, have a seat," Sartoris said. Sartoris had been principal of A.D. Johnston High School for just one year. Although he had been teaching at rival Ironwood High School for the past few years, Sartoris was a graduate of Bessemer High and knew the school inside and out. He and his wife, Agnes, who taught English at the school, lived a few houses away. He bled the blue and gold of Bessemer more than the red and white of Ironwood. When the job opened, he grabbed it.

Bonk sat down in the chair in front of his new boss's desk. As he crossed his legs, his size thirteen shoe banged on the front of the metal desk. He folded in his body as best he could. There was no air conditioning in the building, yet Sartoris was sitting comfortably in his gray suit, white shirt and knotted tie. His receding hairline exposed a scar on top of his head.

"Mr. Sartoris, I'm looking forward to teaching at Washington School," Bonk said. "I'll hold my questions about the classroom duties for Mr. Vispi. In the meantime, I'm hoping you'll tell me about the basketball program here in Bessemer."

Sartoris rested his left arm on his desk and leaned forward. He was no-nonsense guy who had little time for chit-chat. But he obliged the new hire. "Well, John," Sartoris said, "we have had some success in basketball even though football is king around here." Sartoris talked about the U.P. Championship basketball teams from 1947 and 1948. He said that most of those boys still lived in town and were local sports legends.

Bonk seemed impressed and excited that there was hometown spirit.

"Bessemer played in Class B in those years," Sartoris said. "We're now a Class C school due to a drop in enrollment when the mines started closing. In 1952 and 1953, we won the Class C District Championships but fell in the regionals. We had a new coach by the name of Pete Fusi. Hell of a coach. He had one big guy, tall, just like you, on those teams. Jim Beissel was the boy's name. He was 6'7"."

Bonk smiled at the thought of Bessemer boys growing to such height.

"We last won the Michigan-Wisconsin Basketball Conference title in the 1955-56 season," Sartoris said. "We had an all-around athlete named Jim Corgiat. He helped us win the District Tournaments twice. In 1956, we went to Regionals and beat Houghton to snap their 42-game winning streak."

"Imagine a streak like that," replied Bonk.

"But we lost in the Championship game," Sartoris said. "Corgiat ended up playing football for Duffy Daugherty at Michigan State." Sartoris sat back in his chair, tapping his fingers together after proudly sharing that one of their own had made it to a big-time university. "One player can make a difference, Coach," he said. "A big difference."

Bonk smiled. It was the first time someone had called him Coach. He liked the sound of it. "So, Mr. Sartoris, do we have that one player on our basketball team this season?"

Sartoris looked at Bonk, then up at the clock. "Ah, it's getting late. You better head over to Washington School to see Principal Vispi."

Bonk stood and the men shook hands, then Bonk walked to his car, where Alice was still patiently waiting.

"How did it go?" she asked.

"Well, he called me Coach, so that was a new experience."

Miss Gloria Schilling, the 1958 Class Valedictorian at A.D. Johnston High School, and now working as a secretary at Washington School, greeted the Bonks as they arrived for the meeting with Mr. Vispi.

"Welcome, Mr. and Mrs. Bonk. I'm Gloria Schilling. Our principal is eager to meet you. Mrs. Bonk, you can have a seat here while John has his meeting with Mr. Vispi."

Principal Arnold Vispi's door was open, so Bonk walked in. Bonk towered over the diminutive man, but everyone knew that Vispi, a former high school wrestler, could hold his own with anyone who might cause trouble in the school.

Vispi wasted no time getting to the point of the meeting. "John, you'll be teaching science and boy's physical education. You'll enjoy it. Good kids, but if you have any troublemakers, you bring them down here and I'll handle it for you. The priority is teaching. Oh, and coaching freshman football."

"I don't know much about football, Mr. Vispi," John replied.

"Well, you'll be up in E.J. Oas Field for the first two weeks with the varsity squad, so whatever coach John Backman is doing with his team, you do the same with yours."

Bonk chuckled. "Ok, sir. I'll just position myself in the way to see the varsity practice. I'm supposed to meet coach Backman at the Lions Club next week. Or is it the Elks Lodge in Bessemer?"

"Same place," Vispi said. "It's above the Tip Top. There is a B.P.O.E. sign hanging from the second floor of the building. You want the door between Gambles Hardware and the Tip Top."

"Thank you," Bonk said. "That's helpful."

"You do know how to coach basketball, don't you?" Vispi asked.

In 1961, Bonk was playing for the Superior State Yellowjackets, who had earned a slot in the NCAA Small College Basketball Tournament in Brookings, South Dakota. There they met one of the most talked about teams in the nation, the Prairie View A&M Panthers, out of Prairie View, Texas. The Panthers' star player was Zelmo "Big Z" Beaty, a 6'8" All-American.

The Panthers were favored to win the National Championship. But for one game, the upstart Superior State Yellowjackets went toe-to-toe and basket-for-basket with Prairie View. Bonk, the Yellowjackets center, more than held his own against Beaty, blocking Big Z's shots and making plenty of his own. Near the end of the first half, Beaty had seen enough of Bonk's constant pressure inside, so he gave Bonk an elbow in the head. Bonk went down like a felled tree. His head hit the gymnasium floor, and he was knocked unconscious. Big Z was called for the foul and Bonk got a ten count.

With Bonk out of the game, the big upset faded. Prairie View A&M went on to beat Superior State 79-68. They won the National Championship too. Zelmo Beaty was named a first-team All-American, and in 1962 he got the call to the big show. He was drafted with the third overall pick by the St. Louis Hawks of the American Basketball Association, where he led the league in fouls. The next year, Bonk got the call from Arnold Vispi to be ninth grade science teacher at Washington School and varsity basketball coach in Bessemer, Michigan.

Ironically, both Beaty and Bonk were offered the same size contracts that paid $5,000 a year.

"Don't worry, Mr. Vispi, I know basketball, and your program is in good hands," Bonk said.

CHAPTER 3

It was a muggy August afternoon in Bessemer. Nine-year-old Art Boline sat on the steps outside the Tip Top Café, eating a double-scoop vanilla ice cream cone and leaning left or right to allow customers to get by as they walked in and out of the café. The customers didn't seem to mind. Connie Pricco walked by with an arm full of books from the Bessemer Public Library.

"Oh, nothing like an ice cream cone on a hot summer day," she said. Art just smiled.

Connie's little brother Jeff and his buddy Kevin Borseth tossed a pee wee football back and forth on the sidewalk between Gambles Hardware and the Rexall Drug Store. The boys were a bit bored. They were caught between the end of their Little League baseball season and the start of football season when they would watch their favorite high school team, the Speedboys, play under the lights at Massie Field.

"Cubs will be best next season," Pricco said as he caught the football from Borseth. "The Tigers got us this season, but we'll be on top for the next three seasons."

He was talking about Bessemer Little League baseball, not the major league club. Even though Little League was for 9- to 12-year-olds, it was highly competitive and generated razzing between players and arguments among opposing managers and parents.

Players never forgot which team they played for in this league or the name of the business that was stitched on their back. The Cubs were blessed with many natural athletes on the roster, most living on the north side of Highway 2.

There was no youth football league in this town or for that matter in any town nearby. If there had been such a league, young Borseth would have been one of its biggest stars. Taller, stronger and more agile than most kids his age, Borseth was able to compete with boys many years older. If you were drafting a team of any sort, you would make Kevin your number one pick.

Borseth motioned for Pricco to run long into the street towards Ben Franklin. Pricco ran his route. Borseth fired a left-handed spiral that Pricco caught over his shoulder.

"Nice catch, Jeff," said Borseth to his buddy.

As Pricco crossed the street, a car pulled up in front of the Tip Top, where Art was still eating his way through the melting cone. Two men eased out of the car and stretched. Sweat had soaked through their shirts. Air conditioning was a luxury for any car owner in this town. The driver was Harry Rizzie and his passenger was John Backman.

Backman motioned to Borseth.

"Toss me the ball, Kevin," said Backman.

Backman was the head football coach for the Bessemer Speedboys, and the school's athletic director. Rizzie was the area's number one sports fan and sports historian. He rolled beer kegs during the day for Art Boline's father, Bill, a local beer distributor. At night, he was either playing or watching sports in the area.

Borseth tossed the ball to Backman.

"Nice spiral," Backman said. "Someday you could be our starting quarterback. A left-handed QB might throw off the other team. Maybe our guys, too."

Borseth smiled.

"How's that ice cream cone, Artie?" Rizzie yelled to the boy on the Tip Top steps.

"Delicious," Artie replied with a big creamy smile.

Rizzie opened the Elks Lodge door. Backman walked in and up the stairs while Rizzie followed. The men had an appointment to meet the new Speedboys basketball coach.

The Elks Lodge hosted weddings, reunions, Daughters of Isabella Chapter 746 meetings, and high school sports banquets. It was also where the all-important Bessemer Little League draft took place. Young boys waited patiently outside the Elks Lodge door to find out which team had selected them on draft night. Most boys made a team, but a few never got the call. For them, it was a hard lesson to learn that things don't always go your way. A fact of life in Bessemer.

The 6'6" Bonk was pacing back and forth waiting for his athletic director to arrive.

"You're an easy guy to spot," Rizzie said. "We don't have many guys over six foot tall around here."

The joke put Bonk at ease. He laughed, shook hands, then the three took a table near the bar.

"So, you're the new Speedboys basketball coach," Rizzie said.

"Yes, I am," Bonk said.

"My condolences," Rizzie replied.

Bonk looked at Rizzie, trying to determine if he was kidding or not. "Why do you say that?" he asked.

Before Rizzie could reply, Backman chimed in. "Coach, you can't make chicken salad out of chicken poop."

Backman knew what a winning team looked like. He played on Bessemer's championship basketball teams in 1947 and 1948. "We're in a state of rebuilding," he said.

"Unfortunately, we've been rebuilding since 1959," Rizzie said with a laugh.

Backman went on to explain that boys show up for football each August. Great athletes. Easy to coach. But, when football season is done in October, they don't necessarily go out for the basketball team. They opt for activities like skiing at Indianhead Mountain, town hockey, or bar league basketball. Work on their cars or just chase girls.

After hearing this, Bonk was unsure how to respond.

"There have been good teams recently in this town," Rizzie interjected. "But not great teams. The good teams overachieved. Could upset a team or two. Competed hard. But in the end, they weren't good enough to rise to the top and stay there."

Rizzie then explained that since a last-second win in the Class C District Basketball Championship in 1957, the Speedboys were, at best, competitive on the court. Six long years without any type of trophy.

"When you say rebuilding, what do you mean?" Bonk asked.

"Dan Mestnick took over for the legendary Pete Fusi as basketball coach for the 1958-59 season," said Rizzie. "Mestnick told the newspapers they had to 'start from scratch' due to the loss of seven seniors, including our local superstar, Jimmy Corgiat. Mestnick's team finished that season with seven wins and 10 losses. Disappointing but expected, as they were rebuilding, which is just another way of saying 'starting from scratch.' After his team went 7-10 again in 1959-60, Mestnick stepped down to allow a coach with a new plan to take the reins."

Bonk's mind was spinning. He was impressed that Rizzie could remember so many numbers and names.

"In 1960, the school board announced that the basketball coaching duties would be assigned to junior high science teacher Jim Peterson. He had been a star athlete for Duluth Central and the University of Minnesota-Duluth. Peterson also told the newspapers that he was starting from scratch, and his team went 5-13."

"You notice a theme here, Coach?" Backman asked.

"I'm starting to, yes," Bonk replied.

"The next season, 1961-62," Rizzie continued, "the team improved to 8-8. Then last season, 1962-63, Peterson's Speedboys were expected to be underachievers by some in the community. But they were overachievers because they played in the most powerful basketball conference this side of the Mackinac Bridge, the Michigan-Wisconsin Conference."

Rizzie explained that game after game, the 1962-63 Speedboys team, with Bryon Johnson, Tom Manninen, Dick McDermott, Marshall Tillner, Brian Mattson and Louis Marconeri, was competing with some of the greatest players ever to play on the Gogebic-Iron Range. Boys like Rodney Hewitt and Dick DeZur in Hurley, Terry Salmi and Doug Syreini in Wakefield, Cliff Decker and Roland Pakonen in Ironwood. Each an All-Conference selection."

Bonk had heard of some of those players.

"Peterson's team finished last season at 7-10," Rizzie said, "but the Speedboys stunned the conference champion Ironwood Red Devils 60-59 in the season finale. Then, to everyone's surprise, they beat the tournament favorite Wakefield Cardinals 67-63 in the first round of the Class C District Tourney. Underachievers? Not that bunch."

Bonk was encouraged. "Sounds like I've got some talent to work with." he said.

"Unfortunately, you don't," Backman replied. "They all graduated, Coach."

Bonk was not deterred. He considered his words, then made a proclamation. "Thanks for the history lesson, gentlemen. But I know this game, and I plan to make the Speedboys winners."

Rizzie looked straight faced at Bonk before replying.

"Just to be safe, tell the newspapers you are starting from scratch."

CHAPTER 4

Times Like These

My father John Pelissero walked gingerly down the stairs of our family's two-story home, a creak with each step, either from the old wooden staircase or from his aging body. He was 33 and slowed by ulcers, broken ribs, dislocated discs, and the latest setback, diabetes.

Even with his long list of ailments he was still a gifted athlete and highly competitive. He played softball for the Last East Inn Old-timers and coached the Yankees in Little League baseball all summer. He bowled in the mid-200s all winter. He hunted grouse in October and deer in November. He played cards in a league one night a week. He had his toolbox at the ready should a neighbor call in need of some handyman work and would be the first on the site and the last to leave. He was that kind of friend.

And now he was a husband and a father. Five young sons waited patiently for him to descend the steps each morning. In his days as a hometown basketball hero, everybody called him Johnny Pel. My brothers and I, of course, just called him Dad.

"Pull up your sleeve," my mother said to Dad.

With a scowl, he lifted the right sleeve of his white t-shirt, then turned away as his wife, a registered nurse, gave him a shot of insulin. He winced when mom jabbed the needle in his arm. Same scene each morning, going on three years now.

I watched as he buttoned his shirt. With each button, he groaned, indicating discomfort in his fingers. He then fastened the bow tie that Super Valu required him to wear in the meat room.

Seven family members crowded around the kitchen table for

three meals a day. Dad at the head of the table, Mom at the stove. We five boys sitting in our assigned seats.

My brothers and I were each born two years apart. John was the oldest and the best student. Paul was the third boy and considered the quiet one. Gerry was fourth and was the sensitive one. Pete, my baby brother, was a handful. Then there's me, Tom, the second oldest. The anxious one. The one that knew something would go wrong soon and should plan ahead.

There was no talking at the table unless Dad asked a question, which seldom occurred. My brother John said Dad didn't talk because when he grew up his parents spoke Italian and he did not, thus it was hard to carry on a conversation. Good theory, but I had another one. He liked things in order. His meals, work, bowling, and most important, his sons, always in line. He didn't like things to be complicated. If each day was exactly the same, he would be fine with that.

Dad was served eggs and bacon every morning. Mom drizzled the extra bacon grease over his eggs to add flavor. He added milk and two shots of sweetener to his coffee and stirred it with a spoon. He dunked his toast in the coffee, ate his meal, and said nothing.

Mom scooped a ladleful of hot cereal into each of our bowls. We were offered one slice of toast on which she had already spread peanut butter and jelly and cut diagonally. Mom liked things in order too.

Every single morning was the same. We could smell the bacon sizzling in the pan, but we would never taste even a morsel. Mom was on a budget. She had just enough eggs for Dad and couldn't spare a single slice of bacon. She said Dad needed a certain number of calories to make sure his blood sugar didn't get too high or too low. The insulin would do the rest.

The clock on the wall was always set ten minutes ahead. We lived in a world where we were running late, or at least that's what our mother wanted all her boys to think. It kept us on a schedule. Her schedule.

After breakfast she issued commands on where to find our hats, mittens, jackets, and boots. She handed us grocery bags filled with our books and school projects and held open the back door to keep us moving.

On this day, in November of 1963, like every school day, some of her boys walked one block to Washington School and the others walked a quarter mile to St. Sebastian School. No bus, no car ride, no adult supervision. We were on our own, just like every other boy and girl in the neighborhood. Rain, snow, or sleet, my mother's mantra was always the same: "Get moving, boys, or you'll be late."

Winter was settling in. Snow would fall every other day. Cold mornings, some days ten degrees above zero, others ten degrees below. At times, we walked to school with our backs to the wind just to survive the chill from the north.

I was in the third grade at St. Sebastian School, my brother John was in fifth. John was smart, polite, a rule follower and well-liked by his teachers. Even in fifth grade the teachers knew this kid was going somewhere big someday and they reminded me all the time that I should be more like him. A tall task.

St. Sebastian School started in 1920 in what was once the aging Puritan Hotel, which used to be located where the Peoples State Bank building stands today in Bessemer. Rather than build a new school, Father Charles Swoboda and the church leaders thought it better to physically move the Puritan Hotel from downtown Bessemer to Iron Street. In 1917 they moved it on logs, pulled by horses. They converted the old hotel into a school and opened for classes in 1920-21. It served the students well until June 1959.

The new St. Sebastian School held its first classes on September 14, 1959, with 220 students from kindergarten through eighth grade. The teaching staff was dominated by aging nuns from the order of the Sisters of Notre Dame; teaching was their mission work. All the classrooms at St. Sebastian School were the same: tile floors, metal desks with wooden tops, each with a pencil holder carved into the light tan wood. Students could raise the desktop to store his or her books, assignments, crayons and glue. If a kid was lucky, he or she could hide a piece of candy to sneak a bite later.

The blackboards were green, not black. Pinned to the wall and running the length of the classroom was the alphabet; each letter written in perfect cursive in both upper and lower case. Penmanship was a critical part of learning in any Catholic School. Students were graded on cursive writing the same as they were on arithmetic and geography. The teachers had to have perfect penmanship to teach at St. Sebastian.

Mrs. Lucina Vispi, the wife of Arnold Vispi, principal at Washington School, was the morning teacher for the third grade at St. Sebastian School. Mrs. Ellen Carpenedo taught the same students in the afternoon. Both were kindly women with a natural gift for teaching. As neither was a nun, the two ladies were referred to as *lay* teachers.

I was surrounded in class by my buddies, all of us believing we'd be lifelong friends and would live in this town forever, just like our parents did, hanging out with the same people you went to school with. John, Dennis, Jay, Beth, Eleanor, Joanne, Mary and other kids who were named after a Saint or other patriarchs of the Catholic Church. We had to live up to our names.

"Hey Tommy, you going to the game tonight?" asked Jay Maccani. "It's the new coach's first game. They play Ontonagon."

Jay Maccani was up to date on all sports. Ask about a game and he could give you the game and time.

"Of course," I said. "The Polar Bears. That should be a win."

"See you there at 6:00," Jay said. "I want to see the B game, too."

"Gary Niemi and Bill Ryan are gonna start," I said.

Niemi was my cousin. He told my dad that he and Ryan, both juniors, would be in the starting five. Niemi and Ryan were former St. Sebastian Knights basketball players.

Their Knights team normally came out on top. They even won a huge conference traveling trophy: the Father Krysty Trophy. Both Ryan and Niemi had played for the Washington Wolverines as freshmen before heading to high school. Then each rode the bench for the Speedboys as sophomores last season.

"What about Bruce Richardson?" I asked. "Is he playing?"

"I heard he is," Maccani said.

Bruce Richardson was a top-notch player for the St. Sebastian

Knights as well. He could play any position. He, along with Niemi and Ryan, were the nucleus of the 1960-61 St. Sebastian Knights team that was so good.

I had an affinity for any player on the Speedboys that used to suit-up for the Knights. For me, playing for St. Sebastian was the seal of approval of skill and desire to play at the highest level.

"But I thought Bruce had some knee injury." I said.

Without hesitating, my cousin John Stancher, sitting behind me, blurted out: "Osgood-Schlatter."

We all spun around and looked at him.

"Richardson has Osgood-Schlatter disease," he said again. "He grew too fast. He went from being a guard one year to being a center the next. So he had to stop playing until he stopped growing."

I stared at John and thought, *how does he know this stuff?*

Today was like any other school day. Mrs. Vispi, seated at her desk in front of the classroom, communicated the order of activities for the morning. A very rigid schedule that was the same as the day before, and the day before that. Only my father could appreciate a day like that.

Mrs. Vispi announced that our scrapbook project over Christmas break would be titled *Michigan's Winter Wonderland.* That was something new. She said we would cut and paste pictures from newspapers and magazines of winter activities into the scrapbook. We would need to go to the Bessemer Library to research how these activities were important to our community. An easy assignment that I most likely would put off until the last minute.

When the bell rang for lunch, most students grabbed their plaid or black lunch box with thermos and headed to the lunchroom. For the Pelissero boys it was a long, uphill walk home to eat with our whole family.

Dad would arrive from Super Valu with a bag of groceries that Mom had told him to pick up before coming home. He would walk directly to the sink, wash his hands, then sit at the end of the table, where a meal of meat and potatoes was placed in front of him. We all got the same meal, plus one tablespoon of corn, peas or beans. It was the same routine each day.

When dinner was over, John and I would wash the dishes while my dad read the Duluth newspaper sports section. Mom hurried us out of the house by 12:10 p.m. so we could be back to school before the bell rang. Time management was her thing.

"So 6 o'clock, be at the B game," yelled Jay Maccani over the ringing school bell.

"Got it," I said as I closed my locker and ran into the classroom.

Our afternoon teacher, Mrs. Carpenedo, walked slowly up and down the aisles handing out last week's spelling test and a copy of the new spelling words for the week. She had corrected the previous spelling test by circling in red each word a student had misspelled. This week I had two words — and my last name — circled in red. My mother wouldn't be happy.

Debbie Vargovich pronounced each *new* spelling word out loud.

"Respect. Afraid. Surprise," she whispered.

Her friend Jean shushed her. Debbie giggled and read more words out loud. She was interrupted by a knock on the door. Three frantic taps.

When the door opened it was our Principal Sister Mary Andrina, all five feet of her. Her face was flushed, and her voice was somber as she spoke.

"Children, we have very bad news," she announced. "We have just heard on the radio that our President, John Kennedy, has been shot while traveling in a car in Dallas."

A collective gasp sucked the air out of the classroom. Sister Andrina pulled a tissue from her sleeve and wiped her eyes. "We all must pray," she said. "Please put your heads on your desks and pray hard for our President."

Then she left the room to inform yet another classroom of the dreadful news.

As I lay my head down across my arms, I thought, *this can't be true.*

"Please God, make him better," I prayed. "President Kennedy is a good guy. No one shoots the good guy."

We took immense pride that our president was Catholic, like us. The first Catholic ever elected President.

I could hear whimpers and sniffles coming from the girls in the row next to me. Most of the boys lay with their heads facing the windows, stone-faced and not making a sound. We were all in a state of shock.

This same scene at St. Sebastian School would play out across the city in every office building, mine shaft and retail store. One minute it's a bright and sunny winter day. The next it turns into an unimaginable tragedy.

At A.D. Johnston High School, the students were in the gymnasium getting ready for a pep rally for the Speedboys' basketball season opener. The cheerleaders were getting the crowd worked up as they were moments away from enthusiastically introducing their new basketball coach, John Bonk, who would have some inspirational words for the upcoming season.

Mark Martini, a junior and a player on the team, was in the janitor's office with custodian Ranierio "Spun" Matrella, preparing to enter the pep rally and run through some dribbling, passing and shooting drills to the delight of the crowd.

Spun was in his late 50s and married a gal named Edith, though everyone called her Jim. Spun had thinning gray hair, a slight mustache, and a gruff demeanor that belied how soft he was on the inside.

As Martini waited, the radio playing in Spun's office delivered the news.

"This is a bulletin," announced the WJMS newsman. *"The President of the United States, John Fitzgerald Kennedy, has been shot."*

Matrella and Martini looked at each other to confirm they had heard the same thing, then leaned in as the newsman delivered the headline again.

"I repeat, the President of the United States has been shot."

They were not sure what to do next.

"Go tell Principal Sartoris, Spun," said Martini.

"I'm not going to do it," replied the custodian. "You do it."

Both Martini and Matrella left together and found Principal Sartoris talking to Coach Bonk on the basketball court. Martini tapped Sartoris on the shoulder.

"Mr. Sartoris," Martini said, "President Kennedy has been shot."

Sartoris turned to Matrella, "Is this true, Spun?"

Spun nodded. The words wouldn't come out.

"We heard it on WJMS in Spun's office," Martini said.

Sartoris retreated to the janitor's office to listen to the radio. As he walked in, a news bulletin was being read. It was grave news. The President had died from his wounds.

Sartoris gathered himself, tightened his tie and headed back to the gymnasium floor, where he asked the cheerleaders and pep band to quiet down.

Sartoris cleared his throat and then spoke.

"Students and faculty, I have just heard the most tragic news," he said. "Our president, John Kennedy, has been shot and killed in Dallas, Texas."

The sense of shock and loss was immediate and immense. The girls crying out and hugging the person next to them. The boys stoic, yet without the ability to speak.

Sartoris knew there was no way to have a pep rally, much less continue with school for the day.

"It's times like these where we need to seek comfort, and the best place for us is to be home with our families," he said. "I'm going to dismiss students and faculty for the day. I'll have to check with the conference officials about whether the basketball game will still be played tonight. Listen to the radio for any updates on postponement of the game. Everyone is dismissed."

Never had the student body left the gymnasium in such silence. Only the sound of shuffling feet and muffled sobs could be heard as the students and teachers, arms around each other, exited the building.

TEMPERATURES:
24 hr. period to 12 noon: 30; 24.
Previous 24 hr. period: 30, 20.
Year ago: High 30; Low 16.
Boston's snow 20.4 in.
Snow year ago 17 in.

FORECASTS — Snow flurries and turning colder tonight and Saturday. Low tonight in the 20s, high Saturday 35 to 45.

IRONWOOD DAILY GLOBE

45th YEAR, NUMBER 3.

ASSOCIATED PRESS LEASED WIRE NEWS SERVICE

IRONWOOD, MICHIGAN, FRIDAY EVENING, NOVEMBER 22, 1963.

TWELVE PAGES

SINGLE COPY 7 CENTS.

KENNEDY ASSASSINATED

Trooper Is Held In Bank Robbery

Admits Holding Up Suburban Bank, but 'Doesn't Know Why'

CENTER LINE (AP) — A bank thrown by a bank teller led to the arrest of a state policeman on bank robbery charges Thursday night, and the trooper remarkably admitted the alleged holdup, his superiors said.

Andy J. Nabbush, 32, a seven-year veteran of the force, was arrested at the Center Line State Police Post.

"If I could tell you why, I'd tell you — I just don't know," he told Capt. Fred Davids.

Watts teller Pierce E. Hammond Nabbush from the National Bank of Royal Oak after the robbery Thursday afternoon and threw a rock that denied his car, police said.

A citizen told police which way the car had gone, but officers alerted repair shops in the area at Columbus St. called to report the car had been in his repair and gave notice for it rescue number, officers said.

Nabbush, married and father of three children, was arraigned on a bank robbery charge today before U.S. District Judge Fred...

Final Approval Is Given Schema

Modern Language in Worship Is Voted

By GERALD J. MILLER
Associated Press Staff Writer

VATICAN CITY (AP) — The Vatican Ecumenical Council voted final approval today of its first completed schema, providing for modernization of the language used in Roman Catholic worship.

The Roman Catholic prelates put their final seal of strength-ance on the country's liturgy schema by a vote of 2,158 to 19, with 10 left for the document to become the council's first decree in formal promulgation by Pope Paul VI in a public council session.

It is expected to be held next Friday.

The vote was cleared by the named fathers.

NEW PRESIDENT—Lyndon F. Johnson, above, automatically became president of the United States upon the death of President John F. Kennedy, killed by an assassin's bullet in Dallas, Tex. today. Johnson was to take the oath of office as soon as it could be arranged.

Viet Nam Rulers Must Prove They Can Win Backing

No Sharp Changes In U.S. Policies

By FRED S. HOFFMAN
AP Military Writer

WASHINGTON (AP) — Top U.S. officials who assessed the post-coup situation in South Viet Nam repeatedly concluded that new military regime into must prove it can win support of the Vietnamese peasants.

Administration officials who met in Honolulu two days ago with American diplomatic and military leaders from South Viet Nam agreed cautiously that things are going reasonably well so far.

Sources familiar with what went on at the Hawaii conference indicated the report to President Kennedy is unlikely to call for any sharp policy changes.

Ambassador Henry Cabot Lodge, who was among those taking part in the Honolulu talks, will head Sunday afternoon with President Kennedy at the chief executive's country place in Virginia. The enhance-

PRES. JOHN F. KENNEDY

Lives for Half Hour After Hit By Rifle Bullet

Governor Connally Of Texas Wounded

DALLAS (AP) — President John F. Kennedy, thirty-sixth president of the United States, was shot to death today by a high-powered rifle.

Kennedy, 46, lived about 30 minutes after a sniper cut him down as his limousine left downtown Dallas.

Automatically, the mantle of the presidency fell to Vice President Lyndon B. Johnson, a native Texan who had been riding two cars behind the chief executive.

There was no immediate word on when Johnson would take the oath of office.

Kennedy died at Parkland Hospital where his bullet-pierced body had been taken to a frantic but futile effort to save his life.

Lying wounded at the same hospital was Gov. John Connally Jr. of Texas, who was cut down by the same bullet that ended the life of the youngest man ev-

CHAPTER 5

The Show Must Go On

The newsman on WJMS AM 630 read a long list of cancellations due to President Kennedy's death. Yet when they got to the local basketball games, he announced that the Bessemer-Ontonagon game would still be played tonight.

I was relieved to hear this. The somber mood within our home made me want to escape.

"Mom, I'm going to go the Bessemer game, OK?"

She waved me off with a brush of her hand, too busy watching news reports to worry about my comings and goings.

I pulled my boots over my shoes. The jingling of the buckles with each step made me feel like Roy Rogers in his spurs walking down a boardwalk. The evening air was unseasonably warm for November, about 30 degrees and snow was falling. I opened my mouth and let the big flakes land on my tongue.

I walked to the top of Bennetts' Hill, the unofficial name of the street where children's sledding was authorized each winter. I could not resist the urge to take off my boots and slide down the hill in my shoes. So, I did.

I was like a surfer catching a wave. Boots held in each hand to help my balance as I glided down the hill. At the bottom, I slid to a stop. I was quite pleased with my performance, staying upright the entire distance. I brushed the snow from my shoes and slipped on my boots. As I looked east along Longyear Street, I saw two large figures walking towards me. Each carried a satchel. I knew instantly they were Speedboys.

It seemed late for these guys to be heading to the game, but the day had been a blur. The shorter of the two was Mark Martini, proudly wearing his letterman jacket, medals swinging from the letter. The taller one was George Sabol. The guys were neighbors and teammates. Sabol would see some action tonight, but it was Martini who would get the start.

Martini was a junior and a transplant from Stambaugh. He moved to Bessemer when his father was transferred to be Assistant Superintendent at the Peterson Iron Ore Mine. That was fortuitous for Bessemer football fans, as Mark was a natural athlete and a slick and elusive running back. He was the perfect complement to a backfield that featured big, hard running Jerry Corgiat at fullback and agile Jimmy Ippolite at quarterback. Martini wore number 5 just like his hero Paul Hornung, the golden boy of the Green Bay Packers.

Martini walked with a certain cockiness knowing he was the athlete that all the papers wrote about every Friday night. He certainly earned that stride based on his achievements on the gridiron, but could he do the same on the basketball court?

I kept my distance as the two players walked past me. Little guys like me learn early that if you cut off the path of the big kids, you get a fistful of snow stuffed down the back of your jacket.

Both boys had their collars turned up, trying to cover their ears from the winter chill. Snow fell lightly on the top of their heads. Sabol's glasses were fogging, and he often took them off to clean the lenses with the scarf around his neck. The boys quickly outpaced me to the school.

The door to the gymnasium was heavy and rather hard to open for an eight year old. A tall, round man they called Iggy was just inside the door, and he pushed it open for me. Iggy was not his real name. Most guys in Bessemer had a nickname and that name was used so often that you forgot his given name. Iggy was always at the games and regularly kept a scorebook that likely no one would read but him.

The junior varsity game was underway and the gymnasium was a sea of sounds. The bouncing basketball, the buzzing scoreboard, the squeak and screech of sneakers as players cut and pivoted on the hardwood. Cheerleaders clapped and stomped their feet and cheered for their favorite team. Fans applauded the players and booed the referees' bad calls. On Friday nights, the A.D. Johnston gymnasium was the place to be.

I handed a quarter to the lady behind the ticket counter. She smiled and passed a yellow ticket back to me with sage advice.

"Don't lose it, kid."

As I passed the Junior ROTC cadet in full uniform guarding the stairs to the gym floor, I raised my ticket so he could see I wasn't trying to sneak in. The cadet gave me the nod to proceed. No smile, just business.

As I descended the long metal staircase to the gym floor, my boot buckles clanged against the wall, knocking off the wet snow. The steps were a slushy mess. Janitor Spun Matrella was at the bottom of the staircase, mopping furiously to prevent a slip and fall incident.

High school girls sold fresh popcorn for ten cents a bag as fast as they could fill them. Heavy on the salt. The line was long, so I chose to buy a bag later.

I climbed the staircase on the north side of the gym to find a seat in the upper bleachers. Tickets were general admission. No assigned seating, yet there was an unofficial pecking order to who sat where in the stands.

High school students got the lower bleachers on the northeast side. The alumni and player parents took the lower and upper stands on the southeast side behind the home team. The opposing fans took the southwest bleachers behind their team.

My buddies and I were relegated to the upper north side bleachers. Long metal bench seats which were unmovable and uncomfortable. Each painted brown, probably designed by a military man. Plenty wide for big-bottom boys and girls and sturdy enough to withstand a hundred years of wear.

As I got to the top of the stairs, a lady with thin gray hair and rimless glasses leaned down and stopped me.

"Where's your ticket young man?" she asked sternly.

It was Agnes Sartoris, a long-serving teacher and the wife of the high school principal. She had been teaching in Bessemer for so long that my father had been her student. She and her husband John ran the school with an iron fist. They made the rules, and enforced them strictly.

"Where's your ticket?" she repeated.

I reached inside every pocket of my coat and pants in a frantic search for the yellow ticket. Finally, to my relief, I found it, and Mrs. Sartoris let me pass.

My buddies Jay Maccani, John Stancher and Denny Martell were sitting in Row 3 of the upper bleachers directly across the court from the Speedboys bench. We had a perfect view of the action.

First-year junior varsity coach Carl Gregas was shuffling players in and out. Bobby Abelman, Dick Schwartz, Mike Betlewski, Milo Barnaby and others. Each player hoping to impress the coach and get more playing time.

Coach Gregas was new to coaching and he embraced the role. He shouted instructions to his players as he paced up and down the sideline in his tweed sports coat. His boys responded with a gritty effort but still lost by 20 points, 58-38.

Between the JV and varsity games, my pals and I bought some popcorn and warm pop, and read through the game program to get to know the names and numbers of all the new players.

The pep band struck up the Bessemer school song as the varsity team came running out of the tunnel for pre-game warm-ups. The crowd rose to its feet and sang along.

"Fling high the Bessemer banner,

Don't let the standards fall.

Three cheers for Bessemer, for good ole' Bessemer,

The school we love the best of all. U, rah rah!

Bring out the ball boys and blow the whistle,

Fair play will win this game.

For Bessemer's honor must be,

Defend and hail the Gold and Blue."

Hometown spirit was in the air and the Bessemer Speedboys breathed it in.

The team quickly snapped into their drills, looking sharp in their blue warm-up jackets with Speedboys stitched on their backs. Their satin shorts shimmered. All the boys had white crew socks with two blue stripes at the top that were paired nicely with their white high-top sneakers. A couple boys wore knee pads. Bruce Richardson wore braces on both knees.

We watched as player after player gently placed the ball off the glass backboard and into the basket. It looked so easy. The Speedboys moved from one drill to the next. Boom! They jumped into the three-man weave. In the middle, George Sabol threw a chest pass to Mark Martini, then circled around Martini's back. Martini snapped it cross court to Gary Niemi who tossed it back to Sabol as he drove towards the basket. How did they know which way to cut or twist? Somehow it all worked. Sabol laid one in and Niemi got the rebound and started the whole drill over again.

They looked so good, so sharp out there on the floor. Like they had what it takes to beat anyone.

After twenty minutes, the boys returned to the locker room and the cheerleaders took over the court to pump up the crowd. They were the heartbeat of the team and the heartthrobs of the boys in the crowd.

The girls sported blue and white sweaters with a large B and a cheer horn across the front. They wore matching blue and white pleated skirts and bobby socks with white Keds. They each took a turn doing a solo routine, and as they jumped into the air they yelled out their names: "I'm Connie." "I'm Joy." "I'm Marcella." "I'm Jackie." "I'm Patty."

Sweet teen girls. Smiles a mile long. The girl next door that your mom would want you to marry one day. The gals broke into a fan-favorite cheer.

"When you're up, you're up. When you're down, you're down.

When you're up against Bessemer, you're upside down.

Clap your hands, stomp your feet, Bessemer Speedboys can't be beat!"

The two teams returned to the court for the start of the game. The crowd was energized. But then the public address announcer turned on his microphone and asked everyone to stand for a moment of silence for President Kennedy. That changed the mood in the gymnasium immediately. After an agonizing thirty seconds of quiet, the announcer took to the microphone to introduce the starting line-ups with hopes of reigniting the crowd noise.

As a boy sitting in the stands, I imagined it must be one of the greatest moments in a player's life to have his name announced to the roar of the hometown crowd. You earned the start. You were the best. And now everyone in the gymnasium knows it.

After introducing the starting five for the Ontonagon Polar Bears, the announcer read the names of the hometown starting five. The boys stood with hands on hips, rocking side to side, waiting for their name to be called.

As each name was announced, the hometown fans responded with enthusiastic applause, and a Speedboy cheerleader performed an acrobatic move in recognition. The starting lineup included Bill Nemacheck as center, Gary Niemi and Bruce Richardson as forwards, and Mark Martini and Bill Ryan as guards.

"And please welcome the new head coach of the Bessemer Speedboys, John Bonk," the announcer said.

The crowd roared, the buzzer sounded, the whistle blew and the ball was tipped at center court. The Bonk era began.

CHAPTER 6

Downtown

The firehouse whistle blew loudly as I walked downtown. A second whistle would signify a fire and a red fire truck would come screaming down the main street with volunteer firemen in white helmets in tow. But it only blew once. The city blew the whistle at 12:00 p.m. and 9:00 p.m. daily for unknown reasons. Some still believed the 12:00 whistle marked a shift change at the ore mine and the 9:00 was a curfew for those under 16. Another quirk in a small town. For me, it simply meant it was noon, and time to do some shopping.

The drug store corner was a meeting place for kids and teens. No further explanation was needed if you said, "meet me at the corner."

When I got to the corner, 12-year-old Ginny Strelcheck was leaning against the light pole. She held a fistful of Gold Bond Stamp Books. A big rubber band bound them tightly.

Her father, Don Strelcheck, owned the Gambles Hardware store. It was a couple of doors from the drug store. Only the Tip Top Café separated the two businesses.

Ginny lived downtown and was the unofficial leader of the pack of girls who, like her, lived above or behind retail businesses in Bessemer. She and her downtown friends would rendezvous at "the corner," figure out where the boys were and then go mess with the boys' day.

"Hi Ginny," I said.

"Hi Pel," she answered. "Where are you going? Tip Top?"

"Nah, going in here to buy my dad's insulin and then to your father's store to buy my brother a gift for his birthday. How about you?"

"I'm heading to Toyland in Martin's Hardware," Ginny replied, "to redeem these Gold Bond Stamps on something fun."

It is interesting that the daughter of one hardware store owner would redeem Gold Bond Stamps at the competition. But Toyland in the basement of Martin's Hardware was something very special for kids.

Ginny noticed her friend Barb was in front of Martin's Hardware and yelled to her to wait up. She dashed off without saying goodbye to me.

As I reached for the Rexall Drug Store door, Kevin Borseth's sister Joy opened it from inside as she was leaving.

She greeted me while holding the door open with one hand while carrying a bag of Fritos in the other. Tucked under her left arm was a small stack of 45 rpm records. But just like Ginny, she was in a hurry.

The drug store had not changed much in the many years it's been on the corner. Wood cabinets with heavy drawers lined the walls. Locked glass display cabinets with certain items that were there to see, but not to touch. Large globe lights hung from the tin-tiled ceiling. Merchandise and medicine were stacked floor to ceiling, leaving little room to move about the store. The smell of fresh roasted peanuts filled the air.

Bernie Proft, the store manager in his dark blue lab coat, took some cashews from the nut container and climbed a ladder to place an expensive bottle on the top shelf. I didn't greet him, afraid he might drop the bottle.

I went to the counter to get my father's prescription and was greeted by Marcella Boline, the same teen that was a cheerleader for the Speedboys. She kept her hands in the pockets of her white smock, her brown hair curled perfectly upon her shoulders. She was kind and polite, exactly the type of girl a shop owner would want at his front counter.

I requested the insulin, which she retrieved from a refrigerator in the back. I paid $1.98 and checked off the first item on my list. My next stop was Gambles Hardware.

Downtown Bessemer was lively. Shoppers left Kelto-Velin grocery with their purchases. Store clerks took coffee breaks at Tip Top or Dandee Bakery. Men lined up under the big clock on the corner in front of General Insurance waiting for the bus to the White Pine Copper Mine. Friends greeted each other. Everyone was happy and content.

As I entered Gambles, Ward Sliva and Don Strelcheck were talking in the middle aisle. Sliva was the owner of Ben Franklin, Strelcheck the owner of Gambles. As we made eye contact, Sliva poked Strelcheck as he pointed at me.

"Hey, Don, you know who this young shopper is, right?" Sliva asked.

There's a good chance Sliva didn't know who I was, and this was his go-to line when he wasn't sure of someone's name.

"Well, I know it's one of Johnny's boys," Strelcheck said. "But Johnny's got so many, I have no idea which one he is."

I smiled, shrugged, and moved to the next aisle. I preferred not to talk to adults because they tend to ask too many questions of which I had few answers. Additionally, I was focused on my task of finding a gift for my brother Paul's upcoming birthday.

This year I decided to get him a board game. No more toy weapons or plastic soldiers or Lincoln Logs. Now was the time for a game of strategy or luck, if I could find one that fit a seven year old. I had one game in mind. *Candyland*. I figured Paul would like all the bright colors and pictures of the delicious candies.

As I came around the end of the aisle, I looked up and there it was, *Candyland*, on the top shelf on the north side of the store. In fact, there were dozens of games and toys in a neat pile on the shelf. I was in business. But I needed a ladder to reach it.

"Hi there," said a lady as she walked up behind me. "Can I help you find something?"

It was Rosemary Strelcheck, Ginny's mom.

"Yeah," I said. "I need that *Candyland* game up there. But I don't know how to get it down."

"I'm sorry, but that one is on layaway," she said.

"What is layaway?" I asked.

She chuckled. "Well, basically, we lay it aside for someone until they can come in and pay for it. The person's name is on it. You see that name tag attached with a string?"

"Oh," I said. "Can I buy the one next to it? *The Mouse Trap* game?"

"No, that one is on layaway too. All those games up there are being held for someone.

I must have looked confused. She bent down and dropped her voice to a whisper. "Let me tell you a secret," she said. "Sometimes people can't afford to pay us right away, like when the miners are out of work. We hold the item until they are able to pay for it. It is the least we can do during difficult times."

She stood back up and smiled at me. "We have *Monopoly* and *The Game of Life* for sale."

"My brother is only seven, so that's really not gonna work for him," I replied. "I think I'll check at the dime store. Thanks anyway."

As I walked outside, the aroma of freshly baked bread and rolls emanated from the Dandee Bakery. I inhaled deeply and my mouth began to water. Since I had no extra money for a jelly doughnut, I walked into Ben Franklin. The "dime store," as we called it, had an aisle chock full of possible gifts. Many sold for a dollar or less. A paddle with a ball on a string. Year-old baseball cards with year-old bubble gum. 45-rpm records with popular songs not sung by the original artists. Model airplanes with the glue sold separately.

A two-foot-long rubber snake that lay between two glass dividers caught my eye. It was black with a green diamond pattern painted on its back. I thought it was the perfect gift for a seven year old. You could hide it in someone's bed and scare the *bejeebers* out of him or her.

It was an ideal gift, but I couldn't find a price tag on it.

Two aisles over I spotted a clerk who was carefully folding women's underwear and placing them on the shelf. Bras, panties, girdles and many other garments that no nine-year-old boy wanted to see, ever.

I walked up behind her as she was lifting up the last box of lingerie.

"Excuse me, ma'am," I said politely. "Can you tell me how much this is?"

As she turned, I thrust the snake towards her.

She shrieked and threw the underwear boxes in the air. Pink and white underwear scattered about.

A petite lady with glasses wearing a light blue smock came flying around the corner.

"Marilyn," she cried, "what happened?"

Marilyn started to laugh, looking at the mess she had made.

"Oh my gosh," she said. "This little boy held that snake in front of me and I thought it was real." Marilyn kept laughing as she knelt to pick up the underwear. "He needs to know how much it costs."

The lady in the blue smock frowned at me. "It's 99 cents," she said. "You can pay up front."

I sheepishly walked to the front of the store, grabbing a pack of 1963 baseball cards for 10 cents along the way. These two items would be Paul's presents. Stationed at the cash register was a lady with the name tag of Olga. She was a large lady with a commanding voice.

"Oh, you gave Marilyn quite a scare there, young man," Olga said. "I remember when my Bruce brought home a real snake. Now that was a fright. With tax, that's $1.13."

I pushed four quarters, a dime and three pennies toward her. The till opened, *cha-ching*, and she deposited each coin in the appropriate cup and then closed the drawer.

"Have you been to any Speedboys basketball games?" Olga asked. "My Bruce is in the starting lineup."

She was obviously the mother of Bruce Richardson.

I nodded politely and then walked to the front door. Ward Sliva held the door. "Be sure you come back to help keep me in business," he said with a laugh, not knowing the commotion I had caused in Aisle 5.

CHAPTER 7

Making the Wrong Kind of History

The Bonk era had opened with a thud, losing three straight games.

In the opener, the Ontonagon Polar Bears dismantled the Speedboys 56-33. All twelve Speedboys saw action during the first game of the season as the new coach searched for some kind of spark. Mark Martini and Gary Niemi never found their shot. Nemacheck fouled out in the fourth quarter. Bill Ryan's 12 points were the only bright spot during a forgetful evening of basketball in which the Speedboys were outplayed, outshot, and clearly outcoached.

WJMS radio was playing in our kitchen as my mother was preparing to serve breakfast. "Dominique" by The Singing Nun had just finished and the sports announcer started to talk. Mom reached over and turned up the volume.

"*We have Bessemer Coach John Bonk on Coaches Corner this morning,*" WJMS's Bob Olson announced. "*Coach, your team is now 0-3. You lost the non-conference opener and then two losses to the Ashland Oredockers and Hurley Midgets. Both conference losses. Tonight, you continue in league play at home with the high-flying Wakefield Cardinals. What do you expect tonight, Coach?*"

"*Well, all I can say is I hope we do better tonight. We played the Ashland and Hurley teams tough in the first half of each game, but then we faded in the second half. We must get better at shooting. We're only scoring 35 points a game and our opponents are scoring over 60. You can't win that way.*"

"*Are you planning any lineup changes?*"

"*No. Nemacheck, Niemi, Ryan, Martini and Richardson will start again.*"

The smell of burning toast got mom's attention. She leaped towards the toaster and pulled the plug, then proceeded to spread peanut butter and jelly over the blackened bread.

"Mom, can I borrow 40 cents to go to the game tonight?" I asked.

"You can use your allowance money," she replied.

"That's only 25 cents," I reminded her.

"Ask your dad."

Dad was sitting at the table dunking his toast in his creamy coffee. He gave no indication that he heard the conversation or would hand over 15 cents.

"Dad, can I have 15 cents to go the game tonight?" I asked. "I'll use it to get a pop or popcorn. I got my ticket money."

He looked up and gave a huff. His cheeks puffed out as he blew. He leaned back in his chair, reached deep in his pocket, and pulled out a handful of change. He poked and picked at the coins in his palm until he found a dime, which he handed to me. Then a nickel. Never said a word. Just business.

My Dad was not a mean person. Actually, he was beloved by his friends, neighbors and co-workers. They told us often how blessed we were to have him as our father. He was very strict, especially with us boys, and you couldn't help but wonder why he often was moody or less talkative.

My brother John surmised that it had to do with Dad's loss of his own father at a young age. Our grandfather, Pietro, was an Italian immigrant. Spoke little of the English language. And got sick from working in the Tilden ore mine.

When Dad was twelve years old his father was placed in the Grand View Hospital for treatment of tuberculosis. He would be separated from his family for the next five years. Even when my grandmother was allowed to visit her husband in the hospital, my dad and his brother and sister had to sit outside, unable to see their father. Complete isolation. Dad, from age 12 to 17, had to be the man of the house.

"Dad's childhood was cut short," John explained. "Both he and Uncle Bruno had to find work and tend to their garden so their family could eat. He had to stop being a kid. There was no time for goofing off. All Dad knew growing up was hard work. That's why he's tough on us."

Our grandfather died in 1946 when Dad was a junior in high school. I couldn't imagine losing my father at such a young age, nor did I want to find out.

The Wakefield Cardinals fans traveled well. They followed their team to gymnasiums across the Gogebic-Iron Range. When they came to Bessemer, the two towns being less than six miles apart, they packed the gym.

The Speedboys B team won the junior varsity game. A ragged and poorly played affair, the game was the second win for new junior varsity coach Carl Gregas. Greg Hill scored 18 of Bessemer's 34 points in this preliminary game. Hill had real potential to get some playing time on the varsity team later this season. The win was a great beginning to the night for the hometown fans.

But there would be no happy ending.

The Wakefield Cardinals dismantled the Speedboys A team, 81-37. Coach Jim Daniels of the Wakefield Cardinals tried not to run up the score against the hapless Speedboys. He emptied his bench with just three minutes gone in the *third* quarter. Even against the Cardinals reserves, the Speedboys struggled to get the ball across midcourt. They scored just four baskets in the entire second half. Four! That matched the number of losses in the season too.

The *Ironwood Daily Globe* would write the next day that the 44-point margin of defeat eclipsed the 34-point loss to the Hurley Midgets on December 8, 1961. The worst defeat ever for Bessemer. The Speedboys had begun to make the wrong kind of history.

CHAPTER 8

Santa Claus is Coming to Town

"When darkness closed in last night, Bessemer residents were startled by the appearance of a giant lighted Christmas tree, surmounted by a beckoning star, which appeared to rise from the atmosphere, against the darkened sky." (Ironwood Daily Globe –1959)

B essemer Mayor Elmer Sandin suggested at a September 1959 city council meeting that the city consider creating a lighted Christmas tree and a cascading waterfall at the crest of the first bluff as a tourist attraction. One month later, the council voted to move forward with plans to mount an artificial Christmas tree on bluff number one overlooking the town. The waterfall idea didn't make it out of committee. The Christmas tree on the bluff was first lit on November 19, 1959. The tree has been lit every Christmas since.

The 1963 Christmas decorations were installed in downtown Bessemer on Friday November 29. It was an unwritten rule that decorations could not adorn the streets until after Thanksgiving Day. Reindeer, stars and Santa Claus figures were attached to the light poles along the main street. Garland was wrapped around the poles from top to bottom. The downtown area would be festive for the next four weeks.

The Bessemer Chamber of Commerce announced that it had received a message from the North Pole that Santa Claus was coming to town on Saturday, December 7. Santa would parade through this quaint village and arrive at the City Hall at 10:00 a.m., where he would meet with local children and hand out candy. Santa's annual appearance was one of the few organized events for children held each year in Bessemer. The other was the 4th of July children's races and parade each summer.

Our buddy, Denny Kontny, told us that his father oversaw the Santa Claus event. His father, Frank, could easily be Santa Claus. Short. Round belly. At times rosy cheeks. All he needed was a white beard. But Denny dispelled that rumor.

"He's not playing Santa Claus, but he does decide what to do with the extra bags of candy," Denny said with a sly smile.

Denny was as good a friend as we could ask for. He was like an extra brother. If he wasn't at our house, we were at his house. He had two older sisters and no brothers, so naturally he wanted to hang out with us. Plus, he had all the latest toys, gadgets and music. His family even had a color television, which was a luxury for most families in Bessemer. It was more fun playing at his house.

Denny, along with me and three of my brothers, arrived at City Hall half an hour before Santa was to appear. We left the youngest brother, Peter, at home. At age two, he would not last long in line before a full melt down.

It was warm for a December morning, about 20 degrees with light snow falling. The line of kids stretched from the police entrance all the way to the backside of the Last East Inn. Jim Rooni and Jeff Pricco got in line behind us. Then Tommy Maccani, another school buddy, came running up and joined the line.

"Pel, did you go to the game last night?" Pricco asked. "A total stinker for Bessemer, hey? How many losses is that in a row now, four?"

Before I could reply, Rooni answered.

"It's five in a row," he said, "if you count the game they lost last year in the tournament. One plus four is five."

"Yeah, I was there," I said. "It was terrible. If not for Bruce Richardson it could have been worse."

"Worse?" Rooni said. "Didn't you listen to WJMS this morning? It was the worst loss in school history!"

Suddenly, we heard bells jingling in the distance. It was Santa Claus coming up the street. He was standing in the back of a rusty red pick-up truck.

"Hi, boys and girls!" Santa Claus yelled through the police bull-horn he was holding. "Merry Christmas! M-e-r-r-y Christmas!"

"Who is playing Santa?" John asked.

"It's my uncle," Maccani yelled over the excited voices of the children. "Val Maccani. You know, from Val's Bar."

The line finally started to move. We were all excited as we entered the City Hall through the police station door. An officer sitting at the desk smiled and gave us a piece of hard candy. We turned left by the library and walked down the long hall to the Memorial Auditorium, where Santa was sitting in front of the stage.

One little kid after another stood next to Santa Claus.

"What do you want for Christmas?" Santa would ask.

Most kids were too scared to reply. When they did answer, they were usually wishing for G.I. Joes, toy soldiers, Barbies, or Easy-Bake Ovens.

When it was my turn, I walked up to Santa with my four-year-old brother Gerry in tow. But the little guy pulled away, laid on the floor, and refused to engage with St. Nick.

"What do you want for Christmas, young man?" Santa said, turning to me.

"Aw, I don't know," I said. "Maybe a Super Ball?"

According to one of my classmates, the Super Ball was made of synthetic rubber that was compressed so tightly that when you threw it hard at the ground, it would bounce one hundred feet in the air. When it finally came down it would hit the ground and bounce again seventy-five feet in the air. It was a true marvel to boys my age.

"Well, let me see if my elves can make that Super Ball," Santa replied.

He handed me a mesh bag that was shaped like a Christmas stocking, stuffed with miniature Hershey bars, suckers and other hard candies. It was the same type of stocking we got the year before and the year before that. Hopefully, the candies weren't from years past.

Little Gerry finally settled down and got up off the ground. I gave him his candy-filled stocking, and he smiled like he does on Christmas morning when he first sees his presents.

CHAPTER 9

Bennetts' Hill

At 5 a.m., a flashing light lit my parents' bedroom window, waking Mom.

The light came from a large yellow Caterpillar grader driven by Big Dave Brach. He was plowing Beecher Street of 12 inches of new snow that had fallen overnight.

Big Dave lived just two houses up the hill from us. He stored the county's plow in his long driveway, so we were always the first street in town to be cleared. Unfortunately, that meant we were also the first to get out of bed to shovel.

"Boys, get up," Mom whispered. "The plow just went by. You need to get the driveway cleared before school."

The new foot of snow meant Bessemer had over forty inches for the season. It was only mid-December. There would be plenty of shoveling in our future, but the one silver lining was that sledding season had just begun.

Each November the city announced which streets would be closed to traffic so that children could sled. The designated street had to have a reasonable incline with at least two blocks of safe sledding.

In the winter of 1963-64, the city council authorized Yale Street, Iron Street, Mine Street, and Beecher Street for use as children's sledding hills. There were other streets that were unofficial, but authorized streets had orange wooden barricades, called horses, at the ends of the streets to block through traffic.

Our family was fortunate. We had a great view from our front window of the two-block stretch of Beecher Street, closed between Sellar and Mary Streets. We called this Bennetts' Hill because the sledding began next to Beanie Bennetts' family home. It was across the street from our house. Beanie's son, Pat, was one of my heroes. He was an all-conference athlete in football and baseball, and now a member of the Speedboys basketball team.

When Big Dave Brach drew his blade on the grader, he skimmed the surface to a fine honed ice sheet. No sand or salt was allowed on the hill. Once word got out that the plow had cleared the snow from Bennetts' Hill and the orange horse was in place, the neighborhood kids started to appear. In winter, it was *the* place to be. More than 100 kids from the neighborhood, ages 3 to 18, used Bennetts' Hill as their main sledding hill. Kids with nicknames like Bugsy, Toombo, Little Joe and Odie would pull their sled for blocks just to spend a day of zooming down the hill.

On Saturdays, we dressed for an entire day of sledding. Getting dressed was a chore in and of itself. First, we put on wool plaid snow pants with leather patches on the knees. Then came socks, then shoes, then heavy wool socks pulled over the shoes, then a bread bag over the socks to repel moisture, then rubber boots over the bread bags.

We tucked our pantlegs into our boots, which we then zipped or buckled to the very top. Next, we put on layers of sweatshirts or sweaters, followed by a jacket, a knit hat with tassel on top, and a wool scarf, which our mother tied over our mouths.

Lastly, we put on mittens, which we covered with a pair of leather mittens, known as choppers. In the end we were so stiff we could hardly move, but we were outfitted for the elements.

Once on Bennetts' Hill, we joined the other boys and girls at the top, holding our various vessels: sleds, gliders, wooden toboggans, metal saucers and the occasional contraption built by an ingenious father. The classic was the *Flexible Flyer* steel runner sled with a red arrow painted down the middle. You could achieve great speed and agile steering with a *Flyer*.

The kids who used saucers had little control and might spin in circles all the way down. If you didn't vomit by the end of the trip, you certainly were going to think twice about another ride on this trash can cover. Wooden toboggans didn't work well on Bennetts' Hill, but someone would always bring one along. After one failed ride, it was usually stuck in a snowbank for the rest of the day.

I had a wooden runner sled from Montgomery Wards. It looked like a *Flexible Flyer* but performed like, well, a sled from Monkey Wards. Good enough, but not a *Flyer*.

Every kid had a different approach to the sledding hill. Young kids mostly used the traditional *lay-head-forward-on-sled-and-use-your-hands-to-push-off-and-steer* technique. Older kids would take a running start and jump belly first onto the sled. Others would sit on the sled and steer with their feet.

My go-to sledding style was headfirst, steering with my hands. Elsewhere in my life, I was anxious and hesitant, but on Bennetts' Hill I was in full attack mode. Nothing felt better than cold air rushing around my face as I flew downhill on the sled, the tail of my long scarf blowing in the wind behind me.

I could hear the blades scraping the ice as I made calculated turns, never losing velocity as I sped down the hill. It was a freeing experience for me, a daring escapade that I planned and executed from start to finish. On most sledding days, and on most sledding runs, I felt ten feet tall. That is, until I got ditched.

Ditching or tipping another kid off his sled was a ritual of the winter sledding season. If it had been a sanctioned sport in the 1964 Winter Olympics, a kid nicknamed Skeeter would have been the gold medalist. Skeeter could ditch even the most seasoned sledders. He had the best sled, with blades so sharp that even the corner butcher asked him for sharpening tips. His house was halfway down Bennetts' Hill. When he wasn't hunting or trapping in the nearby woods, he was spending countless hours building snow tunnels and forts with secret hatches from which he and his fellow ditchers would surprise unsuspecting sledders.

One moment I was gliding down the hill, then suddenly Skeeter would appear. He'd laugh as he sped past, the blades of his sled spraying ice in my face. One hand steering his sled, the other gripping the back loop of my sled's runner. A quick flick of his wrist and I was flipped, ditched, twirling on my back like an inverted turtle on its shell.

Ditching could have ruined sledding for an anxious kid like me, but fortunately my buddies and I learned to make a game of it. We would try to outsmart Skeeter or outrun him. We would keep track of how many days or how many runs it had been since the last ditching. For us, the challenge of not getting flipped by the world's greatest ditcher only made sledding on Bennetts' Hill that much more intriguing.

Let the winter fun begin.

CHAPTER 10

Coach John Bonk towered over all his players except Bill Nemacheck. Bonk had a deep voice and it commanded respect whenever he spoke. He never used it in anger to get his point across to his cagers. He had a jovial laugh and an easy-going personality that disarmed the people around him.

As the boys took their seats on the bus for the longest road trip of the year to Maple, Wisconsin, Bonk got the attention of his players with a single sharp whistle.

"Listen up, men," Bonk said. "As I told you at the start of this week of practice, our fundamentals are weak. We've worked hard on our passing and shooting. But we've got to get the ball across the half court stripe in ten seconds. Three passes when a team presses. Guards can dribble up with no passes when the opponent sits back."

The team nodded in agreement.

"Now Mark and Bill," Bonk continued, "you've got to pass the ball inside to your teammates. Don't come across that timeline and just drive to the basket. We've got to pass, pass, pass and then shoot. We need good looks at the basket."

The boys all nodded again.

Their opponent, the Maple Tigers, were not particularly competitive in basketball, yet they had more than enough talent to beat the Bessemer Speedboys this season.

The bus trip to Maple was long, cold and boring. The only excitement on this day was when the team passed the Marine Club in Ashland.

"Coach, can we stop at the Marine Club on the way back from the game?" a player asked.

Coach Bonk was very familiar with this restaurant as he grew up in nearby Grand View, Wisconsin.

"Tell you what," Bonk said. "If you boys win tonight, we'll stop on the way back."

The team cheered. They had something to look forward to. All they had to do was win the game.

At approximately 11:00 p.m. the yellow school bus, with its windows frosted over and a sleepy basketball team on board, quietly motored past The Marine Club. There would be no stopping.

The Bessemer boys had gone to the charity stripe twenty-two times in the game and made just four free throws. The Tigers won the game easily, 50-40. Bonk was now 0-5 as a head coach.

The only player who was wide awake on the bus was the team's leading scorer, Mark Martini. He had 13 points tonight. He passed a little and shot a lot.

Martini was intently talking to coach Bonk in the front of the bus. Martini explained how difficult it was at times to be the son of a mine supervisor when many of his classmates were the sons of miners. Bonk let Martini vent and the coach set his own issues aside.

"When my father, Arthur, was reassigned to the mining supervisor job in Bessemer," Martini told Bonk, "I asked him if I could stay in Stambaugh to go to school."

"Why, Mark?" asked Bonk.

Martini took a moment to reply.

"Because wherever my father goes the mines close. I wanted no part of that."

CHAPTER 11

Kick-A-Boots

My mother was a good household money manager. She, like many mothers in Bessemer, used an "envelope system" to manage the family finances. On payday, Mom would allocate cash for different expenses by dividing it into envelopes marked with the business name and due date, then store the envelopes in her sock drawer. On the due date, she sent her oldest sons to make the payments.

Abelman's Department Store was located at the corner of Sellar and Sophie, anchoring the downtown shopping district to the south. The store was bursting with merchandise from floor to ceiling.

With four kids in school, the back-to-school shoe purchases were more than my parents could handle in one lump sum. Abelman's allowed customers to purchase shoes on credit. If shoes cost $8 a pair, you could pay a couple of bucks a month with no extra fees. At least that's what I heard my mom tell Aunt Rosie.

One Saturday, Mom sent me to Abelman's with $2 to pay on her account.

"Ask for Blanche," she said. "And take your brother Paul with you."

The Abelman's front door handle was hard to squeeze open, but if you used two hands you could do it. Inside, it felt like a store from the turn of the 20th century. Its wood floors were unfinished and on the dark walls hung pictures of ancient members of the Abelman family. Dim lighting made it difficult to determine if the t-shirt you had your eye on was blue or dark green. But no one complained.

Various Abelman family members were scattered about the store, each handling their section. Joe, Alice, Frank and Clara

Abelman all knew where to be and what to do. Sometimes Joe's son Bobby, who played on the basketball team, would be wandering about, but not on this day.

As we approached the front counter, Blanche called out to us.

"Pelissero boys," she said. "Oh, I'm glad you are here. I need your help."

She motioned for us to sit in two of the six chairs lined up in the shoe area.

"My nephews are coming to town," Blanche said. "I want to buy them some new winter boots so they can play outside. They are about your age, so I should get close on the size after you try these on."

Blanche brought two identical boxes from the back room. When she opened a box and pulled back the tissue paper, I was sure she had grabbed the wrong item. What was presented to us were black winter boots. Girl's boots.

These boots didn't go over your shoes like the galoshes we wore. I saw this type of boot every morning at school. When the girls arrived for the start of the day, the ritual was the same. The girls would kick off their boots and put on shoes for the school day. Then reverse that process at the end of the day.

The girls called them kick-a-boots.

Blanche slipped the boots on our feet and had us walk around.

"Well, what do you think?" she asked. "Do they slip in the back?"

Paul and I had been taught to be polite.

"Ah, yeah, might need to wear a heavy sock," I said.

Paul just nodded his head in agreement. Not saying a word.

"Do you think my nephews will like these boots?" she continued.

"Ah, sure," I said.

"Well, thank you, boys," Blanche replied. "You've been a big help. These boots will be waiting under the Christmas tree for my nephews."

We smiled back, then kicked off the boots as fast as we could and put our shoes and rubber boots back on.

"Oh, Blanche, we have $2.00 to put on our mom's account," I said.

I reached into my corduroy pants pocket and pulled out the money, promptly dropping it on the floor.

As I picked up the coins, Blanche saw Joe Abelman walking by and asked him to take care of the payment. Joe just nodded and walked us over to the checkout counter where he pulled out this long gray book. He peered through his reading glasses as he ran his big finger down the left side of the book. When he saw our family name, he picked up a pencil and carefully entered the $2.00 payment. He handed me a paper receipt and asked that it be brought to my parents. No smile, just business.

Paul and I quietly walked out of Ableman's and turned towards home. We hadn't taken ten steps when we both burst into laughter.

"Oh my god, did you see those boots?" I screamed.

"Can you imagine the look on their faces when they open those presents on Christmas morning?" Paul cried.

"Kick-a-Boots for Christmas," I shouted. "A boy's worst Christmas present of all time!"

"Glad we could help," Paul said with a chuckle.

Chapter 12

Oh, Christmas Tree

At this time of year, Bessemer families participated in the long-cherished tradition of decorating their home for the holidays. It was hard to beat the lighted Christmas tree upon the bluff or Duray's television tower all aglow with colored lights strung some hundred feet in the air near Highway 2. But the Bessemer residents were up to the challenge and did some of their finest decorating in December.

A family could buy a 6-foot Christmas tree for $2.00. You didn't know when the seller had cut the tree, but it was green and full and beautiful the moment you placed it in your home. All across town, you would see window after window proudly displaying a trimmed and adorned Christmas tree to signal their home was full of good cheer.

Some trees used colored lights; others used white lights. Some sprayed imitation snow on the tree and others bought an artificial Christmas tree that they would display year after year.

We decorated for Christmas on December 15 and not a day earlier. Mom said that's the day you do it. It must have made sense to her, but we were always puzzled by the timing, as other families began putting up their trees the day after Thanksgiving.

This year our father bought a classic balsam fir tree. Dad placed it in a red and green tree stand and tightened the screws around the trunk. He put an eye hook on the wall and attached a wire to secure the tree and prevent it from falling. Mom poured a pitcher of water into the stand to keep the tree fresh.

"I'll be sweeping up needles for the next two weeks," she would say.

Each year, we decorated the tree with the same ornaments that we had used the season before. There was a string of lights with large multi-color bulbs that were very hot to the touch. We had to keep little brother Pete away from the tree to prevent a burn.

Red, white, blue and gold ornaments were hooked carefully upon the tree branches with never the same two colors together. A few ceramic ornaments were placed on tree hooks and then double wound so they wouldn't fall to the floor. Then came the tinsel. The 10-year-old tinsel. The sparkle was gone, but Mom saved 99 cents by having us pluck the long silver strands each year before the tree was tossed out in the yard the day after New Year's.

The final decoration was the tree topper, a simple shiny star with three lights on it, none of which worked. Dad had given up on trying to fix it, and Mom refused to buy a new one, but it was tradition to let it adorn the top of the tree. It nearly touched the ceiling. We thought it was the finest tree on this side of Lake Superior.

Since 1886, the Catholics in Bessemer attended midnight mass on Christmas Eve at St. Sebastian Church. From the tall stained-glass windows to the murals on the ceiling, there was much to admire within the church.

Parishioners marveled most at the manger scene on the east side of the church. It was a large, hand-carved and painted scene depicting the little town of Bethlehem in the background and a road leading out of town to a peaceful manger. A gathering of sheep with a single donkey was placed along a steep path to the stable. The Blessed Virgin Mary and St. Joseph knelt over the manger that held the baby Jesus. Christmas lights in red and green and blue were draped along the entire scene. The colors eerily dark over the town but warm and inviting in the stable itself.

The creche had been created by a janitor at the old St. Sebastian School. Few knew him by his formal last name; anyone who attended the old school knew him as "Joe the Janitor."

Joe lived in the basement of the old school, or at least that's what the students thought since he was always there. They saw him when they went to the basement to use the restrooms. He was usually fixing the head of a mop or a broom. They would say hello as they passed by, and Joe would nod his head, but seldom said a word.

Joe the Janitor was once a wood carver in central Europe before immigrating to the U.S. After serving in both World Wars, he must have decided that being a janitor in the creaky old building was all the excitement he needed.

The parishioners were enamored with his fine artwork and craftsmanship, and many asked if he would create a creche for their family. Joe would always politely decline. Over the years, rumors spread that Joe had created more creches, but most people believed they were cheap imitations made by a lesser artist. After all, there was only one true creche in Bessemer, and it was Joe the Janitor's masterpiece on display each Christmas season at St. Sebastian Church.

When midnight mass concluded, families drove up Main Street toward city hall. Reindeer with red noses, Santas, and snowmen were illuminated and hanging from each lamp post along the downtown stretch of this Upper Peninsula town. Snowflakes fell in the light of a December moon. It was Christmas in Bessemer.

On Christmas morning, children all across town woke their parents early, eagerly hoping Santa had brought their desired toy. Our family shared the same excitement. By 6:00 a.m., brother Paul snuck downstairs on a reconnaissance mission, then reported back to the rest of us. A new red farm tractor for Gerry and a new two-person sled for all of us. There were also two small boxes and one large box for each boy. We appreciated the detailed information provided by Paul.

We sat at the top of the steps waiting for Dad to get out of the bathroom and lead us downstairs. Mom had gone to the kitchen to get the coffee percolating.

When Dad led us into the living room, we were greeted with a neat pile of gift-wrapped presents beneath the tree. It was the most wonderful sight each Christmas.

There was no order as to who opened what and when. The only rule was you opened the little presents first and the largest one last.

"Santa couldn't wrap the sled," Mom said. "But it's for you four older boys. Tommy, you can take Gerry on it this afternoon."

Christmas Day, and I already had my first assignment.

Inside most of the gift boxes were pajamas, long underwear, mittens, or other practical gifts. Mom always bought us what we needed, and she didn't disappoint this year either.

John opened a present from Santa: a Vac-U-Form, which was basically a hot plate with molds a kid could use to make plastic trucks, boats, and fake noses.

Paul got a toy gun that shot rubber bands at a target. Likely, he would shoot at his brothers.

I got a basketball board game with spring loaded levers that sent a ping-pong ball through a basketball hoop. It was called *Bas-ket*.

While Peter crawled into empty boxes, and Gerry tried to ride his new farm tractor, John, Paul and I moved to the large boxes still under the tree.

"Who's going to go first?" Mom asked.

"John," I said.

John slowly opened his large present. It was a pair of after-ski boots: ankle-height, lined boots with a zipper in the front, the perfect footwear to put on after a long day on the slopes. They looked exotic and well-made, maybe from Switzerland or Austria or somewhere. But more likely from Montgomery Wards. We were quite impressed. John would be styling in the ski chalet. He smiled and thanked our parents. Dad didn't hear him as he was busy cutting cardboard boxes with a razor blade.

Mom turned to Paul and me.

"You can open your boxes at the same time," she said.

With great anticipation, Paul and I tore off the wrapping paper in unison. I so hoped it was the Celtics basketball jersey I had requested, and Paul was certain his box contained a matching jersey.

When we pulled off the cover of the boxes, the blood drained from our faces. We could not believe what we were seeing.

It couldn't be.

It just couldn't be.

Kick-a-boots.

In stunned silence, we looked down at the very boots we had tried on at Abelman's for Blanche's nephews. "You didn't know I was playing a trick on you when I asked Blanche to have you try on the boots for her nephews, did you?" Mom said. "Are you surprised?"

"Surprised?" I gasped. "I have never been more surprised in my life."

CHAPTER 13

St. Sebastian Boys

An early memory is of our father walking with us along Sellar Street, holding my brother John's hand with his right and mine with his left. It was 1961, and he was taking us to our first St. Sebastian Knights basketball game at nearby Washington School. Our team would be playing St. Anthony's of Pence.

The Knights were working up quite a sweat running up and down the court in their blue and white uniforms. The skill these boys exhibited was riveting. They could dribble and shoot with such ease and speed. Quickly, our Knights led the Pence team 10-0.

John and I sat upon wooden bleachers next to Dad, who yelled encouragement and direction to each player for the St. Sebastian Knights. Gary Niemi, Bill Ryan, Bruce Richardson, Robert Re, and William Jacobson were on the court. Even our cousin Donny Barbacovi was dressed in uniform and ready to check into the game if his number was called.

Our dad made my brother and me believe we could play for St. Sebastian someday, just like these boys. He said he would work with us on dribbling and passing. He would find a basket that was lower than ten feet so we could learn to shoot. Maybe put up a hoop in the basement at home. The more he talked, the more animated he became. Yet, the real joy was just sitting with him at the game and having a conversation, one that seldom occurred at home.

Bill Ryan, Bruce Richardson and Gary Niemi were my favorite players. I was sure there were none better. The St. Sebastian Knights were winning big, and these three players were the big stars.

Dad leaned over to me and told me to watch Ryan closely.

"Notice how he dribbles the ball low to prevent it from being stolen," Dad said. "Bill's eyes always looking at the opposing player and not the ball. He has a real feel for the game. You can't teach that. See how he drives hard toward the basket and then suddenly pulls up for his jump shot. It's hard to guard a player like that."

It was like that all afternoon. Watching the game. Getting insight from dad. Hoping the day wouldn't end.

The Knights played in the Parochial Grade School Conference and faced other Catholic schools. I learned to loathe those other schools. They were the enemy. The teams you wanted to beat. The St. Mary's Saints were right at the top of the list, but St. Agnas and Holy Family schools in Ashland were a close second. The Knights played St. Ambrose in Ironwood too.

Though the St. Sebastian Knights played in the Parochial Conference, some of their toughest games and losses came at the hands of local public schools, like Erwin, Roosevelt and Ramsay. Dad said the stiffer competition made the Knights better in conference play.

"You learn a lot from losing because you never want that feeling again," Dad said.

The St. Sebastian Knights were coached in 1961 by Mike DeStasio, Jr and James Chiomento. They played at Washington School because St. Sebastian didn't have a gymnasium of their own. But the church had plans for one.

The Bessemer School Board agreed to allow St. Sebastian to use the gym under certain circumstances. The team could practice on Saturday mornings and play their games there on Sunday afternoons.

St. Sebastian did not have the permission to use the electric scoreboard. To compensate for the lack of a clock and scoreboard, the Holy Name Society of St. Sebastian built a manual scoreboard and bought a stopwatch to use at each game.

The scoreboard was placed on the stage. It read HOME and VISITORS, with two sets of numbers from zero to nine under each side. Two grade-school boys with strong arithmetic skills were assigned to sit on each side of the board. When a team scored, one of the boys would move the cloth numbers along the metal rings to match the current score on the floor. When the action was fast, the scorekeepers sometimes couldn't keep up. If the basket was disallowed, then it got interesting as the boys tried to subtract versus add.

The timekeeper had just a stopwatch. On and off with the action, but there was nothing a player could look at to determine how much time was left in the quarter. When the quarter ran out, the timekeeper would blow a whistle to end the action. It was a bit rudimentary, but the players and fans didn't really care. It was part of the game experience.

The Washington School gym was a cracker box. Under the west basket, a stage thrust towards the court. To take the ball out of bounds, a player had to get up on his tip toes with his heels curled against the stage to toss it in without a fault. They attached an exercise mat to the front of the stage to protect the players who might crash into it.

St. Sebastian had cheerleaders too. Like the boys, they shared their uniforms year after year with the next group of girls. Good wool sweaters never go bad, unless the moths or mice find them hanging in an accessible place in the janitor's closet.

The cheerleader's turtleneck sweater was adorned with a big blue S across the front, and the ensemble was completed with a long blue corduroy skirt and white Keds. The girls cheered during breaks in the game. The fight song echoed off the walls.

"St. Sebastian boys are quite complete.

They're 100 percent from head to feet.

They got a smile and a style that can't be beat.

St. Sebastian Boys!"

The Knights won that first game John and I attended, 42-10. I figured they would win all their games. When the season ended in 1961, the St. Sebastian Knights had tied the St. Mary Saints for the Conference Championship with 7-1 records. The teams each took a share of the Father Francis Krysty Trophy that was given to the Conference Champs. As there was only one trophy, the league agreed to allow the St. Sebastian boys to put the hardware in their trophy case that year. It sparkled just like that team.

CHAPTER 14

On The Cover

The Christmas break from school was never long enough. I pushed off the assigned school project until the last day of vacation. With time running out I got busy working on my scrapbook, *Michigan's Winter Wonderland*.

My dad liked to read *Newsweek* and *Look* magazines before going to sleep each night, so he kept a stack under his nightstand. He always read the whole magazine, a little each night. He was so far behind in his reading that Eisenhower was still President.

I dug deep through his magazine pile looking for pictures of children sledding, skiing or skating to put into my scrapbook. I didn't find much to use, except for winter images in ads for cigarettes. One ad for a cigarette company had two people on the ski slopes, a girl that had fallen and a man standing over her lighting up his cigarette. Apparently, before helping a damsel in distress, you light up. I liked it, so I cut it out.

In other magazines, I found action-packed winter activities worthy of the scrapbook. One by one, I cut and glued images to my pages. I labeled each scene with my best cursive. In all, I had eight pages of pictures depicting sledding, snowball fights, igloo living, skating on an open pond, and skiing with a cigarette. The only thing missing from this work of art was the picture for the cover.

I told my mom I had no idea what to use because all the best pictures had been used up already. Mom put her hand to her chin and thought for a minute.

"Wait, I know of something you can use," she said. "I just got an extra calendar and it had a great picture in the month of November. It's upstairs."

Mom sprinted up the stairs. She retrieved the calendar from her dresser and rolled each month over on its spiral spine until she got to November.

"Yes, here it is," Mom said.

It was a beautiful picture of a 12-point buck standing majestically among pine trees with the sun glistening off the deep snow. This was the kind of buck my dad always told me he was hunting each deer season.

"Perfect!" I said. "I'll cut and paste it to my scrapbook cover right now."

"Not now," Mom said. "We have supper ready. Your dad has an Elks Lodge event tonight."

I placed the spiral calendar inside our school desk. Well, it wasn't a real school desk. It was an old television that dad had converted to a school desk. The desktop was a scrap of plywood cut to size, sanded and stained. It worked quite well and didn't cost a dime. Gone was the picture tube, speakers and dials, leaving a space underneath for storage or your feet while doing homework. I placed the calendar in the large storage area.

Supper was always prompt due to my dad's diabetes regimen. Mom helped him manage his insulin needs by having meals at exactly 11:45 a.m. and 5:00 p.m. Everyone else would've called those meals lunch and dinner, but in our house, it was always "dinner" at 11:45 and "supper" at 5:00.

After our supper, it was my turn to wash the dishes and my brother Paul's turn to dry. I'm not sure which was worse: scouring grease from pans or having to dry dishes with a wet towel. As we washed and wiped the last of the dishes and put them away, Dad was in the bathroom upstairs shaving and slapping on some Old Spice. My brother John was up there too, watching our two-year-old brother Peter. Or so we thought.

"Pete, don't move," John screamed. "Don't move! Dad! Dad!"

We heard the bathroom door open like it was ripped off its hinges. Dad's footsteps thudded fast and hard on the floor above us.

"Hold still, Pete," Dad yelled. "Hold still."

Paul and I ran up the steps.

There in the hallway, we saw Dad trying to remove a wire from the corner of Pete's eye.

"I got this, Pete," Dad said calmly, "you'll be ok buddy. Hold still."

Dad gently and successfully pulled the wire from Pete's eye socket. The wire was the end of the spiral binding used on the calendar I had placed in the bottom of the school desk before supper. I unwittingly put the calendar in a place where my little brother could reach it. Somehow, he got the wire caught in the corner of his eye.

After removing the wire from Pete's eye, Dad grabbed the spiral calendar, tore it in pieces and threw it into the garbage. He was huffing and puffing, trying to calm down and catch his breath. He walked back into the bathroom and slammed the door.

My mother was in the basement drying a last load of clothes for the night. When she walked upstairs with a basket of clean clothes to fold, she saw John cradling Pete.

"Why is Peter crying?" she asked.

John explained what had just happened. Mom dropped the basket and covered her mouth with her hand. She pulled Pete into her arms, reassuring him that he was fine, and everything was going to be okay. Mom sat and rocked him until he fell asleep.

"What about my scrapbook cover?" I whispered to mom. "Dad tore it up."

She told me not to worry she would figure it out.

CHAPTER 15

Michigan's Winter Wonderland?

*T*he *Bessemer Herald* reported that the area had been invaded by skiers during the Christmas and New Year holidays. The main draw was Indianhead Mountain, the ski hill between Bessemer and Wakefield. *"All housing facilities on the Gogebic Range were filled to capacity,"* they wrote. My uncle Bruno quipped, "Just like Bethlehem, there was no room at the inn."

"Get going, mister," Mom said.

It was the first day of school after the long Christmas vacation.

"Mom, what about my scrapbook project?" I asked.

"It's in the brown paper bag," she said. "I found a picture for the cover and glued it on. You're all set. Get going or you'll be late."

The school bell rang and we all sat up straight in our desks.

"Good morning, children," said Mrs. Vispi. "I hope you had a wonderful holiday season and did many fun things."

Mrs. Vispi was quite proper in the way she spoke. Polite. Thoughtful. Even though she was an adult, she was someone I could easily approach to ask a question.

"As you know," she said, "today your scrapbook project *Michigan's Winter Wonderland* is due."

There were noticeable gasps in the classroom. A few forgot to bring their project to school today. Others had not even cut and glued a single picture into their scrapbook since it had been assigned a month ago.

I, on the other hand, was totally at ease. My project was secure in the paper bag beneath my desk. While others were anxious, I was relaxed.

"Mrs. Vispi," Debbie Vargovich asked meekly as she raised her hand. "Yes, Deborah?"

"I forgot mine at home," Debbie said. "Can I go home and get it at lunch?"

"Certainly," replied Mrs. Vispi. "Just present it to Mrs. Carpenedo."

Debbie smiled after getting her reprieve. Jean Maki, her friend, poked her in the back and whispered. "I called you last night and told you not to forget to bring your scrapbook."

Debbie giggled and nodded in agreement.

"Children, let's pass your *Michigan's Winter Wonderland* scrapbooks forward," said Mrs. Vispi. "I hope you had fun assembling this project."

Yes, I did. Except for the photo my father tore into a hundred pieces, I found this project enjoyable and easy to complete. Thankfully my mother came to my rescue and found a picture to grace the cover. I felt certain my project was worthy of an A+. Clearly my teacher would see my deep research on the winter scenes in Michigan and note how carefully I had cut and pasted the pictures.

I reached down and pulled the tape off the paper bag. As I removed the scrapbook from the bag, I suddenly could not breathe.

There, in full color, on the cover of my meticulously crafted scrapbook, my mother had pasted a picture of the Arizona desert. In the foreground stood a large saguaro cactus. The sun was setting on red mountains in the background. The desert sand glowed. Beneath the picture were the words *Michigan's Winter Wonderland by Tom Pelissero.*

As I handed it forward, my classmates began to smirk. They each raised their eyebrows, as if to say, "Are you sure this is your project?"

My classmates reminded me about my scrapbook cover all day.

"Hey, Tom, how many inches of snow did they get in Death Valley this year?" one classmate asked.

"Maybe your cover is a mirage because you've been walking in the desert without water," another joked. "Maybe if we look long enough, we'll see snow, too."

"Did they put Christmas decorations on that cactus this year?" another asked.

A kid learns early in life to grow thick skin. You make mistakes, and others remind you about those mistakes early and often. This was one of those moments. The way I coped, the way I made it through this tough day and many more after it, was to have something to look forward to at the end of day.

For me, that something was a Speedboys basketball game.

CHAPTER 16

Area basketball fans were witnessing the greatest competition in years in the Michigan-Wisconsin Conference. Ironwood, Wakefield, Superior East, and Ashland were all vying for the conference championship. Names like McCauley, Peck, Pakonen, Farrell, DeZur, Salmi, Ginolfi and others were lighting up the scoreboard in this talent-rich league. Veteran coaches like Jim Daniels of Wakefield and Gene Farrell of Ironwood were teaching rookie coaches, like Bessemer's John Bonk, a lesson or two.

Against the Ironwood Red Devils, the Speedboys' fiercest rival, they again had trouble getting the ball across half court. Ironwood's full court press caused turnover after turnover for the local lads.

Bill Ryan scored eleven points, but the Ironwood duo of Roland Pakonen and Craig Farrell, with 26 and 22 points respectively, had combined to outscore the entire Bessemer team in only three quarters. *The Bessemer Herald* newspaper headline read, "*Red Devils Maul Speedboys 82–44.*"

On the road against Superior East, the Speedboys scored a season high 51 points, but got drubbed 87-51. The boys also lost 71-43 to Ashland, a nearly identical score in their loss to this same team in November. The conference cellar was all theirs. The losing skid took a break on January 25 when their game against Iron River was postponed due to a winter storm, Mother Nature taking mercy on the Speedboys.

The Speedboys' overall record of 0-8 to start the season may have been a new low for a Bessemer basketball team, but no one was scouring the yearbooks to find out.

Despite never leaving happy, the Bessemer fans continued to pack the gym in support of the blue and gold. The bright spot for

Coach Bonk was that he had mostly juniors on the team. Martini, Neimi, Richardson, and Ryan all had another season ahead, and Bonk had some super sophomore talent in Milo Barnaby and Greg Hill that his assistant coach Carl Gregas was cultivating on the B squad. Bonk had been a winner his entire playing career. Surely next year he would make this team a winner.

There was a lot of basketball left to play on the schedule but not a sure win in sight. The team's best hope was tonight's game against Hurley. The Midgets were 2-5 in conference play. It was a winnable game if the Speedboys could just stop the Midgets' superstar, Dick DeZur.

Speedboys forward Gary Niemi was sitting in the locker room with a copy of the previous day's *Daily Globe* open to the sports page.

"Does it say we'll win, Gary?" asked Bill Ryan as he walked to his locker.

"No," Niemi replied. "As a matter of fact, the *Globe* has us playing Wakefield rather than Hurley."

"Well, they must be thinking ahead," Ryan replied.

"What's our game plan tonight against the Midgets?" Niemi asked.

"We need to share the ball," Ryan said.

Tension was not uncommon among teammates on any team. The Speedboys were a mix of 16-, 17- and 18-year-old boys. Each was highly competitive. Each, at times, felt he was wise beyond his years. Mark Martini and Bill Ryan were no different. Each wanted to win badly, though neither had tasted victory yet. Both guards wanted the ball in their hands, causing tension that would spill over onto the court.

Hurley's DeZur scored his first field goal immediately after the opening tip-off. A minute later he scored again. After that second basket, the ball bounced on the sidelines as guards Ryan and Martini looked at each other.

"Mark, take the ball out!" Ryan yelled.

"I'll get the next one," Martini replied.

As the referee started counting to five, a frustrated Ryan picked up the ball and threw it in play to Martini. Martini dribbled the length of the court, got a screen from Nemacheck and threw an underhanded layup that bounced off the rim. A Hurley player grabbed the rebound and threw a long outlet pass to his teammate Gordon Gimski, who laid it up and in.

Hurley now led 6-0.

Again, the ball just bounced along the end line. Ryan waited for Martini to pick it up and toss it in. Martini didn't budge. The referee counted to five, then blew his whistle for an inbounds violation on the Speedboys.

Ryan was fuming.

"Mark, you've got to take it out next time."

Martini shouted back, "My job is to bring it up the court and make a play."

"Knock it off," said teammate Bruce Richardson. "We're on the same team."

On the ensuing possession, Hurley's Robert Klosno hit a shot from the corner. As the ball went through the basket, Richardson batted it out of bounds and up the tunnel, hoping to buy some time for Ryan and Martini to decide who was throwing the ball in. The referee blew the whistle to stop play and retrieved the ball. When he came back, he handed the ball to Richardson and told him if he did that again, he would be called for a technical foul.

"Got it, sir," Richardson replied. "Mark, take it out."

Richardson bounced the ball to Martini on the end line. Martini reluctantly in-bounded the ball to Ryan. Ryan promptly dribbled the ball up the court and fed Niemi in the corner. Niemi put up a shot that hit the rim and bounced out towards the top of the key, where Ryan grabbed it and immediately put up a shot in traffic. It found the net. With 1:57 remaining in the first quarter, the Speedboys were finally on the board.

Another Midgets basket made it 10-2. Richardson took the ball out. He tossed it into Martini, who dribbled up the court and popped a shot from the top of the key. *Swish!*

The buzzer sounded to end the quarter. The Speedboys trotted to the sidelines down 10-4.

"Boys," coach Bonk said, "I'm not sure what's going on out there with the in-bound plays, but we have one enemy. That's Hurley. Don't fight each other."

The mild-mannered Bonk was perturbed. He looked at his starting five. "I think you boys need to sit for a while," Bonk said. "Barnaby, Hill, Pann, Lind and Sabol, check in."

The reserves leaped off the bench to get into the game. The fresh five brought a new level of energy on the court.

Back on the bench, the original starting five talked among each other. They were not used to being sidelined.

When the second quarter ended, Hurley was up 23-14. The Speedboys reserves had held their own. Bonk was pleased with the spark his bench players had provided and the message it sent to his original starters.

The second half was more like roller-derby than basketball. Both teams played rough, throwing elbows when someone tried to drive past them to the basket. The referees wore out their whistles. Richardson, the football star, knocked Hurley players around underneath, drawing four fouls.

Niemi finally found his shot, hitting from the corner and driving to the basket along the end line to draw fouls. Ryan and Martini left their first half differences behind and played like teammates. Bill Nemacheck was present and accounted for: one field goal, two free throws, two fouls, and two rebounds.

But the night belonged to Hurley's Dick DeZur. He tallied 30 points, just three fewer than the entire Bessemer team. The Midgets went back to Wisconsin with a 60-33 victory and a 3-5 record in conference play. The Speedboys were dead last in the M-W conference.

The road to victory would be paved with many punishing losses, as was the case with the trip to Wakefield three days later where the Cardinals beat the Speedboys 79-47, a game in which no Speedboy scored in double figures. Bessemer's Bill Nemacheck, playing his best game of the year, was the high man for the team with nine points.

John Bonk, the rookie coach, was now 0-10 to start his coaching career. A dark cloud hovered over his team.

CHAPTER 17

The Paperboy

His right hand opened the door and with a quick toss of his left the *Duluth News-Tribune* newspaper was trapped between the back door and storm door. The paperboy had done his job.

His name was Mickey LeClaire; our neighbor and Mr. Reliable. Mom and Dad marveled that Mickey *always* delivered the paper by 6:30 a.m., regardless of the weather.

"You want to look up to someone," Dad would say, "be like Mickey."

Mickey delivered both morning and afternoon newspapers to earn money. To carry the cloth bag, you had to have strong shoulders and a sturdy back. But most importantly, you had to have ambition, drive, and a sense of responsibility.

The local paperboys were skilled, especially in winter. It was at that time of year that it was important to keep the newspaper securely loaded between the storm and main doors of a home so a strong wind wouldn't spring it open and scatter the morning news throughout the neighborhood. The newspaper boys learned how to do it quickly. *Pull, toss, close.* On to the next house and repeat.

Mickey was an alarm clock for many. *It must be time to get up, the paperboy was here.* Mickey had to stay on schedule as he had school after his route was complete. He got up at 5:30 every morning, in all types of weather, to pick up his bundle of papers at Dewey's Café.

The *Duluth News-Tribune* newspaper came in on the Greyhound bus. Mickey would grab the papers, load his bag and he was off on his route. It was 6:30 a.m. when he tossed the paper between our doors, and finished his route by delivering the news to most houses down Sellar Street to where it ended at Steiger's Sawmill. Most kids had no idea that he did this every day, twice a day, for maybe $20 a month. He needed the money. Mickey's father Robert LeClaire had died in 1960. Leaving behind his wife Leone and three young children.

In many ways, I think that is why my dad admired Mickey. Both my dad and Mickey had lost their fathers when they were very young. As the oldest child, each had to grow up fast and take responsibility for much of the work around the house. Each had to help his mom, when he would rather be playing ball with friends. Dad and Mickey had a lot in common.

I was old enough to remember Mr. LeClaire. They lived just two houses up the hill and my folks visited often during his illness. Their home was cozy. There was always a pear sitting on the top of their refrigerator. That pear stayed there until it was ripe, then replaced with a green one and the process started over again.

From the kitchen, I could see Mr. LeClaire lying on their living room sofa covered with a plaid wool blanket and making small talk with my folks.

Dad once told me that Mr. LeClaire, whose first name was Robert, was a very good athlete in high school and Dad had the pleasure of watching him play. Mr. LeClaire worked as an electrician at the Peterson Mine. Yet now, he had trouble walking and talking. Mom said that cancer had made him sick.

His voice was soft and low. He would laugh, then cough and then swallow hard and go silent. He would smile now and then at the stories being told, but all knew he wasn't well. He would cringe in pain, but say he was fine.

Mickey's mom, Leone, would chat with whoever visited knowing that there was not much she or others could do about her husband's pain. My mom, the nurse, would ask all the right medical questions. My dad, the friend, would keep things light and talk about sports. Dad would pat him on the arm to reassure him things would be alright.

But as a kid, I didn't know what to do. We were always told not to talk. Just be good kids while around Mr. LeClaire. Should I just ask his daughter Maripat to go out to play?

Sadly, it wasn't long after one of those visits in the summer of 1960 that Mr. LeClaire died.

"Don't go up to Maripat's house today," Mom said. "Her dad died."

I remember seeing the sadness on Mom's face.

When you are young, you are quite aware of everything around you, even though adults may not think you understand. You understand happiness. You understand anger. You understand sadness. You understand pain. What you can't quite get your head around is death itself. The person has just gone away, leaving a lasting emptiness. Resting heavily upon loved ones' shoulders.

Yet, for Mickey, the dependable paperboy, there was work to do. He would be the one to deliver the news. His father's obituary would be in the next day's newspaper.

Pull, toss, close. On to the next house and repeat.

Chapter 18

Salute

A.D. Johnston High School Principal, John Sartoris, was presented with 13 large American flags by VFW Auxiliary in early 1964. The new ones replaced the out-of-date 48-star flags in each classroom. The VFW Auxiliary raised funds with various projects to purchase flags. The presentation at the high school was part of the VFW Auxiliary's "Americanism Program." The goal is to provide new American flags for every classroom in the city.

From our vantage point in the upper bleachers, my brother John and I saw dad arrive at the Speedboys game against Maple at the end of the third quarter. He walked in through the southside gymnasium door, then stood along the railing near the stairs to watch the rest of the game.

He wore a black corduroy jacket that looked like a letterman's coat with buttons that snapped up the front. The coat was lightly insulated and he usually kept the collar flipped up. His ears were bright red from the frigid winter temps, but the man refused to wear a hat.

It was a rare Friday night appearance for him. Watching his alma mater play basketball, even for one quarter, was just the break from work he needed. The Maple Tigers had the game well in hand by the time he set eyes on the court.

In the fourth quarter, with the Tigers leading 54-30, Maple coach Al Forsythe pulled his starters to not run up the score against the hapless Speedboys. Bessemer's Mark Martini scored easily against the reserves, but the game was already out of reach. The Tigers won

64-50. Martini, Bruce Richardson and Gary Niemi all scored in double figures, but in the end it was another forgettable night. The Speedboys were still winless.

As we made our way across the east side of the gym floor to the steps, we heard a loud whistle. We looked up to see Dad waving to us. He usually didn't wait, but on this night he must have been feeling sociable.

"Come on," he yelled. "I'll take you to the Legion for a pop."

We walked to the American Legion Post 27, just a block away. Many fans, a good number of them veterans, stopped by the Legion after ballgames. Any game; football, baseball or basketball.

As we entered the crowded bar there was a steady stream of people greeting Dad.

"Let me buy you a cold one, Johnny!" one patron yelled.

"Not tonight, I've got my sons with me," Dad replied.

"How many boys you got now Johnny?" another asked.

"Enough for a basketball team!" Dad said with a laugh.

"Good to hear," the guy replied. "We need one."

We found a table in the corner. Dad ordered an Orange Crush and Coca-Cola for my brother and me and a Stroh's from the tap for himself. He gave the bartender 30 cents, then picked up all three glasses from the bar and walked slowly through the crowd to our table, trying hard not to spill.

As Dad placed the glasses on the table, my brother John was trying to pronounce the words on a sign that was hanging in the bar.

"Gedda-Cychosz American Legion Post 27," John said. "Dad, what does Gedda-Cychosz mean?"

"That's not a word," Dad said. "It's two names."

"Who are they?" John asked.

"Well, they're two important military men from Bessemer."

Dad leaned in as it was becoming hard to hear in the crowded bar.

"The name *Gedda* represents Corporal Peter Gedda," he said. "He was one of the first men from around here to die in World War I. Died in France in 1918, but the Army didn't get his body back to Bessemer until 1921. By then the American Legion was already named for him."

Dad reached for his beer, leaned back in his chair and took a swig. He looked around and waved to a buddy who was belly up to the bar. The buddy raised his glass in salute. Dad did the same back to him.

"What about the name Cychosz?" John asked. "Is he another soldier from World War I?"

Dad leaned forward in his chair.

"Have you learned about Pearl Harbor in school yet?" Dad asked. We nodded.

"Well, on December 7, 1941, the Japanese bombed our naval base at Pearl Harbor in Hawaii. They destroyed most of our fleet there in one attack. One of those ships was the Arizona. On that ship was Seaman First Class Francis Cychosz from Bessemer. He died instantly in the attack."

"Did they get his body back?" I asked.

Dad paused for a moment.

"He was buried where he died," he said. "On the ship. At the bottom of the harbor."

"Did you know him?" I asked.

"He was older than me," Dad said, "graduated in 1940, so I was about your age when I watched him play ball. Great athlete. He played football right over there at Massie Field."

He pointed in the direction of the high school football field, then reached for his beer and took another drink before continuing his story.

"He was a very good running back. First team All-Conference. Played with Bob LeClaire. Both were fun to watch play, in any sport really. In basketball, Cychosz had a sweet set-shot. They don't teach that shot anymore. He was one of the high school boys I looked up to when I was growing up. Made me want to be a Speedboy."

"Dad, what about our neighbor Joe Bria?" I asked. "Wasn't he injured in the war too?"

"Yes, he was. Shot in the back. That's why he limps so badly today."

As Dad told it, Joe was injured in World War II. He was one of the few men from our area that hit Omaha Beach on D-Day on June 6, 1944. Joe saw all the horrors on the beach at Normandy that day. For forty days, he and his regiment pushed forward into France, fighting the German army all the way.

They secured the city of Saint-Lo and got a few days of rest. Then the Germans made a surprise attack and Joe was shot in the back, leaving him paralyzed. If not for the quick work of field medics who found him badly wounded, Joe wouldn't have survived.

After multiple operations, Joe was left with the scars of war: partial paralysis of his right leg, a drop foot, and constant leg pain. He was just 26 years old.

"But you never hear him complain," Dad said. "Resilient, tough, but kind."

Dad, took a long, slow drink, then set down the empty glass before speaking.

"You can either wallow in your misery or adapt to your current state and make something special happen. When the odds are against you boys, you devise a new plan. That's Joe, and really that's the spirit of this town."

CHAPTER 19

It's Ed Sullivan's Fault

Over the last 80 years, the local communities have experienced both exhilaration and desperation. They counted on two things. One, that the iron ore mines would run at full capacity, keeping their men employed. And two, the resilience of the town folk to withstand any layoffs or shutdowns. The iron ore mines and their management often had the upper hand against workers.

So it came as welcome news that the copper mine in White Pine, Michigan was expanding and would be hiring experienced miners, with a goal of extracting one billion pounds of copper from the mine by 1965.

Pickands, Mather & Co., operating the iron ore Geneva Mine, quickly responded to the news of the copper mine expansion by increasing their miners' work schedule from four days to five, with the hopes of keeping their best men underground.

But the buzz in every school hallway, in every café, in every barbershop, on every sledding hill in Bessemer was the upcoming appearance of The Beatles on The Ed Sullivan Show.

The four mop-tops from Liverpool had garnered the admiration of the high school and junior high teens, especially the girls. The conservative crowd, which included just about every man over thirty, was not too pleased that these four rock-and-roll musicians had the guts to wear their hair over their ears.

Our father was one of those guys. Heck, he was still struggling with the popularity of Elvis Presley.

"What's wrong with these kids today?" he would ask. "Don't they like swing music anymore?"

The Beatles had released one album called "Meet The Beatles." Every rock-and-roll fan in the country wanted it. The Johnson Music Store in Ironwood was selling the album for $2.99 and the 45 rpm for 78 cents each and couldn't keep either in stock. Our local radio station, WJMS, didn't have a show to play The Beatles songs, but management announced they were working on it.

After sundown, I could dial in WLS AM 890, a real rock-and-roll radio station out of Chicago. I would place a transistor radio under my bed covers and keep the volume down low so my anti-Beatles parents couldn't hear it. Every hour, the WLS disc jockey would play "Please, Please Me" and the flip side "Til There Was You." I loved every second of it.

I wasn't trying to be rebellious by listening to The Beatles. I just wanted to be like my buddies who in one way or another got to listen to this new sound. The Beatles would be to me what the Glenn Miller Orchestra had been to my dad. My kind of music.

Ed Sullivan promised viewers that The Beatles would play at least three new songs on this Sunday's show. I would have to wait until Sullivan introduced the band to America on CBS to hear them.

When Sunday night came, my dad was sipping a beer and reading the newspaper while my brothers watched Walt Disney.

I made my move.

"Dad, can we watch Ed Sullivan at 7:00?" I asked.

Without even looking up from his paper, he said, "Why?"

"Um, because they're going to have The Beatles on there and I want to see them."

He pulled down the paper from in front of his face. I could tell what was coming next by the scowl on his face.

"There is no way we are watching those finks on TV."

Anyone my dad didn't like was a hoodlum, a jerk or a miscreant, but most often a fink.

"Why not?" I asked. "All my friends are going to watch them. We've been talking about it all week. People are getting together. Jeff Pricco told me that his sister Connie was meeting a bunch of friends to watch it on the television at the Bessemer Bowling Alley too."

Dad was having none of it.

"Listen, it's because of goofballs like Ed Sullivan that we have all these issues in our country," Dad said. "Now we have rock-and-roll that doesn't even sound like music, and boys wearing hair like girls. It's Ed Sullivan's fault, I tell ya."

"But Dad, just because I want to watch them doesn't mean I will wear long hair. I just like their music, like you like Frank Sinatra or Perry Como…"

Dad cut me off. "Now those are real singers," Dad said. "This is just a bunch of "yeah, yeah" songs. You can't understand a word they're saying."

"Dad, I'll be the only kid in Bessemer that didn't see them."

"Lucky for you. Now go up to your room and do homework or something."

There was no convincing him on the topic. I went upstairs, trying not to cry. After hearing the discussion, my brothers realized they couldn't watch The Beatles either, so they followed me upstairs. Except for our two-year-old brother Pete, who was asleep on the floor in front of the TV.

When the clock struck seven, I quietly snuck back downstairs to the kitchen. To my surprise, I could hear the voice of Ed Sullivan coming from the living room.

"Ladies and gentlemen, The Beatles," Sullivan announced.

I tiptoed into the dining room and around the table, where I had an angle on both the TV and my dad as he sat on the sofa.

The Beatles began with "All My Loving." It was hard to hear the song above the screaming of girls on the television and my father's cursing.

"Christ," he said. "Look at those long-hair finks. Who in their right mind would listen to these idiots?"

The Beatles looked like they were having so much fun, almost as much fun as I was having watching them from my secret hiding spot. With each shake of their heads and flick of their hair the girls screamed. The Beatles smiled and laughed and tried to sing above the shouts of the adoring television audience. I connected with each lyric they sang.

Dad kept up a steady stream of cursing but didn't turn the channel. He couldn't help himself. During the song "She Loves You" I saw him tapping his foot to the beat.

After The Beatles were done singing, Ed Sullivan said, "Wasn't that just great?"

"Your ass," Dad answered him.

Dad had seen enough. He got up, stepped over Pete and turned off the television.

"What a bunch of finks."

He then reached down and carefully scooped up his youngest son from the carpet and held him in his arms. He gently placed a kiss upon Pete's forehead.

"You don't need to hear any more of that music Peter," Dad whispered. "You'll go deaf."

Dad walked quietly up the stairs, little Pete cradled warmly in his arms.

CHAPTER 20

Barbershop Fodder

By mid-February 1964, the plight of the Bessemer Speedboys became the talk of the town. As conversation fodder, the team's inability to get into the win column, now at 0-13, was a more popular topic than The Beatles. In the local barbershops, this meant Speedboys banter was at a fevered pitch.

Our father got his hair cut at Guglie's Barbershop, so naturally we went to Guglie's, too.

Domenic "Guglie" Gugliemotto had hung his red, white, and blue barber pole outside his one-chair shop on Sellar Street since 1949. He and his family, like other shop owners downtown, lived upstairs of the business.

In the barbershop, Guglie had a wall chart hanging over the waiting room chairs with pictures of various haircuts for boys and men: the Butch, the Flat Top, the Duck Tail, and so on. The poster also said the barber would give you a different cut if you told him how you liked it. Yet Guglie never asked me how I wanted my hair cut. He just buzzed it into a crew cut, because that's the way my dad wanted it.

"That'll be 25 cents," Guglie would say.

Each customer who came through the door of Guglie's barbershop got a friendly hello, then took his seat to wait. He would pick up a newspaper or magazine and just bide his time. When one customer was done, Guglie would yell, "Who's next?" The honor system took over and the next person in line popped into the barber's chair.

A Saturday morning at Guglie's meant picking up a nickel or a dime from busy guys who wanted to move to the front of the line.

"Hey, are you Johnny's boy?" one guy would ask.

"Yes," I would reply.

"How about I give you a dime so I can sneak ahead of you?"

"Sure."

Before I knew it, I was an hour behind my scheduled cut but had an extra thirty-five cents in my pocket. Thirty-five cents went a long way at the Tip Top or in the summer at the Root Beer Stand.

One Saturday, the next customer who hopped into the barber chair sported a mustache and wore a nice suit. Cuffed pants and shiny shoes. Tie knotted. I didn't know where he worked, but he definitely didn't work in an underground mine.

"What do you think of our Speedboys basketball team?" Guglie asked the gentleman.

"Well, Guglie, seems like they should be a lot better," the man said, "but they're missing some players that could have helped them this year. Jim Hoffner moved away. Paul Busch decided to play hockey. The Speedboys don't have much height, and Busch is about 6'5" last time I saw him."

"I thought Busch was hunting and trapping with his dad out at their camp." said Guglie. "That's what I heard."

"I'm sure he's at the camp too," the man said with a chuckle. "But a 6'5" kid that can dunk could help this team."

A high schooler sitting next to me in the waiting chairs decided to chime in.

"They cut the boys from Ramsay first," he said. "They favor the boys from Washington School and St. Sebastian School. Busch is from Ramsay."

The man seemed surprised.

Guglie would repeat that Ramsay story for the next few weeks to other customers. Whether it was true or not, it was good barbershop fodder.

Guglie kept clipping the hair around the man's ears with his long scissors. You could hear each snip clearly across the room.

"Are you cutting the new coach's hair?" the man asked.

"No," said Guglie. "I understand he drives back to Grand View, Wisconsin to get his hair cut."

The man laughed.

"Well, he better figure out how to coach soon or he'll be staying in Grand View.

"Do you want a shave today?"

"Yes, but leave the mustache," the man said. "It makes me look sophisticated at the office."

Everyone laughed.

Guglie used a lever on the side of the barber's chair to lay the customer back, then raised him up a bit by pumping a pedal on the floor.

"I read that the Washington School freshman basketball team was winless too," Guglie said. "It was in the paper today. They went 0-10 for the season. Wakefield won that conference. Ramsay was in that same league, and they had four wins."

He placed a hot towel on the mustache man's face, then gathered foam from a black dispenser sitting on the shelf to his right. The cream was heated and smelled like menthol. He removed the towel and lathered the customer's cheeks and chin, careful not to get the foam in the mustache. He finished up with a barber's brush, touching up the lather around the man's nose and ears.

"I told you before, there are some good players from Ramsay," the man said. "The Ramsay school kids are just not playing when they get to high school. Is it the same in Ironwood? Do the Roosevelt and Erwin boys choose not to play basketball for the Red Devils?"

"I never heard that," Guglie said, "but it's been a long time since they had a grade school program in Bessemer to get these kids interested in playing basketball. John Backman always says he going to start one, but it doesn't happen." Guglie said. "I know my boys would like to play."

Guglie dabbed here and there on the man's face to fluff up the foam, then reached for a straight razor. He honed the razor on a leather strap that hung from the shelf. He smacked his razor back and forth on the strap — *slap, slap slap* — until it was ready for cutting.

He turned the man's head to the left, raised his sharpened blade, started cutting at the right sideburn. You could hear the blade cut across his face — *scratch, scratch, scratch* — shearing away all the thick whiskers as he dragged the razor in careful strokes. He moved swiftly but with flair, wiping the blade clean on a towel laid across the man's chest.

The high schooler sitting next to me wanted to add a little more to the basketball dilemma.

"You can't play basketball at Washington School unless you are a freshman," he said. "It would have to be a special situation to allow a seventh or eighth grader to play on the freshman team."

"Well, there's your problem," said the man in the chair.

Guglie finished the shave, wiped the man's face clean, and thanked him for his business.

"Who's next," Guglie shouted.

CHAPTER 21

We Just Want to Play

Freshman Jim Milakovich peered through the window on the south side door but saw no one inside. The light was on in the gym, a sure sign that the janitor had not yet swept the gym floor.

He shook the door, rattling the padlocked chains. It worked. Spun Matrella, the janitor on duty, poked his head around the tunnel entrance and looked up in Milakovich's direction. But he couldn't see anyone.

Milakovich gave the door another shake.

Spun climbed the stairs to see who was in such a desperate need to enter. The young boy smiled and waved through the frosted glass. Spun just shook his head in disbelief.

"You never give up, do you kid?" Spun said. "You're going to get me in trouble if I stay much longer. I'm supposed to have these lights off soon."

"Thanks, Spun," Milakovich replied. "I'll only shoot 10 minutes or so. My freshman basketball season is over and, well I need the work. Our team didn't win a game."

"Seems like a theme around here," Spun replied.

They walked down to the gym floor. As Spun swept the floor with his long dust mop Milakovich took his shots: layups, jump shots, free throws. When Spun came sweeping close to where he was shooting, Jim would just dribble to the other basket.

School District Superintendent Walter Newman was driving home from a meeting and noticed that the lights were still on in the gym. Always the penny pincher, he parked his car and went to turn off the lights. As he entered the gym door, he could hear the *thump, thump, thump* of a basketball.

"What's going on here?" he shouted from the upper deck.

"Oh, Butch, I was just finishing up," Spun stammered. "I let this boy in to shoot for a bit as I would be here anyway."

"That's against the rules," Newman said. "Who is paying for the electricity bill?"

"I was gonna be here anyway," Spun replied. "Jim, sorry you need to go now."

Milakovich nodded and left the court without a word of protest. He headed up the staircase with his tattered basketball tucked under his arm.

"This better not happen again, Spun," Newman said.

"Yes, sir."

We loved the game of basketball, and with all the gyms in town locked up and off limits, we learned young to make do with what we had. We would play basketball anywhere we could: outside, inside, in a garage, in a basement. Anywhere in town we could get a few friends together and find a rim it was game on.

Sometimes you had to shovel snow off the court before playing. Other times you had to shovel during the game. Sometimes the snowbanks were out of bounds, and other times they were in play. We adapted to any and all surroundings.

Art and George Boline had installed a basketball rim inside the family garage; no backboard, just the rim. The garage had a concrete floor. Here and there it was cracked and uneven and caused the ball to fly off in different directions when a player dribbled. Nonetheless, it was indoors, so to speak, free of ice, snow and the northerly winds. In the Boline garage, the basket was just six feet off the ground, so you kept your shot flat. If you tried to lob an arcing shot, it would hit the ceiling and be called out of bounds. It all worked well until Kevin Borseth went up for a dunk and tore the rim from the wall, which happened more than once. The brothers Boline would nail it back up on the garage wall and the game continued.

At our buddy Denny Kontny's house, the basket was on the outside of the garage next to the street, eight feet in the air with a nice backboard. Denny always had money for a new net, and it was installed each January. The most important part of "Kontny's Kourt" was the driveway. It was flat and wide, so the court extended nicely into the adjourning street.

A drawback was that you had to look both ways for traffic after a rebound before you took the ball back out. The games at Kontny's Kourt usually came to an abrupt end each spring when his mother's tulips came poking through the ground.

We Pelissero boys called the basketball court at our house "Pel Gardens." You know, like Boston Gardens. Dad built and mounted a square backboard above the garage door. It was square to be just like the Speedboys' backboards, except ours was plywood, not glass. We painted it green and painted a shooter's square on it to target bank shots. The net was always frosty, sometimes frozen. On the coldest of days, the ball would get stuck in the frozen net and we would need a long stick to knock it out. Our rim was ten feet off the ground, basketball regulation height. However, our slanted driveway changed the actual height of the rim. Ten feet at the rim became fifteen feet as you got farther down the driveway. But we adapted. That's what Speedboys do to play the game.

CHAPTER 22

Bonk sat on a chair in his coach's office, leaning forward to lace up his white, high-top basketball shoes. The radio droned in the background.

"In local basketball action this Friday night, the Ashland Oredock-ers will welcome the Wakefield Cardinals to their gymnasium. Maple will collide with Superior East. The Ironwood Red Devils, currently in first place in the conference, will take on the lowly Bessemer Speedboys at Luther L. Wright High. The Speedboys have lost all 13 games this season. Ironwood needs this win to stay..."

Bonk turned off the radio. He finished lacing up, grabbed a whistle and hung it around his neck. As he was heading out to practice, there was a knock at his door.

"Coach, can I have a few minutes with you?" asked Mark Martini.

"Sure, Mark," said Bonk. "Come on in."

"Coach, I know we're trying to find a way to win a game. I think we have to change what we're doing."

"OK," Bonk chuckled. "What would you do?"

"Stall!" said Martini.

"Stall?"

"Yes, stall. We'll only shoot if we have a layup. I've seen it run on television by some of the colleges and it works well against great teams. We have Ironwood this Friday, right, and it seems to me we need a different plan. One they're not expecting."

"Well..." Bonk said rubbing his chin. "We would have to practice it. But at this point I'm willing to try anything."

As a young coach, just a few years older than his players, he was still open to ideas. After 13 straight losses to start his coaching career,

110

Bonk was hardly set in ways like a veteran coach in the league.

That afternoon at practice, Bonk announced to his team that they were going to play *stall ball* against Ironwood.

Martini smiled.

"Listen up," Bonk said. "Here's how it works." He ran his team through the details of the stall offense. "Dribble up the sideline, flip the ball to the player coming back out. Look inside for Richardson or Niemi or Nemacheck to be open, and if they're not, do it all over again. Martini to Niemi to Ryan, then do it again."

Bonk had the starters practice the drill again and again.

"Unless you get an open layup, hold the ball."

Martini understood, but his teammates were confused.

"So, we just hold it for eight minutes unless we get a layup?" Bruce Richardson asked. "Just hold it?"

"Yes, it's a total ball control offense," Bonk replied. "The final score might only be 10-8, but that's okay. The goal is to keep the ball out of the Red Devils' hands."

Richardson shook his head. He was not buying it.

The Speedboys won the tipoff in Friday night's game in Ironwood and immediately put the stall ball offense on full display. They held the ball for the first three and half minutes of the game. Dribble in, dribble out. Pass in, pass out. Look for a cutting forward or a lonely center for a layup. Not there? Start over again.

Martini finally found an opening, cut hard to the basket, got a pass from Niemi, and laid it in for two. The Speedboys had a lead over the host Red Devils halfway through the first quarter, 2-0. The Speedboys were onto something.

The Red Devils scored on their first possession, then stole the ball from the Speedboys twice, scoring both times. Ironwood led 6-2.

Bill Ryan was able to clear the pressing Red Devils and started the stall tactic again. Ryan dribbled in on the left side and bounced the ball into Richardson. Rather than pass it back out to Ryan, Richardson put the ball on the floor, made a nice move around his opponent, and banked in a jump shot from ten feet out.

Bessemer Coach Bonk called a timeout. He stopped Richardson as he came off the court.

"Why did you shoot?" Bonk asked. "We're trying to hold the ball. Unless you have a layup, pass the ball back out."

"Coach, if the ball comes into me, it's not going back out," Richardson replied. "I made the basket, OK?"

Bonk pointed to the bench. He sent Larry Pann into the game to replace Richardson for the rest of the first quarter, which ended with Ironwood leading 10-6.

Stall ball continued to work in the second quarter for Bessemer. They were keeping it close. By halftime, Ironwood was ahead, but only 23-17.

"Ironwood can't score if they don't have the ball," said Coach Bonk to his team in the locker room. "Let's keep it up."

The Red Devils increased the pressure in the third quarter, but Bonk's team continued with their four-corner offense. Boos started to rain down from the stands from both sides. Red Devil fans wanted to run up the score. Speedboys fans were perplexed and let the coach know it.

"Hey coach, aren't you supposed to *shoot the ball* in basketball?" one fan shouted sarcastically from behind the bench. "I think that's how you win the game."

Bonk tried to act like he didn't hear the complaints, but eventually they got to him. He called a time-out midway through the third quarter, put Richardson back into the game, and encouraged his team to make quicker decisions and take more shots.

That was another coaching mistake. The Red Devils scored at will.

On defense, Ironwood collapsed on Bessemer's big guys inside. Martini fell back into his old shoot-first, pass-second mentality, even though stall ball had been his idea. He finished with 10 points, as did Bill Ryan.

The Speedboys lost 67-41 and fell to 0-14.

Richardson touched the ball twice in the second half. He scored both times, each basket further fueling his growing displeasure with Bonk's coaching style.

❖

The Speedboys hosted Superior East at the A.D. Johnston gymnasium the following Friday night. Superior East had the talent you would find on a small college team rather than a high school squad.

The Speedboys looked on during warmups, sizing up their chances against Superior East's height, speed, and strength. To send a message to their opponents, each member of East's starting five stuffed the basketball through the basket for all to see.

Their two superstars, Tom McCauley and Bob Peck, were especially impressive. But Bessemer's Bruce Richardson was not visibly intimidated. He was childhood friends with McCauley and Peck, both of whom came to Bessemer and stayed with the Richardson family for summer baseball tournaments. All three boys had the same competitive fire inside.

The Speedboys held Superior East to only three points in the first five minutes of the game, using the same stall ball strategy they had used against Ironwood. Their ball-handling had improved immensely, but their shooting had not. Even when they got easy layups, they missed many.

The talent-rich Superior East five soon took over. McCauley and Peck relentlessly drove to the basket, pushing their old pal Richardson around. He racked up four fouls in the first half alone. Bill Nemacheck fouled out in the third quarter. When the final buzzer sounded, Superior East had four players who scored in double figures and the Speedboys had four players who had fouled out.

The final was 82-50. It was the Speedboys' 15th loss of the season and the one that cemented an undesirable distinction for both the team and the town: the first winless regular season in Bessemer's high school basketball history.

CHAPTER 23

The 1963-64 basketball season ended as it began: the Bessemer Speedboys lost to the Ontonagon Polar Bears 64-44 in the Class C District Tournament.

In John Bonk's first year as coach, he managed to lose 16 straight games. When the Michigan-Wisconsin Conference announced their All-Conference awards in April, no Speedboy made the first or second team. Mark Martini, the Bessemer guard, received an honorable mention.

The ray of hope for local sports fans was that Bonk was losing just three players from this team to graduation. The returning players had all received valuable playing experience.

To commemorate the end of the season, the Bessemer Lions Club put on their annual basketball banquet in the Elks Lodge in downtown Bessemer.

The President of the Lions Club, George Waters, had asked his officers and board members to be there early. Waters was a financial auditor for the firm Ernst and Ernst, and a stickler for decorum. He gave club members assignments for setting up the meal and serving the players, coaches, and parents, and he expected all to fulfill their designated roles with diligence and grace.

From his seat at the head of the banquet table, Waters checked his watch, then leaned toward the microphone in front of him. "I need my Tail Twister," he said. "Is Harry Rizzie here?"

The Lions Club Tail Twister's responsibility was to spread harmony, good fellowship and enthusiasm, and to serve as the banquet's master of ceremonies. They chose the right man for the job when they appointed Rizzie. He had an innate ability as a public speaker and the talent to make people laugh.

"At your service *El Presidente*," Rizzie replied.

President Waters, unamused by Rizzie's reply, banged the gavel on the table to get the banquet started. Then, Waters welcomed everyone and informed the guests that the meal would now be served, with a program to salute the athletes following the dinner.

High school principal John Sartoris was the Lions Club Secretary. He brought a salad to Coach Bonk, who was seated at the head table with President Waters on his left and Superintendent Walter Newman on his right.

As he set the salad in front of Bonk, Sartoris leaned in.

"Coach, how many lettermen do you have this year?" Sartoris asked.

"We've got thirteen, John," replied Bonk.

"Seems like a lot of letters after a winless season," Sartoris said. "Remember only ribbons or bars for those who have the letter from another sport. We don't have the budget to buy more letters."

Bonk did not reply. He believed his team was deserving of their letters and the recognition that comes with it, budget or no budget.

Bonk had prepared a short speech about the value of hard work and how it leads to success. He also planned to announce a few important changes to the basketball program. He turned to Newman, who was midway through his salad.

"Walter, at my high school in Drummond, the coaches kept the gym open on Saturday mornings and all summer long so that players could practice their basketball skills whenever they wanted," Bonk said. "Open gym is what made me into the player that I was at Drummond. I would like to do the same thing here in Bessemer, and I would like to announce it tonight. What do you think?"

Newman nearly choked on a cherry tomato. He wiped his mouth with his cloth napkin and gathered his words before responding.

"John, I know you mean well," he said. "But the cost of everything to run our school is through the roof. Plus, we have construction workers there all summer putting in glass blocks to replace the old drafty windows. I'm sorry the answer is no."

Bonk paused for a moment before responding.

"We have talent in this town, Walter, and yet we went 0-16," Bonk said. "The Drummond high school boys made it to State last year."

"Coach, I know it's been a tough year," said Newman. "We want to do everything we can for these boys. The budget is just too tight. I will make it an agenda item at our next school board meeting, but for now the answer is still no."

Newman stabbed at his iceberg lettuce with his fork.

Bonk sat back in his chair, drumming his fingers on the table, thinking about his speech and what he would tell his team.

When people were finishing dessert, President Waters banged the gavel three times, then asked Harry Rizzie to get the program started.

Being master of ceremonies at a banquet for a team that had lost every game was hardly an enviable job, but Rizzie read the room perfectly. He started by thanking his fellow Lions Club members for their service, ribbing a few of them with some good-natured teasing to warm up the crowd. Then he shifted to talking about the Speed-boys, assuring the team that things would get better, while slowly building toward his punch line.

"Few teams can say they had a perfect season," Rizzie joked, "but you guys pulled it off at 0-16. If you keep this up, you can re-place the Washington Generals and go on the road with the Harlem Globetrotters."

Everyone laughed. All in the room knew the hapless Washington Generals lost every game to the Globetrotters as part of the show.

For the Speedboys' faithful, Rizzie's opening lines had set the right tone for the evening. Rizzie then introduced the Speedboys head coach.

Coach Bonk adjusted his black rim glasses.

"Good evening," he said. He spoke slow and low, choosing each word carefully to be sure he didn't make the players feel bad about their season.

"First, I want to say I'm proud of you boys. You let a first-year coach lead you this season. I had no experience as a coach, and it showed. I'll work hard to be better prepared next season, and I know you will too."

The audience applauded politely in response to the young coach's humility.

"Second, thirteen of you have earned a varsity letter this season," Bonk announced. "Wear it with pride. I'm excited about next year and getting many of our core players back, but I want to thank our seniors for their leadership. Sixteen losses was no way to end a basketball career, but I know you gave it your all. That's all a coach can ask of his seniors. Come on up to the stage and get your letters, boys."

The three seniors, Bill Nemacheck, Pat Bennetts, and Brian Lind, walked to applause and received their letter.

"Third, I was looking back at our scoring this season, and it was pretty balanced. Mark Martini had 163 points to lead our team. Mark was 17th in the league in scoring and received an All-Conference Honorable Mention. Next year, Mark will be our team captain. He certainly earned it this year with his performance on the court. Congratulations, Mark."

Martini smiled and raised his hand, acknowledging the applause from the crowd.

His father Arthur Martini, who was assistant superintendent of the Peterson Iron Ore Mine, was beaming from ear to ear. He understood the influence a leader can have in a community and was proud of his son's achievement.

"There's one last thing I have to say tonight," Bonk said.

He paused, then took a deep breath before continuing.

"Men, if you want to improve your game, you have to play more. Even the best coach can only teach you so much. There is simply no better way to improve your game than to play more basketball. So, get together with your friends this summer and shoot."

"Can we get in the gym this summer?" shouted one of the players.

Bonk looked over at Newman and then Sartoris. Neither made eye contact with him.

"Well," Bonk said. "I'm working on that. For now, I'll just say thank you again to all the players for your efforts this season. To the families and to all Bessemer basketball fans in the room, thank you for your support. Have a good night."

After the banquet, Speedboys player Bruce Richardson approached Coach Bonk near the coat rack.

"Coach," he said, "I appreciate the things you said up there tonight. The players needed to hear something positive, and what you said was very kind."

"You're welcome, Bruce," said Bonk. "Thank you for hanging in there through a tough season. I'm excited about next year. You, Gary, Bill, and Mark are all coming back. It's not every year a coach gets four of his starting five back."

"Coach, I won't be playing basketball for you next year," Richardson said.

"But why, Bruce?" the coach asked.

Richardson spoke to Bonk like he was his peer and not his coach. Honest and straightforward.

"You really want to know?" Richardson said. "Well, Coach, let's start with this. You are easily influenced by other people's ideas and opinions. And look where it got you."

Bonk was taken aback by what he was hearing from his young cager. When the coach gathered himself, he tried to sound as reassuring as he could.

"Bruce, the season just ended," he said. "Give it some time. We can all use the down time to reflect on the season and come back ready to go next season."

"Coach, you aren't listening," Richardson said. "I'm done."

Second Quarter
1964-65 Season

CHAPTER 24

Around 1880, a young man in the employ of the Milwaukee Lake Shore and Western Railroad was part of a surveying party that was literally cutting its way through the Gogebic Range, making a trail for the venturesome and daring pioneers that subsequently made possible the development of the region. His name was Albert D. Johnston. An educated man born in Manitowoc, Wisconsin in 1860.

When Johnston first saw the area that would soon become Bessemer, it was nothing more than trees and rocky bluffs. Not one human had put up a homestead, at least not one that he could see. By 1884, the railroad had reached Bessemer and the town began to take shape. Little did anyone know that the young man who had first cut his way through the forest would one day become one of its most important community leaders.

Johnston was elected clerk of Gogebic County in 1898 and he made Bessemer his permanent home. He was a director of the First National Bank and helped build the Bessemer Electric Company. He was the first chairman of the County Road Commission and was responsible for much of the trunk highway system in the area.

Johnston was a sportsman too. When he arrived in the wilderness of Bessemer back in 1880, deer, grouse and brook trout were plentiful. By 1920, he was concerned that the area had been overhunted and overfished. He set out to get laws passed to shorten the hunting and fishing seasons in the spirit of game and fish preservation. He was successful. He even led an effort to plant fish in streams and lakes that were foreign to the area to help increase the enjoyment for the many sportsmen.

But his most important role was that of President of the Bessemer Board of Education. He set the standard high in this town. He made sure the most qualified teachers were hired, and that the faculty and students had the finest educational facilities in which to learn. He was at the helm when the new Bessemer High School was constructed and opened in the fall of 1908.

In acknowledgement of Johnston's many years of leadership and service to the Bessemer School District, the high school was named the *A.D. Johnston High School* in 1914.

Johnston's impact on Gogebic County and Bessemer was immense.

Yet, just like a Greek tragedy, his death came suddenly and without warning.

On October 4, 1923, while returning to his hunting camp at Sylvania Lodge on Clark Lake, Johnston lost control of his automobile on the state highway between Watersmeet and Taylor's Siding. His car rolled and Johnston was pinned underneath. He was pronounced dead at the scene. The 5,400 people of Bessemer were left in shock.

The city of Bessemer was built by men like A.D. Johnston. Men with pioneering spirit. Men respected for their integrity. Men of worth. Brave men who blazed the trail for the next generations to come.

A.D. Johnston had set the bar high and encouraged others to jump over it.

As promised to coach John Bonk, Superintendent Walter Newman placed the request for a grade school basketball program and open gym on the Bessemer Board of Education meeting agenda. But he had a more pressing issue on the list first.

"It has come to my attention," Newman said, "that several blackboards in our classrooms are pitted and have deteriorated to a point at which it is difficult to see what is written thereon, resulting in student eye strain."

Newman noted that the boards are 57 years old, and some are even older having been transferred from the old Olcott School building.

"Slate boards are expensive," Newman continued, "so I propose we resurface the boards. The cost will be 35 cents per square foot."

A motion was made to do one classroom and then assess if it was satisfactory before moving on. The motion passed and Cadger Chalk Board Resurfacing Company would be contacted.

Newman moved to the next agenda item. "Earlier this month, Coach Bonk approached me about supporting the reestablishment of a basketball program for boys fifth through eighth grade. As you know, we eliminated the grade school program when the ninth grades were transferred from the junior high category to the freshman team organization."

Newman continued to say that Coach Bonk wants a program that is organized by two teams. One has fifth and sixth graders, and the other seventh and eighth graders. The teams would practice on alternative nights from 6-7:30 for four months.

"Since regular coaches have full schedules," Newman said, "it is my suggestion that two ex-Speedboys living in Bessemer who are interested in coaching be hired for $100 apiece. In addition to teaching fundamentals, the intramural program would provide activity and interest for the students and give them constructive activity."

The board acknowledged that they had received the request but tabled the idea for further study and action.

When coach Bonk heard that the school board had tabled his idea for grade school basketball, he blew a cork. He walked into the office of athletic director John Backman to make the most consequential request in Bessemer sports history.

"John, I came from a winning basketball tradition at Drummond High School," Bonk said. "We could walk into a gym nearly any night of the week to shoot baskets with our friends. We would have 3-on-3 games where we worked on all our skills. We learned to love the game with that kind of freedom."

"Your point is, Coach?" Backman asked.

"My point is," Bonk continued, "that this administration is setting our basketball program back a hundred years by not allowing boys, especially grade-school-age kids, to have a good place to practice the game. Heck, Ironwood has five grade schools in a basketball league learning the game every year. They are light years ahead in teaching the basic fundamentals of the game."

"What are you proposing?" Backman asked.

"If the school board won't help me, then I need you as Athletic Director to help establish a youth basketball program where they get to learn the game. Dribbling, passing, shooting, defense and rebounding. Superintendent Newman wants a chaperone. But I want coaches, not a free-for-all. Men who know and love the game. Men who want to see the Speedboys of the future compete and win."

Bonk seldom was worked up. But he was now. He was frustrated by the roadblocks that the administration had put in his way. He had good athletes on his team, but they lacked the fundamentals that came from years of practicing the game *all year long*. He was adamant about a change. It wouldn't help his team next season, but it would in the years to come.

"Well, coach, I support you," said Backman.

Bonk was shocked. It was the first hint of hope he'd gotten for his idea from anyone in Bessemer with influence.

"But I'm also resigning," Backman said, "to move to a school downstate."

Bonk's heart sank. He slumped down in a chair in front of Backman's desk.

"A former Speedboy, Jack White, is going to replace me," Backman said, "and he's just the kind of guy who would support a program for our boys. Let me set up a meeting with Jack and we can discuss this more."

And he did just that.

Backman passed along the idea for a youth basketball program to the incoming athletic director in June 1964. He told White it was his first priority. White was a good soldier and knew how to follow orders.

The directive said to move quickly to organize a grade school basketball program for fifth through seventh grade boys that meets weekly to teach the fundamentals of the game. The objective was to train our athletes at a young age to be better prepared to compete in the older grades.

Assignment received and process underway.

White asked Coach Bonk and Harry Rizzie to meet him at the Elks Lodge in Bessemer to discuss the details.

After a couple of beers, Rizzie agreed to lead the intramural program on the condition that it meets *two* nights a week, not one. White and Bonk appreciated that Rizzie would give that much time to the young boys. White got approval from principal Arnold Vispi for the use of the Washington School gym two nights a week.

Word spread quickly throughout the schools and neighborhoods that Bonk was starting an intramural basketball program. The school district was investing in the future for a change. There was great enthusiasm and interest.

CHAPTER 25

Bruce Richardson removed his helmet and plucked a clump of grass from his facemask. He turned to look back at the scoreboard and smiled. Visitors 25. Home 6. The visiting Bessemer Speedboys football team had closed out their Michigan-Wisconsin Conference season with a decisive victory over their rival, the Hurley Midgets.

Richardson knew that the next day the *Ironwood Daily Globe* would write that running back Mark Martini had another great game, with over 100 rushing yards and two touchdowns; that Martini was a shoo-in to be on the All-Conference team after another stellar season. The paper would write that Gary Niemi had a nice two-way game with a crucial interception and touchdown reception pass from Speedboys quarterback Jim Ippolite. He also knew there would be no mention of his play in the story. He was fine with that.

In his final game as a senior, Richardson had helped his team on both sides of the ball. He had done his job. His team won. That's what mattered most to him, and he was satisfied. No headlines were needed.

As Richardson walked towards the team bus, he pulled off his number 41 jersey and slung it over his right shoulder pad. Basketball coach John Bonk was standing next to the bus and greeted Richardson as he approached.

"Nice game, Bruce," said Bonk. "You worked hard out there. A great way to end the season with a win."

"Thanks," replied Richardson as he reached for the handrail to enter the bus.

"See you Monday for the start of the basketball season," Bonk said.

Richardson stopped on the second step and leaned back out of the bus, still holding the railing. "Coach, I told you before, I won't be there on Monday. I'm done. I'm not playing basketball this season."

Richardson continued up the steps onto the bus. He found a window seat and joined his teammates celebrating their 10th straight football win over Hurley. The player watched through the window as Bonk's 6'6" frame disappeared into the darkness of night.

By Monday morning, the entire coaching staff and administrators had heard from Coach John Bonk that a key player for the upcoming 1964-65 Speedboys basketball team had decided not to play. This news didn't sit well with any of them.

When Richardson got to school on Monday, he didn't get too far down the hall before athletic director Jack White grabbed him by the arm. White had just coached Richardson in football and saw how competitive he was on the field. He was shocked Bruce wasn't reporting to the first basketball practice that day.

"Hey, what's this about you not suiting up for basketball this year?" White asked. "Are you kidding me?"

"No, I'm not kidding," Richardson said. "I'm done with basketball and I told Coach Bonk as much. If you want to know why, ask him."

The athletic director looked at Richardson intently, searching for some sign of misgiving. But he could find none. Richardson had made his final decision.

"Well, if you aren't going to be doing anything on game nights, will you run the clock for the basketball games?" White asked. "I'll pay you."

Richardson chuckled at his sudden turn in good fortune.

CHAPTER 26

Time to Take Cover

On election night, November 3, 1964, my father was laying across the family's well-worn burgundy davenport reading the *Ironwood Daily Globe*. A cigarette was burning itself out in the ashtray next to him. Walter Cronkite was on Channel 3, announcing that the presidential election results would be in soon and CBS would be first to have the results.

"Dad, did you vote today?" I asked.

"Of course," Dad replied nonchalantly turning the page.

"Did you vote for Lyndon Johnson or Barry Goldwater for President?" I asked.

"I never tell anyone who I voted for," he replied. "It's my private business. It's a secret. I don't even tell your mom."

"Mom said she voted for President Johnson, so I figured you did, too."

He turned the page on the *Daily Globe* and didn't respond.

Soon, Cronkite reported the early results, which heavily favored Johnson. My father sat up, dropping the paper in his lap. He seemed pleased. Cronkite announced that it appeared to be a landslide. A big smile spread across my dad's face.

"Dad, why do you think people don't like Goldwater?" I asked.

"Well, one, he's a Republican," he stated. "Kennedy was a Democrat and there are a lot of people that voted for Johnson because he was Vice President under Kennedy. And two, Goldwater is a nut."

I knew I shouldn't ask the next question for fear it would trigger a lecture on presidential politics, but I couldn't resist.

"Why is he a nut?" I asked.

"He's a nut because he would get the whole world blown up in a nuclear war with the Soviet Union," Dad replied. "You remember how close we came to nuclear war two years ago when the atomic bombs were in Cuba?"

Two years earlier, in late October of 1962, my classmates and I were all sent home early from school. Even at the age of seven, I could sense the fear that my teachers were feeling. Sister Leonita had a radio on in our classroom, even during quiet reading time. I overheard the broadcaster say that if the bombs were fired, nearly one-third of civilization would be destroyed, much of it in the United States.

My stomach clenched with anxiety, even more so than usual.

As soon as they released us from school to go home and hide, I walked as swiftly as I could to get to my parents. I glanced up at the sky, looking for rockets, but the sky was blue. The fluffy white clouds did not match the dismal outlook for the day.

As I crossed the railroad tracks, I felt guilty for not waiting for my classmate Mary Corona. She was still on the other side of the highway watching for cars to pass before she could cross.

My guilt got the better part of me. I stopped and waited. And waited. And waited some more; my fear building with every passing second. Mary finally crossed the highway and climbed up the hill near the tracks. She spotted Adam Modjewski, the grandfather of our classmate Roy, coming out of a little building that sat along the railroad tracks.

"Hi, Grandpa Modjewski," she said. "Isn't it a beautiful day?"

The world was about to end, but Mary didn't want to be rude.

"Come on, Mary!" I yelled at her.

"Oh, I've got to go," Mary said to Grandpa Modjewski. "Have a nice day!"

She hurried to catch up with me and we walked swiftly.

"Those leaves just won't give in to winter, will they?" Mary said looking up at the trees. "I love autumn. Don't you, Tom? All the colors. I love the crackling and swishing of leaves beneath my feet."

"The leaves have all died Mary," I said. "Just like us if we don't get home soon."

The world was about to end, and all Mary could see was beauty. I knew she was trying to make me feel better with her positive thoughts and uplifting words, to relieve my anxiety and convince me that maybe things would turn out alright. And I did feel a bit better walking with her. But when we reached Beecher Street, and our homes were in sight, I ditched her like a bad sandwich.

"See you, Mary," I said.

"See you tomorrow, Tommy," Mary shouted.

I charged up Beecher Street in a full sprint, hoping to outrun the incoming missiles.

My four brothers were already huddled in the basement with our parents when I got home. Mom had the radio on and we all listened intently. National news reporters were giving the play-by-play of negotiations between President Kennedy and Soviet Premier Nikita Khrushchev.

My dad explained to us our plan for surviving the attack. He said we would be safe in the new basement he had just finished this past summer, but we may have to stay below ground for many days. We would hide under the work bench in case of debris falling. We would drink water from the many jugs he and mom had filled and stashed nearby. If our water supply ran out, we would drink the water from the back of the toilet.

Then a breaking news bulletin came on the radio. Mom shushed us and turned up the volume.

"The President of the United States, John F. Kennedy, has just announced that the blockade of Cuba by our Navy has turned the Russian ships around. The Soviet Union has agreed to dismantle the nuclear weapons that are in Cuba. I repeat, the threat is over."

Relief washed over my parents' faces. They smiled and hugged, and so did my brothers and me.

The next day the sky was blue again, the clouds were gone, and we returned to school like any other day. Mary had been right all along.

Chapter 27

Wimpy

Good news was always welcome in the Gogebic-Iron Range area. When strikers ended a 48-day walkout and returned to work at the White Pine Copper Mine before the holidays, residents rejoiced. Over 1,400 members of the United Steelworkers Local 5024 were left idle until they reached this new agreement with management. The economic impact was severe for families and businesses in Bessemer, Wakefield and Ironwood while the men walked the picket line. But was it worth it?

White Pine management announced that the terms of the new three-year contract provided wage increases of seven cents per hour now and six cents per hour on Sept. 1, 1965, and another six cents per hour on Sept. 1, 1966. The miners also received an increase in insurance, major medical and a retirement plan. All in all, the miner's walkout succeeded in providing approximately 36 cents per hour in wage and benefits over the duration of the contract. However, the mine lost 17 million pounds of copper production during the strike.

Wimpy backed the coal truck into our yard. It was early November and the ground was already frozen, so the weight of the load did little damage to the yard. He hopped out of his truck and walked directly to the coal bin chute on our house, a window with two latches that you spun to loosen and pull the window off.

"Hi, Wimpy," my mother said as she leaned out the back door. "Looks like we need a half of a load today. Should last us until March."

"Okay, Mary Lou," Wimpy replied. "The price just went up over $13 a ton. A half load is smart. Just like the copper mine, they're paying the coal miners more too, so I guess now we're all paying for it."

Wimpy was a slight man, but far from wimpy. When he wasn't doing the back-breaking work of hauling coal all around the county, he was working on the city garbage truck each week. Lifting metal cans, dumping them in the back of the truck, hopping on and off the truck as he rode on a step connected near the back end. It was like his life's work was to prove his nickname was wrong.

Mom told my brother John and me to get inside the coal bin and be ready for the load to come in.

"You have to use the shovel to spread the coal as it comes down the chute," Mom said. "If you don't, it could knock down the far wall of the coal bin. We can't let that happen. I'll help you."

When we opened the coal bin door, the cold air from outside blew black dust into our faces. Wimpy had already loaded the metal chute though the window and pointed it down to the floor. He leaned into the window and asked if we were ready.

"I think so," my brother replied.

My mom came in to help.

Wimpy put one hand on the lever to release the coal down the chute, and with the other hand placed a handkerchief to his mouth so as not to breathe the dust.

The coal *shush-shush-shushed* as it poured down the chute. It came a lot faster than I expected, first filling the void in the back side of the room, then piling higher and higher. We pulled and pushed and scraped with our shovels trying to spread hundreds of pounds of heavy black rock across the floor of the room. Mom seemed to know how to do it. She had a good rhythm and we tried to keep up with her pace.

"Don't let it hit that wall," she yelled. "Your dad will have a fit it that wall bows out."

"Well," I asked, "why don't we have Wimpy come when Dad is home?"

Mom didn't reply. She just kept shoveling and spreading.

Finally, Wimpy pulled the hammer back to shut off the load. Black dust billowed around him as he walked to the window. When he arrived, his forehead and cheeks were caked with soot. He wiped his face with the handkerchief.

"You all good there, Mary Lou?"

"Yeah, Wimpy. Thank you."

All three of us in the coal bin were a filthy mess, but Mom kept right on working. She walked out of the bin, opened the top of the red stoker, and heaved in four or five shovels full of coal. She closed the stoker and walked directly to the boiler. She put a towel around her hand as she grabbed the handle of the boiler door and opened it.

She reached down and picked up long metal tongs to grab one of the red-hot lumpy ash clinkers inside and quite efficiently dropped it into a metal can. It sizzled and smoked.

"You have to be really careful," Mom said. "You could burn yourself if you don't move slow."

John and I would perform this dangerous process constantly throughout the winter. Open the stoker, shovel in the coal, pull out the hot clinkers, and repeat. We didn't think anything of the work involved or even the risk. Mom preferred a house heated with coal over one heated with oil or gas, so coal it was. We brothers didn't care one way or the other. Just as long as we could get our cold, wet feet on a heat register at night, life was good.

CHAPTER 28

The 1964 Michigan-Wisconsin Conference All-Conference Football Team was announced in the *Ironwood Daily Globe* on November 12, and the Bessemer Speedboys were well represented. Tom Fafford, an outstanding guard, and pile-driving fullback Jerry Corgiat were selected to the first team offense.

To no one's surprise, Mark Martini, the 5'11" 175 lb. halfback, was also selected for the first team offense. He had played both offense and defense and kicked extra points. Martini would now take his award and talent to the hardwoods as captain of the 1964-65 Speedboys basketball team.

Six lettermen returned to play on the Bessemer varsity squad for Coach John Bonk's second basketball season, but none of the boys grew much over the summer. The tallest man on last year's squad at 6'4", center Bill Nemacheck, had graduated, while 6'1" forward Bruce Richardson had decided to sit out the season. That left seniors Mark Martini, George Sabol, Larry Pann, Gary Niemi and Bill Ryan, all less than six feet, to decide who would play center.

One sophomore with high potential was 6'1" Richard Syrjala. Coach Bonk felt it was prudent to place Syrjala on the varsity immediately. Others working out with the varsity and trying to garner playing time were seniors Don Johnson and Greg Hill, along with juniors Milo Barnaby, Mike Betlewski, Bill Velin, and Bob Abelman.

It was a team with a lot of work to do.

The junior varsity, under second year coach Carl Gregas, had some promising young players, including sophomores Jim Milakovich, Don Barbacovi and Bill Joki. Each was happy to play some serious minutes on team B, with the hope that the experience would get them a shot at team A in the future.

Before the first game, the local newspapers ran stories rehashing the Speedboys' first winless basketball season in school history. It had been 629 days since the last recorded Bessemer victory back on March 6, 1963, in the district tournament.

The reporters agreed that the goal for the Speedboys' coming season was merely ending the long losing streak. To do so, the Speedboys would have to rely on their quickness, especially against the stronger and more experienced teams such as the Ashland Oredockers, who they would travel to play in the first game of the season.

Bill Ryan had one of his best games as a Speedboy against Ashland, as he scored 16 points. Yet, 10 of his points came in the last quarter against the Oredockers' second string when the game was already out of reach. The Oredockers won big, 96-47.

As the *Ironwood Daily Globe* wrote, "*the Oredockers had too much height for the short Speedboys and made good use of the fast break in outscoring the visitors by a decisive margin every period. The rout allowed Coach Bonk to use all 12 players and gain valuable playing experience.*"

The 17th straight loss under Coach Bonk and the 18th straight loss for Bessemer dating to March 1963.

CHAPTER 29

I Got a New Record

Music was the lifeblood of any growing boy and girl. As you age, your musical preferences evolve. Hearing your favorite music gave you extra energy. Pep in your step. Except at my parents' house. They were dead set against any rock and roll music being played in our home. "I don't want to hear any of that Shindig or Hootenanny music in this house," Mom would say. Both were the names of television shows that featured popular music. We were exiled to the 1950s to listen to Perry Como, Dean Martin, Frank Sinatra or another of our parents' favorite Italian crooners.

You can imagine my excitement when my classmate Mary Corona invited me over to hear a brand new 45 rpm record that she had just purchased at Johnson Music Store.

"Be there at 3:30 after school," Mary said.

Mary's parents' house doubled as a business. Not unusual for a small town like Bessemer. Her mother, Theresa, was a hairdresser and operated Theresa's Beauty Shop in one half of their home. Teachers, neighborhood moms, and even the nuns from St. Sebastian School all went to Theresa's Beauty Shop.

As I approached her house, I noticed there were two doors. Door One led to the beauty shop and Door Two, I assumed, led to the living room. I knocked quietly on Door Two. It opened. But not by Mary. It was her father. He didn't say hello. He just looked down at me.

"Yes?" he asked finally.

He probably thought I was selling greeting cards door to door and he was about to say no.

"I'm here to see Mary," I said with a stammer.

"She's not here," he said.

Of course she's not. Invite you over and then get wrapped up in a conversation with all the people she met on the way home.

He stood there looking at me. His whiskers were gray and his hair a bit unkempt. His eyes were puffy like I had just woken him from a nap. He pointed to the sofa and told me to wait over there. As he walked away in his stocking feet towards the kitchen, I saw a red polka dot handkerchief hanging from his back pocket. He mumbled to his wife Theresa in the beauty shop, something about a boy here for Mary.

Mr. Corona seemed gruff, but aren't most fathers in this town? You stood up straight when you addressed any adult. It was about respect for your elders. I tended to look at the floor when I encountered the man of the house. Thus was the case today.

Mary told me that her dad was a veteran of WWII. He had been a bricklayer, one that any contractor or neighbor would be proud to hire. After the war, he did stonework for the Peterson Mine, but currently there was little work at the mine. So, on this afternoon, he was the greeter at Door Two.

I had been at Mary's for ten minutes patiently waiting to listen to her new record. But no sign of her. I could hear the conversations in Theresa's Beauty Shop as the ladies chatted away about this and that and paged through their magazines. It was hard to follow the conversation as they interrupted each other often or finished one another's sentences. There was a strong smell of peroxide. At least one customer was getting a perm in the beauty shop.

Finally, I spotted Mary walking down the path in her red winter coat, her shoulders just above the snowbanks.

She chose to go through Door One into the beauty shop and happily greeted her mother's customers.

"How was school today, Mary?" her mother asked.

Each customer looked up from their magazine to listen to Mary's response. It was a bright and cheery reply.

"Oh, Sister Camille read The Boxcar Children book to us today," said Mary. "You know how much I love chapter books. Maybe we should have a boxcar in our backyard."

All the ladies in the shop gleefully supported Mary's idea.

One customer commented on Mary's red coat. How perfectly it fit her. Such a lovely color. Theresa replied that all girls should have a red coat because it is so cheery.

Mary walked into the kitchen and gave her father a hug. He finally managed to smile now that his daughter was home. He held her tight with one arm and a coffee cup in the other.

"I love you, Daddy."

Mary came into the living room and opened the top of the record player. She was ready to do the next item on her list, which was to play the new record for me.

"Do you always go through the beauty shop when you come home?" I asked.

"Yes," Mary said. "My mom wants me to do that. I don't always want to, but someday when I'm older I'll appreciate that my mom taught me to be cordial to guests and not be rude."

My goodness, I never thought of things that way.

"Tommy, this is the record I wanted you to hear," Mary said. "I play it over and over again. When our friend Eleanor is here, we hold wooden spoons like microphones, and we sing and dance to the song. It's called Downtown and it's sung by Petula Clark," Mary said. "Don't you just love the name Petula?"

It was more of a statement than a question, so I didn't answer her.

She turned on the record player and slowly dropped the needle on the record. There were a few seconds of scratchiness and then the song began to play.

It was snappy and fun, just like Mary. She turned up the volume so we could hear it better. She swayed back and forth in her pleated skirt keeping time to the beat of the music.

When the song finished, she said "Doesn't that song make you want to go to downtown Bessemer right now? See all the shops and watch the people?"

Once again, a statement, not a question. I shrugged like any boy would do, which looked like an answer but wasn't.

"I've got to go," I said. "I need to shovel our path before my dad gets home."

"Okay, Tom Terrific," she said, "maybe next time I can come to your house to listen to your records. Wouldn't that be fun?"

I didn't want to say that the newest record in our house was the soundtrack from stage production of Hello Dolly.

Many parents, like Mary's, were just fine with allowing their children to listen to cool new music or wear the latest styles. Sadly, my parents were not. They believed that rock and roll music had given us a society where juvenile delinquency was on the rise and young men dodge the draft. They wanted to keep their boys in line, so my parents chose our music too.

Yet, all I wanted to do was listen to my kind of music, not theirs. It was no deeper than that.

CHAPTER 30

Uncle Ern

The discussion around our Thanksgiving dinner table was seldom robust. Normally, our family ate in silence. The only sounds were those of serving, cutting, and eating the meal. We would devour a 26-pound turkey along with mashed potatoes, stuffing, cranberry sauce, olives, carrots and other fixings in a matter of twenty minutes. If a conversation got started, it centered on the misfortunes of the Detroit Tigers, the amazing Green Bay Packers' championships, or the construction of the new ski hills. Politics were off the table.

Our grandfather was Leonard J. McManman, son of Irish immigrants and original pioneer settlers in Ironwood. He was the 8th child of 14 in the McManman family that had lived in the mining village of Jessieville. He was the Probate Judge in Gogebic County and a dyed-in-the-wool Democrat. He was a powerful figure in the Michigan Democratic Party and was a delegate to the Democratic Presidential Convention in 1948 and 1952. When there was an opening on the Michigan Supreme Court, the name of Judge McManman was brought forward by the power brokers.

He was married to our grandmother Nina O'Leary, also the daughter of immigrants. She was the 4th child of nine in the O'Leary family and the perfect partner to the stoic judge. She was prim and proper and told us often to "throw our shoulders back and stand up straight" or "act like a nice young man." Status in the community was important to her husband especially during election season. She certainly didn't want her grandsons to turn out to be juvenile delinquents.

No one spoke at the Thanksgiving dinner table until our grandfather, the Judge, was ready to do so, that is unless his older brother Ernest was present. Uncle Ern, as we knew him, did not heed the unwritten family rule of "speak only when spoken to."

Ern began asking questions phrased as statements shortly after taking his first mouthful of sweet potatoes.

"I understand they're closing the Peterson Mine next year," Uncle Ern said.

Uncle Ern had worked in the Newport Mine in Jessieville for many years before retiring. Mining was his life. Well, mining and drinking. He drove a flatbed truck making deliveries. It had Pickands, Mather & Co. painted on the door. Like many miners who were single and lived in a boarding house, he worked all week, received his pay on Friday, and spent the weekend drinking. By Sunday morning, he had spent his money, and the cycle started over again.

Thankfully, Uncle Ern had been retired for years from both mining and drinking. He neither asked for nor was offered a drink at the Thanksgiving dinner table.

"Seems that Pickands, Mather & Co. are determined to shut down all of the iron ore mining in our area," Uncle Ern said. "I think January 28th they're closing the Cary Mine, or was that the Geneva mine?"

My dad jumped into the conversation to bring clarity to the question.

"They plan to close the Cary in January and Geneva in February," Dad replied. "They'll put 450 men out of work."

Our grandfather, the Judge, listened but didn't speak. He just kept eating, dipping his white turkey slice into the rich gravy. However, I had seen this scene play out before. The Judge was on a slow burn as he listened to his big brother ramble on about the mines. He was a tea kettle slowly heating up on the stovetop. But Uncle Ern was oblivious to the kettle boiling.

"I read that they plan to move Arthur Martini to the Peterson Mine from the Cary Mine after they close it next year," Uncle Ern said. "That means the Peterson Mine will likely close next. No doubt about that. Since that blast killed the two miners there last year, the place has not been the same."

Ern identified with the working man, that miner underground and his dangerous plight.

His brother, the Judge, identified with management and the difficult task of running an efficient mining operation.

"It was proven to be an accident," the Judge said firmly. "The mine incident was investigated and the company cleared."

Uncle Ern poked his fork into a dark piece of turkey on his plate and brought it to his mouth. Before he took a bite, he asked the folks at the table another question. "Do you know how many tons of ore they took out of the Cary and Geneva mines this past year?"

The Judge was starting to fidget in his chair. He reached for his Chesterfield cigarette in the ashtray beside his plate. It had a long ash but was still lit. He put it in his mouth, took a drag and the ash fell on his white shirt and tie. He brushed it off while his brother continued to talk.

"I read in the Daily Globe that they took 1.4 million tons from the ground at Cary and Geneva this year," Ern said.

We all acted amazed at the story. We had no idea if that was a lot or a little, but Uncle Ern would certainly give us more details.

"Do you know how much iron ore we took out in 1919?"

The Judge started to jab at his dressing, trying desperately not hear any more of this mining story.

My brothers and I tried to hold back our giggles. We could see that the scene was about to unravel.

"We took out more than seven million tons!" he exclaimed.

Forgetting the rule not to speak, I had to ask for more details.

"Did your mine do most of that Uncle Ern?" I asked.

"Oh, no. I worked in the Newport Mine. That mine opened in 1886 and the Geneva Mine opened in 1903. We were like brother mines. Do you know how many tons of ore we took out of those two mines?"

That's when the kettle boiled over.

"Who the hell cares," the Judge blurted, "how much iron ore came out of the ground!"

The room fell silent. My mother's eyes shifted nervously from her father to her uncle and back again. My grandmother, Nina, pursed her lips in disapproval.

"Leonard, your language around the children," she said.

Uncle Ern was unphased by his brother's outburst.

"We took out 55 million tons," he said. "Yes sir, those were the days. Those were the days."

Chapter 31

The thumping of the bass guitar, the booming kick drum and crashing of the cymbals penetrated through the thin walls of the White Birch Inn onto the main drag. The whistle from the fire hall blew at 9 p.m., just like it always did. It was going to be a tough night to sleep in the upstairs apartments along Sellar and Sophie for the Abelmans, Strelchecks and Guglielmotto families.

Ginny Strelcheck had a room with a view from the family's upstairs apartment that was kitty corner from the bar. She sat on the floor and looked out the window, with her chin resting on her arms against the windowsill. If she couldn't sleep, she might as well take in the revelry at the local bar.

One by one, the patrons opened the door to enter the White Birch, and a big splash of sound came spilling onto the street. It was Saturday night of a long Thanksgiving weekend and The Galaxies were tearing up the place to the delight of the over-21 crowd.

It was a night of rockabilly and rock and roll.

There was a time when The Galaxies were the biggest band in this corner of the world. Their hit songs played on the radio, they performed around the area and even toured across the Midwest. They were on the verge of a big break out; caught somewhere between a community dance band and performing on TV's American Bandstand.

But then life hit. One member went off to college, another got married, and at least one needed a good paying day job to support his family. By 1964, when The Galaxies got together at the White Birch Inn, it was for fun. This gig at the smoke-filled bar put a few bucks in their pockets, brought out the ladies and gave them the chance to do what they really wanted to do: play rock and roll.

The four young men who made up The Galaxies were Danny Sullivan, Greg Winn, Andy Abraham and Bernie Michelli. They mirrored the sight and sound of Buddy Holly and the Crickets, right down to the band's white topcoats and ties and that rock-a-billy sound.

In 1959, Andy Abraham, went to Duluth to see the Winter Dance Party tour featuring Buddy Holly, Dion and the Belmonts, Richie Valens, the Big Bopper and some other up-and-comers. He was blown away by all the acts.

Buddy Holly's final words on stage that night were that they were off to play in Appleton, Wisconsin. The reality for Holly and the rest of the Winter Dance Party tour was that fate would intervene, and the bus would make a bone-chilling detour to Hurley and Ironwood.

It was January 31, 1959, and temperatures had plunged to a frigid -30 degrees. The Winter Dance Party tour bus traveled through wicked weather all the way from Duluth to Ironwood on Highway 2. It turned on Highway 51 and headed towards Hurley and the famous Silver Street, known for its raucous bars and strip joints.

According to newspaper accounts, when the tour bus was about ten miles south of Hurley, near Pine Lake, the engine started to make a horrendous noise and suddenly the engine blew. The bus came to a slow and final stop. They were not heading to Appleton or anywhere else for that matter. The Winter Dance Party tour was literally frozen in time.

On the coldest day of the year, Buddy Holly, Dion and the Belmonts, Ritchie Valens, and the "Big Bopper" J.P. Richardson, who were just a bunch of guys from Texas and New York, were freezing their butts off in the dead of night, in the middle of nowhere.

According to the Iron County Miner newspaper, "an orchestra" had been stranded on Highway 51 and a passing motorist contacted a local sheriff's deputy to come to the band's aid.

The deputy was able to make some quick decisions and get the drummer, Carl Bunch, to Grand View Hospital in Ironwood. Although Bunch was wearing six pairs of socks to keep warm, he was suffering from a suspected case of frostbite.

The rescue cars took the remaining musicians to Club Carnival in Hurley, one of the few places still open late on a Saturday night. It was after 2 a.m. and no alcohol could legally be served, so the bartender would fill up coffee cups and serve the crowd. Coffee in some cases, whiskey in others. No local cop was the wiser.

The occasional drummer at Club Carnival was The Galaxies' own Bernie Michelli from Bessemer. No one is sure if Bernie was on the drum kit that night at the club, but if he had been he may have solved the Winter Dance Party tour dilemma.

A phone call came into Club Carnival that informed Holly, DiMucci, Richardson and Valens that their drummer, Carl Bunch, did indeed have frostbite and would need to remain in the hospital for treatment. He wouldn't be leaving with them in the morning for the next stop on the tour.

Just like that, the tour had no drummer. Fate could have intervened if Michelli had been on stage that night displaying his chops on the drums. Then, maybe, just maybe, Holly would have said, "Hey, how about we ask this guy to tour with us?"

The world will never know.

The tour adopted a plan presented by singer Dion DiMucci. He convinced the other musicians sitting in Club Carnival that the best drummer on the bus was Carlo Mastrangelo, who played with Dion and the Belmonts. So DiMucci suggested that Mastrangelo play drums for Buddy Holly. Then, Buddy would play drums for Dion. And Ritchie Valens would play drums for the Big Bopper. They all agreed.

The bandmates were given a ride to the St. James Hotel in Ironwood to stay overnight. They would board a train in the morning for Green Bay as the Appleton show had been cancelled due to their layover in Hurley and Ironwood. The tour would leave their drummer Carl Bunch behind at Grand View Hospital. Afterall, the show must go on.

Word spread in town, thanks to the Ironwood Daily Globe's "Hospital Notes" section that Buddy Holly's drummer "Carl Hugh Bunch, Odessa, Texas" was confined to a bed at the local hospital. Fans of Buddy Holly snuck into the hospital to meet the drummer as he was still a few days from being released.

As fate would have it, on February 3, 1959, Buddy Holly, along with Ritchie Valens and the Big Bopper, boarded a small plane in Mason City, Iowa to fly to their next gig in Moorhead, Minnesota. They never made it. The plane crashed in a cornfield in Clear Lake, Iowa.

Once word of the fiery wreck hit the Ironwood Daily Globe and WJMS radio, fans that knew that Holly's drummer Bunch was still in Grand View Hospital began to arrive there by the dozen to offer their condolences.

Bunch was in a total state of shock from the news of his fellow musicians' deaths. But he found solace in the sympathies offered by local youth of the Gogebic Iron Range area, who dug rock and roll and understood his loss.

Due to the number of fans stopping to see the drummer, the Grand View Hospital nursing staff had to enforce "visiting hours" rules to keep the greasers and bobby soxers from clogging the hallways. And they did, sending the fans out of the hospital into the cold of a U.P. winter night.

But it's easy to imagine, if fate had intervened, that one admirer, a local drummer, would discreetly ascend the rear staircase to the hospital's second level and quietly gain access to Bunch's room. The two drummers would chat about their favorite musicians, songs and venues. Just two guys who loved to play, discussing their craft. But mostly, they would talk about the devastating blow the music world was dealt, when three young musicians played their last note.

CHAPTER 32

Hope Runs Eternal

I waited for my buddy, John Hellman, to come from the end of Sellar Street so we could walk to the Bessemer gym for the home opener against the Hurley Midgets. I looked down the road but didn't see any kid walking my way, just the headlights of an oncoming car.

As the car passed our driveway, to my amazement, John was crouched behind it and hanging on to the back of the bumper. When the car stopped at the stop sign, he let go and the car kept going with the driver oblivious to the young boy who had been holding on.

"What the heck are you doing, John?" I asked.

"Hitching." he said with a smile. "Just hitching a ride."

"How are you able to grab the car bumper without the driver knowing?"

John was happy to fill me in as we walked to the gym. "When a driver comes to a full stop at the stop sign, you sneak up behind the car and grab the bumper. Then stay in this low crouch and skate all the way to your destination or until the driver wonders why his car has such a drag."

"My dad would kill me if I tried it," I replied.

"I once hitched from my house to Abelman's," John said, "but when I let go my choppers were frozen to the bumper and the car took off with them. My parents had to buy me a new pair. They were not happy."

We pulled open the big door on the south side of the gym. The junior varsity game had already started.

"That'll be 40 cents each," said the teen girl behind the ticket booth.

"It's supposed to be 25 cents for kids if we come to the B game," I replied.

"Take it up with the principal."

I was too scared to argue about it for fear a ROTC cadet would have me physically removed. John chose the safe route as well.

We found our appointed seats in the upper bleachers on the north side of the gym. No one checked our tickets to prove we paid, so we felt like we were getting away with something. Yet, the security detail was all around us. They walked up and down the aisle with scowls on their faces. Did they just dislike children or were these teachers upset that it was his or her night to patrol the bleachers?

The junior varsity team had Jim Milkovich, Don Barbacovi and Bill Joki playing the entire first quarter and into the second quarter. Gerry Drazkowski and Louie Menara were getting some serious minutes too.

"Hey, isn't that Bruce Richardson at the scorer's table?" John asked.

"It is," I said. "I heard he isn't playing basketball this season."

"Man, he was good, plus he was over six foot," John said. "He would be the tallest on the team."

The game program confirmed it. Only one player over six foot, Rick Syrjala. The boys were not growing like trees in Bessemer.

The late arriving crowd filled the bleachers on both sides of the gym. The JV team had shown they had some talent and were fun to watch. Little Don Barbacovi was getting the ball up the court with efficiency and finding Milakovich or Joki open for set shots or drives to the basket. Drazkowski was using all his girth to pull down some rebounds.

The JV game went back and forth. The cheerleaders and fans applauded the effort, but when the final buzzer sounded our junior varsity boys had lost to Hurley's JV, 61-47. Gary Gotta was the big scorer for the Midgets B team. Hope ran eternal for Bessemer fans that one day these young boys would help bring a championship back to their hometown.

The pep band made their entrance from the tunnel and onto the court, being careful to walk along the north side of the floor and not leave scuff marks with their shoes. Sharply dressed band director Fred Tezak was the last one out, carrying his sheet music and baton. The band wore gold sweaters with three stripes on one sleeve and the letter B sewn over the lower pocket. Their instruments sparkled as if the band had spent the last hour polishing the brass. They would play familiar instrumentals, the same ones they played last year and the year before that. Never a current hit song from The Beatles or Beach Boys.

The crowd waited patiently for the 1964-65 Speedboys to appear. All eyes focused on the tunnel, which was crowded with people pushing in and out. The JV players were walking out with satchels and wet hair, men heading in to have a smoke in the boiler room, cheerleaders with pom poms and signs going in both directions. It was a mishmash of bodies, yet it was all part of being at the A.D. Johnston High School gymnasium when a perennial rival, like Hurley, was in the building.

"Ladies and gentlemen, your Bessemer Speedboys!" the public address announcer exclaimed into the microphone.

With that announcement, the crowd rose to their feet while the band struck up the school fight song. Everyone sang as Speedboys captain Mark Martini led his teammates onto the court and into their pregame drills.

For the home opener, the team was dressed in white uniforms with blue trim. Each wore matching low top Converse sneakers, except Rick Syrjala and George Sabol who chose high tops. They looked like a team, but the question on every fan's mind was could they play like a team?

The man in black was second-year coach John Bonk. Black sport coat, black pants, and a black tie with a starched white shirt. His coke-bottle glasses with black frames matched his black hair. He looked dressed for a funeral, but was praying it wasn't.

Bonk stood five inches above any of his players. A clear sign to the competition that there were plenty of points for them inside the lane tonight.

The varsity cheerleaders were dressed in their blue sweaters and matching blue and white skirts that hung below their knees. There was not one mark on their newly purchased Keds.

Their faces were familiar. Joy Borseth, Jackie Burt and Marcella Boline were returning cheerleaders with newbies Bernadine Drazkowski, Sue Pricco and Florence Switzer joining the squad. They would jump and tumble and yell all night; hope upon hope that they could cheer the Speedboys to victory.

Staff Sergeant Adrian Anglim inspected the members of the Junior ROTC color guard that would step onto the court. He reminded the color guard how to present the flag once the guard made it to center court. Sgt. Anglim was emphatic about every detail.

"Ladies and gentlemen, please stand for our National Anthem," the announcer said.

Principal John Sartoris and the rest of the teachers on security detail patrolled the gym to be sure all boys and men removed their caps and all fans stood. Everyone complied.

The color guard marched onto the court. Only the clicks of their heels could be heard.

They stopped at center court and did a slight pivot and then the leader directed the presentation of arms and the American flag. The band struck up the National Anthem. It was big and bold and beautiful. Everyone in the gym sang loud and proud. When it was complete there was a rousing cheer as the color guard marched off in tight formation.

"Ladies and gentlemen," said the announcer, "I have your starting line-ups for tonight's game between the Bessemer Speedboys and the visiting Hurley Midgets."

He announced the fierce line-up of the Midgets. John Sicchio, Gary Miller, Barry Hautala, Herbert Perlberg and David Schimke. Their coach, Bill Zell.

The fans who had traveled from Hurley cheered loudly. No one louder than Marco Gotta who had just watched his son, Gary, deliver a win for the Hurley JV team.

"And now for your hometown Bessemer Speedboys!" the announcer said.

All Speedboys fans jumped to their feet. Pom poms were waving. Fists were thrust in the air. Applause rained down. The sound was deafening.

The Speedboys starters were announced as Mark Martini, Bill Ryan, Gary Niemi, Milo Barnaby and George Sabol. Their coach, John Bonk. Rick Syrjala would be at the ready if Hurley got out to a quick lead.

Bruce Richardson, last year's starting forward, was sitting at the scorer's table and gave no indication that he wanted to be out there. He was focused on his job as timekeeper. No smile. Just business.

The starting five got in a huddle at the free throw line and said a few encouraging words, then broke to center court for the jump ball.

Sabol jumped against the taller Perlberg of Hurley. The ball was tipped to Perlberg's teammate, who dribbled past his Speedboy defender and scored. And then they did it again. And then again. Before you could spell S-y-r-j-a-l-a, the score was 12-2 in favor of Hurley.

Syrjala checked into the game.

With sharp passing and good patience, the Speedboys made a comeback. Ryan found his range and hit a couple of neat jump shots. With the defensive rebounding of Syrjala paying dividends, the Midgets found there were no longer easy second chances underneath. Martini drove the lane multiple times for easy baskets and the scrappy Speedboys had tied the score at 12-12.

The Speedboys moved from a man-to-man defense to a 2-3 zone. They sagged inside to deny the easy points in the lane and forced Hurley to shoot from 10 to 15 feet out. The Midgets were less accurate from that distance.

Milo Barnaby hit a shot from the left corner. Ryan hit one from the right corner. Syrjala grabbed multiple offensive rebounds and put them back up and in. Suddenly, the lovable losers were leading the Hurley Midgets 21-14 at the end of the first quarter. A 20-point swing in a matter of minutes.

Coach John Bonk didn't know what to say to his lads, as they had never led after the first period — or any period that he could remember — during this entire losing streak.

"Just keep doing what you're doing," the coach said. "Number 13 doesn't like to guard anyone, so Milo, you take him to the basket."

On the other side, coach Bill Zell lectured his Midgets. He pointed intently at Sicchio.

Sicchio was an all-conference end in football. One of the best to ever play in the Gogebic Iron range area. His 6'1", 185-pound frame enabled him to screen out opposing players and allowed him to grab easy rebounds. He'd be playing college football in the future, but tonight his basketball skills were on display.

Whatever his coach said to him, it hit home. It was brutal for any Speedboy that dared to play down low in the second quarter.

With Sicchio controlling the area around the basket and feeding the ball to Gary Miller, the Midgets erased the deficit and went on an 18-6 run to take the lead at halftime, 32-27. Yet, it was the Speedboys that walked with a spark in their step as they made their way to the locker room. The local fans were proud of the effort.

"I thought we had them," I said. "Let's hope we give the same effort in the second half."

"They looked better," said John, "at least they did in the first quarter. I'm gonna get another pop."

He walked up the steps and down the aisle to get to the refreshment stands at courtside.

"Jim, how many points for Milo?" I asked Jim Rooni sitting nearby.

"Six," said Rooni. "Same as Martini. Same as Ryan." Rooni was always keeping score. He would file this scorecard next to all the others when he got home.

"So, you're saying that 18 of our 27 points came from three guys?" I asked.

"Yup. But Gary Miller has 14 points for Hurley," Jim said. "Stop Miller, stop the Midgets."

Jim sounded like a basketball analyst at that moment.

It was the tale of two periods. The Speedboys were great in the first quarter, stone cold in the second quarter and down at the half. The third period was just like the first. They made up the deficit with great shooting from Ryan and Martini and outstanding rebounding from Syrjala and Sabol, and only trailed by seven at the end of the third quarter, 46-39.

Beating Hurley appeared to be a real possibility for Bessemer fans.

"Get aggressive," Bonk yelled to his team. "Stop that easy shot inside."

And Bessemer did. To the tune of 24 personal fouls and three players fouling out in the fourth quarter. Martini, Syrjala and Niemi were all gone.

With three key players on the bench, Ryan was the only scoring threat still on the court. Yet, he scored just one basket in the fourth quarter. The *only* basket the Speedboys would score in the final period.

The final score was Hurley 62, Bessemer 41.

On Friday night, December 4, the Speedboys played the Wakefield Cardinals, a Michigan-Wisconsin Conference perennial powerhouse. No one in the Cardinal gymnasium, including the Bessemer fans, who had traveled the five miles to watch the game, expected the losing streak to end that evening. And predictably, it did not. Wakefield beat Bessemer 86-56.

For the Speedboys it was their third loss of the season and their 20th consecutive loss since March 1963.

Wakefield coach Jim Daniels shook hands with Bessemer coach Bonk.

"It's time we talked," Daniels said.

CHAPTER 33

The Range Restaurant in Bessemer was like many small-town restaurants. It adapted to the needs of the community. Dinners were prepared for groups up to 30, like the Ladies' Bowling League year-end banquet or a rehearsal dinner for a wedding party. Some days the power brokers in town would meet there over lunch and carefully plot the next move to address the mine closings or the influx of skiers to the new ski hills.

Mainly, it was a place for coffee and a doughnut to start the day off right for local folk going to work. On this morning, it was an unlikely meeting of rival coaches to chat about basketball.

"Black coffee, Coach?" Jackie Burt, a server on the early shift, asked John Bonk as he sat down at a table.

"Yes, Jackie, that would be wonderful," the coach replied. "You cheer all night for the game and get up early to be here to work on a Saturday?"

"I enjoy it," Burt replied. "Life is so much better when you embrace it. I like to be around people and this job gives me the opportunity to do that when I'm not in school or cheerleading at the games."

"Well, I wish I could give you more to cheer about," Bonk said.

"Oh, we all know you'll end that streak soon," said Burt, as she walked over to pour coffee at another table.

The door to the Range Restaurant opened and Wakefield's coach, Jim Daniels, walked in. Bonk stood and motioned Daniels to join him.

They shook hands and sat down together. Jackie moved to their table and poured Daniels a cup of coffee. Daniels dropped a cube of sugar into his cup, poured in a little cream and stirred it with his spoon.

"Thanks for taking it easy on us last night, Coach," Bonk said to Daniels.

"Call me Jim," replied Daniels. "I don't take it easy on anyone and I won't in the future either, but the game was well in hand so I got some of my young guys in. Your team was very feisty at the beginning and gave us some problems, but I think my guys were planning for an easy game and were just lackluster for the first half."

"Well, I thought our guys fought hard," Bonk said. "But when your Cardinal team can go on those runs of 13-2 and so on, we just don't know how to stop it."

Daniels nodded in agreement.

"John, I want Bessemer to be good. There is no place in our conference for teams that are push-overs. Bessemer was always a competitive team. It isn't now."

Daniels took a sip and then continued.

"You have to develop basketball players young. You have good young men on your team, but they're football and baseball players. They're strong, tough, and aggressive. But they don't have finesse. They go hard for the rebound but commit a foul. They take a shot from ten feet when they could have had a layup. They play physical and ignore the mental part of the game."

Bonk just sat quietly and listened.

"Coach, you need a youth program, and you need it bad," Daniels said. "You've got to develop these boys in the right environment with the right mix of fundamentals and decision making."

Daniels spoke from experience. Their youth program was one reason the Wakefield Cardinals basketball team had been successful. Daniels coached teams that won the Michigan-Wisconsin Conference and the Class C District Championship four times. His team played in the U.P. Regional Championship game in 1958, 1961, 1962 and 1964. The Cardinals finally broke through and won the U.P. championship in 1964 and took their first trip downstate under Daniels to play in the state tournament. Daniels knew it all started with teaching the fundamentals of the game at an early age.

"Well, you'll be happy to know that we'll be starting a youth basketball program at the fifth-, sixth- and seventh-grade levels beginning this month," said Bonk.

"That's a great start, John."

"Fundamentals will be taught every single night," Bonk said. "I saw at my first practice last season that the fundamentals were lacking. I didn't realize how good this conference was and how it exposed our flaws."

Daniels waved Jackie over for a coffee refresher.

"Why did you insist on meeting me this morning," Bonk asked. "Why during the season?"

Daniels poured creamer into his fresh coffee and stirred as he thought about how to reply to Bonk.

"I wanted to meet you today, but not because of our game last night," Daniels said. "I wanted to meet you because of what I saw at the junior varsity game."

Bonk bellowed his big deep laugh.

"Oh, why do you say that?"

"John, our JV beat your JV team 88-24," Daniels said. "Your JV scored just eight points in the second half. Eight. You don't have a bench. It's as empty as your coffee cup. My JV players were ninth graders last season and went 10-0 while your ninth graders went 0-10."

Bonk nodded.

"Don't get me wrong," Daniels said. "I love to beat Bessemer. And I plan to beat Bessemer every time we play. But we don't get better unless we're facing the very best talent game after game, season after season. The Bessemer Speedboys have got to get better."

Bonk nodded. He couldn't dispute it.

"Thanks, Coach," said Bonk. "I mean, Jim. You know, I couldn't agree with you more."

"Your youth program should start paying benefits in five years." Daniels continued. "But you should consider giving your juniors and sophomores more playing time now."

With that, the coaches shook hands, exchanged phone numbers and headed out the front door. They each left a 5-cent tip for their waitress. Jackie pocketed the money as she cleared the table.

Chapter 34

No Vacancy

"Big Powderhorn Mountain opens next week," said John Novascone. "Where are the skiers going to sleep?" Novascone, the publisher of *The Bessemer Herald* newspaper, had been asking that question for the last two years in his weekly column. He was convinced that ski tourism would be a boon to the local Gogebic-Iron Range economy that was suffering from the steady loss of iron ore mining jobs.

WJMS radio advertised the western U.P. of Michigan as "Big Snow Country." There were many skiing venues in this part of the area for all levels of skiers.

Many Bessemer children had learned to ski on Mussatti's Hill on the eastern side of Bessemer while others had only skied the trail down from Miners Mesa above Tourist Park. Most did not have the money to ski the "big hills" at Indianhead Mountain in Wakefield or Whitecap Mountain in Iron Belt, Wisconsin.

Fortunately, Louis Gheller, an Italian immigrant, along with Paul Steiger and other local investors, were building a major ski destination in northwest Bessemer named Big Powderhorn Mountain. Together with the other ski hills, the new 115-acre resort would soon attract skiers by the busload to the area.

Which brings us back to the question posed by the *Herald's* publisher.

"Where is everyone going to sleep?"

The small towns in this part of the Upper Peninsula of Michigan were not prepared for the number of beds needed to house the many skiers each weekend. There was a mad scramble in Hurley,

Ironwood, Bessemer and Wakefield to provide enough housing for the impending onslaught. The local motels literally had *No Vacancy* signs hanging all winter long.

A few local citizens agreed to open their homes to the overflow of skiers, charging $5 per night, per person.

Bessemer resident Ann Massie would welcome a skier or two, female only, and provide coffee, juice, and Dandee Bakery rolls in the morning and a clean bed at night. All for $5.00. It was nice supplemental income for a widow.

Her son Joel would answer the phone and enter the reservations. Mrs. Massie reported that skiers from all over the world came to ski in the area and to stay at her little weekend bed and breakfast.

But Mrs. Massie's two-bed accommodation had little impact on the larger demand for room nights. Now, Big Powderhorn Mountain would open.

"Where is everyone going to sleep?"

In Bessemer, the entrepreneurial spirit of the local shop owners turned this problem into an opportunity. The businesses quickly converted vacant or underutilized spaces into sleeping accommodations.

Don and Rosemary Strelcheck turned their flower shop at the corner of Sellar and Sophie into four modern sleeping compartments they called the *Motel-ette*. It had showers and a kitchenette, and it slept ten or more people.

Bernie and Helen Proft lived upstairs at the corner of Mary and Moore. They converted their vacant lower level into a skier sleep paradise for twenty. Simple cots and mattresses covered every inch of the lower level. The Profts focused on youth groups that came to the area by the busload. Bernie often had to get up in the middle of the night to discipline the young skiers, but it was all part of the experience of offering sleep accommodations.

John Novascone of the *Herald* entered the room and board business as well. He converted his farm, the Tenderloin Beef Cattle Ranch, into a year-round facility that had sleeping quarters for up to 22 people per night.

Even the abandoned Barber School in Yale found new life. The Barber School had not been used since 1960, when the fire marshal gave the Bessemer school district the alternative to either upgrade to meet state fire codes or to close it down. Superintendent Carlo Heikkinen chose the latter. Now, local volunteers opened up the old yellow brick firetrap to house up to 125 youth, rebranding it the Bessemer Indianhead Hostel, or "The Hostel" for short.

Even the Gogebic County Jail would let a poor skier or two stay the night if he was down on his luck with nowhere to sleep, provided the jail had vacancy.

Big Powderhorn Mountain officially opened to the public on December 11, 1964.

When we got back from Sunday Mass, we loaded our ski gear into the Ford wagon after lunch. My brother John and I were selected for the maiden voyage to this new ski destination. We each placed a dime in our jacket pocket so we could get some hot chocolate, if it was available.

We followed the snow-covered road near Powdermill Creek to get to our destination. We were not used to seeing new construction in Bessemer. When Dad pulled up, a huge Alpine-style chalet stood at the bottom of the hill. It was magnificent. We watched as skier after skier slalomed down the hill. The ski slopes flowed right to the new chalet.

"Louie Gheller was smart," Dad said. "He built the chalet at the bottom of the hill rather than the top like those stumblebums at Indianhead. You don't have to ride the cold chairlift back up the hill just to go home."

Another statement by Dad explaining the brilliance of Bessemer people.

Dad helped us get our skis and poles out of the back of the station wagon. He pointed us to the chalet, then slapped the tailgate shut and drove off, never concerned for a minute that we didn't know where we were supposed to go. There was no hand holding in Bessemer. Just figure it out boys. And so we did.

Big Powderhorn Mountain sold tickets on the south side of the building next to the ski runs. We got in line behind the other half-day skiers and waited for the opportunity to buy our bunny hill pass. The line was long yet moving at a reasonable pace.

Louie Gheller stood behind the ticket counter, holding a large stapler. He was sporting a powder blue turtleneck, a dark gray windbreaker buttoned at the top, and a light blue baseball cap with the mountain's logo on it, a gunpowder horn.

When we got to the front of the line, Louie was just finishing a story about how they were able to build the ski resort in one and a half years.

"Hi Louie," I said.

Calling Mr. Gheller by his first name seemed natural and he didn't seem to mind.

"Ah, hello there little man," Louie responded. "You ready to ski the big hill?"

I could feel my cheeks flush and my voice catch in my throat. I didn't know what to ask for — a ticket for the chairlift? Thankfully, my brother John interjected.

"We're only going to ski the bunny hill today, so we need two tickets for the rope tow."

"Ok," Louie said. "Helen, take care of these two boys."

Mrs. Helen Boline was the mother of our good friends Art and George. Both of them were skiers and would soon spend many afternoons and evenings on the slopes, waiting for their mom to finish work. Helen was decked out in a yellow dress with white button earrings and a pearl necklace. Her golden hair was wrapped in what ladies called a beehive. We had never seen her hair out of the hive. I'm not certain Art or George had either.

Helen was one of the first people that Louie Gheller hired. She was dedicated to any job at hand, whether it be the ski hill, the ladies' club, or her backhand in the summer at the ladies' tennis league in Wakefield. She was always serious and stayed on task.

Helen, without even looking up from the cash register, said, "That will be $1 each."

"Thank you, Mrs. Boline." I said.

She looked up and smiled, recognizing John and me. She handed the tickets to Louie.

As John stood in front of him, Louie grabbed the bottom of John's jacket, pulled it tight, and then stapled the ticket to his jacket. We saw this from some of our friends in school. They had multiple tickets stapled to their jackets, reminding one and all just how many times they had skied.

I was up next.

But before Louie took care of me, Dante Pricco and his brother Teenie came down the hall with bags full of freshly baked bread. Oh, the bread smelled so good. Louie and the Pricco brothers started talking in Italian and laughing out loud. They seemed happy to be speaking their native tongue.

When the Priccos moved on, Louie turned back to the job at hand. I stepped up to Louie and he tugged on the bottom of my jacket, wrapped the ticket and slipped the jacket into the jaws of the stapler. He squeezed the stapler twice. It made a gigantic sound. However, when he removed the stapler the ticket fell to the ground.

"Helen, I'm out of staples," he said.

Without even taking her eyes off the register, Helen handed a box of staples to Louie.

Louie struggled to load the stapler. The line grew longer.

"Helen, I don't know. This just isn't working," he shrugged as he handed her the stapler.

With military precision, Helen hit one button, slid in a row of staples and snapped it shut. She handed it back to Louie and said, "Next."

Louie motioned to me and said "Come, come."

He grabbed my jacket, slapped on the ticket and snap, snap, I was stapled.

"Go, ski, ski," he said. "I will join you soon."

Dad told us that Louie Gheller was a man of the people. He wanted to be on the slopes and skiing through the powder with his friends. All he ever wanted to do was ski and teach others how to ski. He had created a magnificent winter paradise, but ironically, he would be trapped behind a desk most days with an avalanche of paperwork. A sacrifice Louie was willing to make to create jobs for local residents and a winter getaway for visitors.

When we got outside and strapped on our skis, we finally set eyes on Big Powderhorn Mountain. Never had we seen such a spectacular sight. Dad said it was built by local people with local money. He liked that.

There were two chair lifts, one on each side of the brand-new chalet. The lifts were painted red and the seats were wood with steel sides. There were no safety bars, and Art and George said you had to be prepared when the lift made a sudden stop so you wouldn't be thrown off. We didn't have to worry about that today as the bunny hill was our only challenge, or was it the rope tow?

Skiers took the rope tow at his or her own peril. Imagine a big hunk of two-inch-thick rope on an endless loop, moving at a speed of five miles per hour, swinging through a large pulley on former telephone poles.

There was an art to using the rope tow. Most first-time users did a faceplant. Their error was grabbing the rope and squeezing it tight. That tight grip immediately thrust your body forward while your skies dragged behind. Some kids didn't let go and were dragged for a few dozen feet. Many considered quitting at that point. Eventually, a knowledgeable 12 year old skied up to the tow and gave the newbies instructions. We listened intently.

"Allow the rope to glide through your mitten or glove like this," he instructed as the rope sped thru his leather chopper.

"Then, slowly grasp the rope, squeezing ever so slightly until you start to move. Once you feel yourself moving, grab tighter and ride to the very top. Let go at the top and you are ready to ski down the hill and do the rope tow all over again," he said.

Smart kid. But I did notice that the inside of his chopper was worn away. Apparently, as the rope flows through your gloved hand, it rubs off the material. It was like a rug burn for your winter glove.

Since this sage advice came from a big 12 year old, we took his words to heart. John and I got our turns to grab the rope and did well. The girl behind us grabbed on as instructed but got scared and let go. Her mitten, firmly attached to the rope tow, continued up the hill.

We skied all afternoon and it was exhilarating.

CHAPTER 35

Future Stars

*T*he *Bessemer Herald* announced the boys intramural basketball program was starting next week and would be held two nights per week through March. The program was designed for fifth, sixth and seventh graders. The *Herald* said interested boys should bring with them a white t-shirt, gym shorts, white socks, an athletic supporter, and sneakers, causing an immediate run on P.F. Flyers at the Bootery Shoe Store in Ironwood and jockstraps at Abelman's.

Over 60 boys showed up for the new basketball program in December of 1964. The noise in the Washington School gymnasium was ear-splitting with basketballs bouncing and boys yelling with excitement.

We were dressed in our white t-shirts and shorts, but a few boys showed up in blue jeans and were told to bring the right attire for the next session. One boy forgot his sneakers and was relegated to playing in his stocking feet. But all of us were enthusiastically chasing each other around and throwing up wild shots at the baskets as we waited for the instructor to take control.

Harry Rizzie blew his whistle and gathered all of us at midcourt. He explained that the purpose of the new program was to teach us the fundamentals of the game. He said that for 90 minutes a night, two nights per week for the next four months, we would practice bounce and chest passes, left-handed dribbling, right-handed dribbling, and shooting. Any given drill might last 15 minutes at a time, the intent being to build the muscle memory of executing the perfect pass or accurate set shot. We were excited to be playing basketball indoors. The drills were a bonus.

"Alright, boys, make two lines that run the length of the court. Face each other. Now, I'm going to teach you the chest pass and the bounce pass. We'll do the same with dribbling and shooting. Over and over again until you get it right."

Each boy concentrated hard during the various drills. Some boys were naturals at the game and others had never touched a basketball. But it was the place to be. Sweating, yelling, and running about with sheer delight. We were playing the game that we had all dreamed about.

When I got home after that first night, I was exhausted but on cloud nine. I wanted to share everything about the night.

My family was watching the Bob Hope television special. There was a haze floating in the room and six butts in the ashtray, so I could tell Dad was relaxing, watching his favorite show with a brandy and water and a pack of smokes.

My brother Paul was sitting close to the television on clicker duty. He had to turn from channel 3 to channel 6 upon Dad's command. *Click, click, click* and you were on channel 6; three times the other way and you were back on 3.

The television knob had broken off about a month ago, but dad had attached a pair of vice grips to the channel peg and it worked just fine. Sometimes Dad needed the vice grips to work on a project, so on those occasions we were stuck with either channel 3 or 6 until the vice grips were reattached.

I didn't care much for Bob Hope. I liked his specials when he was entertaining the troops, but this wasn't one of those nights. It was his usual campy humor, and at some point, someone would get a pie in the face.

We only had one television, so there was no choice but to watch what dad had on, like Bob Hope. I decided to head upstairs to my room.

I plopped down onto my twin bed. I leaned over and turned on the radio to listen to the Speedboys game. It took a moment for the radio to warm up. Slowly the sound increased to a reasonable level and the voice of Bob Olson, the sports announcer for WJMS, became clear.

"The Speedboys have a win on their minds. The Maple Tigers led by big Obe Saari had a 13-point lead just a few minutes ago. Now, it's down to nine."

I loved listening to radio broadcasts. Our television downstairs was black and white, but Bob Olson's radio play-by-play seemed to be in color. You could use your imagination as Olson described the dramatic scenes occurring on the basketball floor. It was certainly better than watching some campy television show.

Olson was a master at describing the action and convincing listeners that even the winless Speedboys were about to pull the upset. His voice was made for radio.

"Bessemer's Milo Barnaby has gotten hot and the Tigers have gone cold. Ryan and Sabol are pressing the Tigers' inbound pass. Coach Bonk, who is just a few feet in front of our broadcast table, is yelling to his team not to press. To get back. However, Sabol and Ryan are either not hearing his directions or not listening to their coach."

The crowd noise appeared to be getting louder on the broadcast as the Speedboys made a furious comeback. I put my ear right next to the radio speaker to hear clearly.

"Dave Arnold passes the ball in for Maple, but HOLD ON, it's stolen by Ryan. Ryan passes it to Sabol, and he lays it in. 65-58 Maple. Ryan is yelling to his teammates to press, keep pressing. Coach Bonk is still yelling to his team to get back. Obviously, miscommunication between coach and player."

"OH! It's stolen again by the Speedboys. Ryan shoots and hits from five feet out. Could this be the night that the Speedboys end their 20-game losing streak?"

I jumped out of bed and began pacing the room. I turned up the radio louder.

"There are 23 seconds left on the clock. Khalar, who has four fouls, is taking the ball out for Maple. He gets it to Johnson. The Speedboys are still pressing the Tigers apparently against the wishes of Coach Bonk, but the Speedboys are out of timeouts so he can't get his message to his team. Wow! Ball is stolen at mid-court by Ryan again. He passes it to Barnaby who goes in for the layup, the shot is no good, but he was fouled by either Khalar or Arnold, I'm not sure which one. It's Khalar. He is protesting

the call, but heads to the bench. Khalar will have to sit with five fouls. And Barnaby heads to the charity stripe with 13 seconds left, shooting two. Wow! Makes you wonder what would have happened if Bessemer had pressed Maple earlier."

"Come on, Milo!" I yelled at the radio. "This is our night."

"Barnaby, number 12, calmly steps to the line. Takes a couple of dribbles. Sets and shoots. Swish. It is now 65-60 Maple. Bill Ryan is talking to Coach Bonk in front of the bench. Barnaby gets the ball from the referee, dribbles twice and puts up the second free throw and it rolls around the rim and IN. That's 21 points for young Milo Barnaby. 65-61, the Speedboys trail by just four with 13 seconds remaining. Wow! We got a dandy here."

Olson was breathlessly enjoying the rare opportunity to broadcast a game in which the Speedboys were still competitive in the fourth quarter. He knew the place would go crazy if Bessemer pulled it out.

"The Speedboy B team won a thriller by one point earlier tonight; can the varsity join them finally in the win column? Maple tosses the ball in. 10 seconds, 9 seconds, they get it across the timeline. The crowd is yelling, "Foul! Foul!" Maple gets it inside to Arnold; he goes up for the shot! And makes it. And he is fouled by Ryan. That's five on Ryan. There are just three seconds left on the clock. Sorry, Speedboy fans, it's not happening tonight. The Tigers are going to win it, and the Bessemer Speedboy losing streak will be extended to 21 games."

I turned the radio knob off as hard as I could. Somehow that made me feel better.

I heard my dad laughing downstairs apparently at some dumb joke told by Bob Hope. I got up and headed downstairs to see what was so hilarious.

"Dad, the Speedboys lost again," I said.

"Tell me something I don't know," Dad replied.

"It was close though. Like 68-61. It was pretty exciting."

"Martini do all the scoring again?"

"No, actually George Sabol and Milo had a lot of points. I think Milo had 21 and George had 12 or something like that."

"Well, I'm sure George Sr. will be happy to hear that his son had a good game. I'll have to say something to him at smear night."

"It's their 21st straight loss," I said. "Do you think they'll ever win a game?"

"Oh, they'll win as soon as they play as a team. I've had a few beers with Coach Bonk at the Elks Lodge, and he's a really nice guy, but he is so green as a coach. He was a great player in high school, but some guys just can't teach others. He may be one of them."

"I heard the announcer say the B team won 49-48 in a real thriller," I said. "I wish I had been there."

"Well, that's good to hear. I'm sure cousin Donny had a good game then," Dad replied. "Glad he's learning to win on the B squad and not sitting on the bench for the varsity."

Mom had to chime in.

"Sitting on the bench for the varsity is what cousin Gary Niemi did as a sophomore," she said, "and you see where that got him. He needed to play like Donny on the junior varsity."

"Yeah, I guess," I replied.

Dad lifted his empty glass towards me and twirled the ice cubes around on the bottom.

"Tommy, mix me another one," Dad said. "Easy on the water. Paul, turn the TV to channel to 3."

Paul grabbed hold of the vice grips and turned the channel three clicks.

"It's Gomer Pyle," Paul said.

"Geez, turn it back," Dad yelled.

CHAPTER 36

Letters To Santa

On Saturday night the week before Christmas, I was doing my homework on a new school desk my father had built. This one was an old 1940 era sewing machine. Dad didn't bother to remove the guts of the machine. Just placed a nicely finished pine board on top. Also, he had not removed the band wheel or the treadle, which was the foot-operated lever mechanism that powers the machine. While doing our school assignments, we rocked the treadle back and forth, in a way getting a leg workout while we learned. Kind of ingenious.

As I worked on my homework, WJMS was playing in the background. During the week before Christmas, Santa Claus came on the radio and read letters that had been mailed by children to the North Pole.

It was hilarious to hear about the toys children wanted, and it was even more fun when Santa read a letter from some kid you knew from Bessemer. The program was good company when you were doing something as monotonous as fourth grade arithmetic.

"Ho, Ho, Ho! Merry Christmas, children. This is Santa Claus at the North Pole ready to read more letters from good boys and girls."

It sounded like Santa, but I was quite certain it was Bob Knutson, the newsman on WJMS. He read the news and also served as host of the "Trad-E-O" show, where people called in to get rid of their junk to some unsuspecting customer.

"Well, let me see whose letter we will read first. I have four letters from a lot of good boys and girls. Let's see… the Olson family, the Webber family, the Schultz children and the Pelissero boys."

My mouth dropped open. *Oh, my god*, I thought. *Oh, my god.* Who sent a letter to Santa from the Pelissero boys? We would be judged mercilessly at school the next day by a jury of our peers.

My brother John rushed into the room.

"Did you write a letter to Santa?" he yelled.

"No! Not me," I yelled.

Mom solved the mystery with one quick line.

"Hey, boys, come down here," she said. "They're going to read the letter on the radio that I sent to Santa."

It's one thing to give your parents a list of gift ideas. It's quite another way to have it broadcast to the world.

"Ho, ho, ho. It's always good to hear from those Pelissero boys in Bessemer," Santa announced.

Brother Paul and Gerry sat at the kitchen table, all smiles to hear their name on the radio. I was looking for a bucket to puke in.

"Dear Santa, We have been good boys this year. But our mother would like us to clean our rooms more often. We will try to do better next year and she will inform you. We would like the following toys and games from your workshop. Little Pete would like a Bozo the Clown talking doll. Gerry would like a G.I. Joe Action Figure. Paul would like the game of Sorry."

I was sweating. Oh, my god. What did Mom write in that letter? This was awful. But there was no stopping Santa.

"Ho ho ho, let's see what the two older boys would like from Santa. Tom would like the game of Scrabble," Santa announced.

"Scrabble?" I yelled. "I can't even spell!"

"That's why Santa is bringing it," Mom replied.

I'm not sure what is worse. Getting *Scrabble* or having it announced on the radio that I wanted it.

"Shush, they're going to read John's wish now," Mom said.

John sat on the steps, hands over his eyes, humiliated that a sixth grader was about to have a Christmas wish announced by Santa.

"Ho, ho, ho, Johnny would like a Magic 8 Ball so he can predict the future.

Well, let me look at my Magic 8 Ball and ask will the Pelissero boys have a merry Christmas. The Magic 8 Ball says, It is definitely so.

Well, Merry Christmas and Happy New Year, Pelissero boys. I'll get my elves working on these requests right away. And be sure to clean your rooms to make your mom happy. Ho, ho, ho."

The telephone rang not fifteen seconds after Santa's proclamation, the first of many phone calls that evening. When I answered it, all I heard was laughter on the other end of the phone, and one word.

"Scrabble?" the voice said. "Scrabble?"

It was one of my friends, not sure who, but he was belly laughing so hard that he may have injured himself. I just hung up.

Ho, ho, ho.

CHAPTER 37

"*Welcome to Coaches Corner on WJMS 630. This is Joe Blake filling in for Bob Olson, who is on vacation. First up this morning we have Coach John Bonk of the Bessemer Speedboys on the telephone. The Speedboys are mired in last place in the Michigan-Wisconsin Conference with a 0-5 record. They have Ironwood next. Coach, you haven't played since December 19th when you lost to Ontonagon. What have you been working on during the winter break to get your boys ready to play the rest of the conference schedule?*"

"*Well,*" started Coach Bonk. "*I have been working with Rick Syrjala and Don Johnson over the past week trying to improve our rebounding. Don and Rick will provide more height to our line-up and hopefully grab more offensive rebounds. We normally get one shot and then we head back down to the other end. We need some second chances.*"

"*Are you saying Johnson and Syrjala will start this Friday against the Ironwood Red Devils?*" Blake asked.

"*No, we'll probably go with the same lineup before we went on break. Gary Niemi will play center. Bill Ryan and Mark Martini will be the guards, and George Sabol and Milo Barnaby will be the forwards.*"

"*Barnaby has really been coming on, wouldn't you say Coach? He had fifteen against the Polar Bears.*"

"*Yes, I'm really excited to see this young man step up. His quickness and shot selection is very helpful to our team. Heck, he has great jumping ability, so I may use him at center, too.*"

"*Coach, the Ironwood Red Devils are down this year, only 1-4 in the conference. What do you think of your chances against them?*"

"*I don't know what a 'down year' means in this conference. All these teams are good enough to beat anyone else, even in a down year. We need to stop Kangas, Finco and Carli.*"

"Good luck, Coach," said Blake.

Coach Bonk's wife, Alice, was pouring her husband a cup of coffee as he hung up the phone.

"Maybe I should start Don Johnson tonight?" he said to his wife. "I need more rebounding. No, no, I'll just go with what I told them on the radio."

Alice couldn't hold it back anymore, so she finally said what was on her mind.

"John, maybe it's time to play the younger guys."

"Why do you say that, Alice?"

"Well, you continue to lose and sometimes by a lot. Maybe you should give the sophomores and juniors a look. After twenty some losses, you can't be worse off."

John laughed.

"I've been thinking the same thing," he said. "But it's a double-edged sword. I hurt the seniors in order to give experience to the younger guys. It's a no-win situation."

Alice put the coffee pot down on the kitchen stove and sighed.

"John, it's been a no-win situation for one and a half seasons."

That night the Bessemer Speedboys faced 32 minutes of full court pressure from the Ironwood Red Devils. Bessemer's starting five was held without a field goal for nearly the entire first quarter. It never got better.

Even in a down year, the Ironwood Red Devils basketball team had little trouble breezing to their second conference victory, winning 74-51 and handing Bessemer their 23rd straight loss. Adding to the misery, starting guard Bill Ryan suffered a severe ankle sprain. He would need x-rays and his return to the team was in doubt.

Did Coach Bonk have the guts to turn this team over to sophomores and juniors? It would be a very tough decision for the young coach; one that could cost him his job.

CHAPTER 38

Varsity vs. Junior Varsity

After-school cartoons, featuring *Bozo the Clown*, had just concluded when mom called us for supper. Once again, our Bozo button number had not been picked for the prize drawing. "*Better luck tomorrow, kids,*" Bozo would say.

"Time to eat," she yelled. "We're having barbecues and potato chips."

As we walked into the kitchen, Mom had the radio on and turned up plenty loud.

"*And time for Gogebic Range News,*" the WJMS newsman said. "*A member of the Bessemer Speedboys basketball team was injured this morning in a two-vehicle accident on U.S. 2 in Bessemer.*"

Mom pulled in a quick breath, holding it, and put a dish towel over her mouth knowing there was tragic news to be announced.

"*Milo Barnaby, a junior at A.D. Johnston High School and a member of the varsity basketball team, was injured as he drove to school during whiteout conditions just west of Anvil Road in Bessemer. Barnaby ran his 1960 Impala into the back of a truck driven by an unidentified man from Wakefield. Barnaby sustained a broken nose and facial bruises in the accident. The other man had no injuries. The Michigan State Patrol ticketed Barnaby with driving too fast for conditions. Due to his extensive facial injuries, Barnaby was ruled out of playing in Friday night's game by Bessemer coach John Bonk. In other news…*"

Mom turned down the radio slightly and finally took a breath. She was relieved that no one was killed. She started to serve the barbecue, but I could tell her mind was racing.

❖

The barbershops needed fresh conversation fodder, and they got it with the misfortune of Speedboy Milo Barnaby. No one in Guglie's could agree on the extent of Barnaby's injuries and at times it got a bit exaggerated. Most understood he had a broken nose and facial bruises. All agreed that with him or without him, the Speedboys were likely to lose again, this time to league-leading Superior East.

And lose they did: 76-37. Their 24th straight defeat back to March of 1963.

At Saturday morning practice, Coach Bonk began testing the idea of giving more playing time to his younger players. Instead of running the usual drills, he and JV coach Carl Gregas decided to have the varsity scrimmage the junior varsity. Niemi, Martini, Johnson, Syrjala, and Sabol were skins for the varsity and Milakovich, Barbacovi, Joki, Drazkowski, and Menara were shirts for the JV. Others would play as well.

The whistle blew, then a jump ball at center court and off they went. The JV team was a little nervous, and the varsity stole the ball early and often, jumping out to an early 4-0 lead. However, before long the younger team's offensive chemistry began to click. Don Barbacovi, a sophomore, discovered confidence in his ball handling. He found Jim Milakovich, a 5'9" sophomore, on the left side of the court. Milakovich faked Johnson to the right, took a cool left-hand dribble, drove to the basket, and laid it in with ease. Repeatedly, Barbacovi, Milakovich and Joki got open and made their shots.

For the varsity squad, Martini took shots from beyond the free throw line with little success. Niemi got good looks from the corners but couldn't find the net with any consistency either. Bonk tried different combinations for the varsity, rotating in Mike Betlewski, Bobby Abelman, and others. The results were mixed.

Bonk and Gregas allowed the two Bessemer teams to go at it with as little stoppage of play as possible, except to call an occasional foul. There was no scoreboard, but when the final whistle sounded, both teams knew who won.

CHAPTER 39

Bonk wrestled with his decision all weekend long. He didn't come to a final determination until late Sunday night. Then, on Monday morning, he drove to work through falling snow, arrived at school, and immediately called a team meeting.

He asked the varsity players to leave their homerooms and head to the locker room. There they would discuss the future of the team.

Slowly the players walked into the locker room. All were there except Bill Ryan and Milo Barnaby. Ryan was still nursing his ankle sprain and Barnaby was recovering from his broken nose.

"Do you know what this is all about?" George Sabol asked teammate Mark Martini.

"No idea," whispered Martini.

Bonk opened by thanking the seniors for giving their all. He thanked them for their perseverance and spirit despite losing all the games he had coached.

The players started to think their coach was about to resign.

Then, Bonk dropped the bomb.

"It's time for a change," he said. "After looking over the past year and half and understanding the competitiveness of our Conference, and after witnessing the junior varsity defeating the varsity in a scrimmage last Saturday, I've decided to make a change. I plan to promote some junior varsity players to play on the varsity for the rest of the year."

The seniors stared at their head coach, not yet comprehending what this meant for their careers. But they could count, and there were only 12 varsity uniforms.

"We need to get our sophomores some varsity game experience so that next season we'll be competitive," Bonk said. "The more they play, the more they'll learn, and the more we'll have a chance to win again. Now, I know this is hard for you seniors to hear, but we have to start now and not wait until next year."

Bonk met eyes with the seniors in the room.

"Seniors, there's a chance you won't play another minute the rest of this season."

Bonk let that message hang in the room.

One boy held back tears, another shook his head in disbelief, and others just stared blankly.

"You can choose to stay and help the team, or you can choose to leave the team," Bonk said. "We are going nowhere at this point, and we need to build from the ground up. I plan to promote Milakovich, Barbacovi and Joki, and consider a few others. It's all part of a bigger plan to bring winning basketball back to Bessemer."

Bonk looked over the stunned faces, but he just kept on trudging through the bad news for seniors.

"At least three of you have to give up your uniform."

One senior stood up, gave a wave of disapproval, and walked out of the room while Bonk was still talking. The player had made his decision. Bonk didn't react. He kept talking.

"We're rebuilding our basketball program at all levels in this town. Last month we started an intramural program in the grade schools. We've authorized eighth graders to play on the freshman team at Washington School. And we are going to elevate the best of our freshmen players to the junior varsity team. Someday, I hope you'll understand."

Bonk paused momentarily.

"We start preparing for the Oredockers at 4:00 this afternoon."

Bonk left the room, trailed by junior varsity coach Carl Gregas, who ran to find Milakovich, Barbacovi and Joki to give them the news before one of the varsity players broke it to them.

The juniors returned to class, but the seniors stayed behind to mull over their personal decisions. Two senior benchwarmers said they felt relieved. Basketball was no longer fun for them. They immediately handed in their uniforms to the team managers.

Senior Gary Niemi spoke to no one. He quietly left the locker room, walked up the stairs, and headed back to class. His career as a member of the Bessemer Speedboys was over; he would reluctantly hand in his uniform at the end of the school day.

Mark Martini sat down in front of his locker and leaned back against the cold metal grates. He looked up toward the ceiling and sighed.

George Sabol sat next to him.

"Mark, what's your plan?" Sabol asked. "You gonna quit or ride the bench?"

Martini sat forward and quickly responded.

"What, and go home to my mother after school each day?" Martini said. "Are you kidding me? I'm still the captain of this team. I need to teach these younger guys how to play. It will pay off."

"Well, if you're gonna stay, Mark, then I'm gonna stay," Sabol said.

CHAPTER 40

The Masked Man

Milo Barnaby's broken nose from his car accident on January 12 was worse than he thought. He had refused medical treatment at the scene of the accident, but after a few days, his mother insisted he contact Dr. Donald Davidson. The good doctor still made house calls, but in this case he needed Milo to come to his clinic for an x-ray after school. There might be more than a broken nose going on.

When his appointment was over, Milo walked up to Washington School to see Joe Jurasin, the shop teacher. Dr. Davidson hoped that the creative instructor could fashion a protective mask that might allow Milo to continue to play basketball.

Milo explained to Jurasin that when Dr. Davidson looked at his x-ray, he pointed out that Milo's nose was broken at the very top and that if it got hit in the same spot again it could push the bones up into his brain. It could be fatal.

Jurasin and Milo agreed that a mask that covered the upper part of his face would provide the most protection.

"Mr. Jurasin, I want to play ball," Milo told the teacher. "As soon as next week."

"I'll get right on it, Milo," Jurasin said.

The shop teacher would create a protype by the next day and then, if that worked, produce the final version before the next game.

Milo had no idea what the mask would look like or if it would work. He put his trust in the shop teacher.

On Friday night, my buddies and I gathered in our usual spot in the upper deck of the gym. This was a mix of fourth-, fifth- and sixth-grade boys. Sitting in front of me were Kevin Borseth, Mike Massie, Jimmy Rooni, Jay Maccani, and Jeff Pricco, each had his chin on the metal railing watching the Oredockers warm up. We were all in the intramural program on weeknights and hoped one day to represent Bessemer on the court.

As I looked at my buddies, I could imagine a starting line-up of Borseth at center, Rooni and Massie at the forwards, Pricco and Maccani at the guards. But I also saw myself competing for a spot in the starting five, somehow beating out Pricco or Maccani through hours of practice and keen focus on the fundamentals of the game.

It's good to dream. To imagine. To one day walk off the snow-covered driveway court with the frozen net and onto the hard-woods of our school gymnasium. We would proudly wear the blue and gold of our hometown team and hear the roar of the crowd as they announced our names. The fans would cheer with every basket we made and pat us on the back for the victories that would undoubtedly come from our effort. Maybe even a championship someday. Imagine what winning would do for this town.

On this night, we would live vicariously through our favorite sophomore players, who got the call up to the varsity.

Kevin Borseth stood and stretched out over the railing to try to see the Speedboys in the tunnel.

"Here they come!" he shouted.

The Speedboys, dressed in their blue and gold warm-up jackets with Bessemer embossed across the back, exploded onto the court, led by their captain, Mark Martini. The crowd stood and cheered as the boys ran to half court and then turned and broke into the two-line layup drill, the upper classmen in the shooting line and the under-classman in the rebounding line.

For the first time, we saw the new faces of the underclassman. But nowhere in sight was Gary Niemi or Bill Ryan. The rumors must have been true. Bonk was going to play the young guys, and some seniors would sit or quit. Gary and Bill must have walked away, or at least it seemed that way tonight.

"Hey, look at Milo!" yelled John Stancher. "What the heck?"

Milo Barnaby was sporting a clear plexiglass face mask that wrapped around his nose and ran up to his forehead. It was like a hockey goalie mask as it had two eye holes and two breathing holes below his nose. It didn't look too comfortable to wear, but Milo was making the best of it, enough so that he earned a spot in the starting lineup, along with seniors Martini and Sabol, and sophomores Rick Syrjala and Jim Milakovich.

The game was never in doubt. Ashland got out to a 7-0 lead and never looked back. The Speedboys were unsteady, undisciplined, and overwhelmed by the taller, more experienced Oredockers. The young guys making their debut on the court made mistakes, but you couldn't question their effort or their heart. They even made the game close at one point 14-13, but that didn't last long. By half time, our Speedboys were down 43-20.

As the game moved along, Barnaby struggled with his protective mask. During timeouts the crowd saw him spray water on his number 12 jersey, then suck on the jersey. He was struggling. He had to wipe the mask as it was fogging up. But Milo played through the discomfort, and somehow found the net and scored nine points for the night.

In the second half, Coach Bonk sat seniors Martini and Sabol and gave Don Barbacovi and Bob Abelman some playing time. Sophomore Milakovich scored seven in his starting debut. Little Don Barbacovi got plenty of minutes but seldom got a shot off and finished with zero points and two fouls.

Milakovich, Syrjala, Barbacovi, Abelman, and Milo Barnaby. Was this the future five?

The game ended in another crushing defeat with an 85-48 loss, the 25th straight for the Speedboys since March 1963.

More ominous was the streak in the annals of Michigan high school basketball history. White Pigeon High School had held the longest losing streak at 61 games, that is until three days prior (January 19, 1965) when they broke the streak by beating Coldwater St. Charles High School for their first win since 1961. With that win, the current longest losing streak in Michigan high school basketball was placed firmly on the backs of the Bessemer Speedboys.

A heavy load for the youth movement to carry.

CHAPTER 41

Like the Hand of God

One Tuesday night in late January, ahead of a major winter storm, Sister Superior at St. Sebastian School cancelled classes for the next day. My father dropped me off at my grandparents' house to help clean out the stacks of *Ironwood Daily Globe* newspapers that stood in the corner of their single-car garage. The storm never came, but my assignment to clean out the garage stood.

In the early 1940s, residents had been encouraged to save their newspapers and then deliver them by the bundle to the local War Drive center. Many years after the war, my grandmother was still saving the paper, tying stacks with twine and storing them in the garage. Unfortunately, moisture also found its way into the garage, making it a haven for mildew and mold.

The paper on top of the stack was dated February 18, 1956. When I reached for it, the twine knot in the middle snapped. I pulled the sports page delicately out of the moldy stack and found this headline plastered across the top of the fold:

"Bessemer Wins M-W Championship"

According to the story, the 1956 Bessemer Speedboys beat the Ashland Oredockers 76-55 to win their first Michigan-Wisconsin Championship since 1948. The 1956 team had a scoring machine in Malcolm Gustafson and a budding superstar named Jim Corgiat, plus a coach named Pete Fusi, who would become legendary for winning titles in basketball, baseball and football in Bessemer.

Reading the story of their dominance in the championship game made me strangely nostalgic for something I had only experienced secondhand through my father's stories: the joy of victory.

Meanwhile, the 1964-65 Speedboys were finding new ways to lose.

The youth movement that Coach Bonk had instituted brought with it inexperience, and the youngsters were no match for the older, more mature teams in the Michigan-Wisconsin Conference.

Against the Hurley Midgets, Jim Milakovich scored a season high of 13 points. His left-handed jump shot served him well when he was given time and space to set up. But the team succumbed to the full court press of the Midgets, losing 86-57.

The next week, playing at home against the Wakefield Cardinals, the Speedboys jumped out to a 6-0 lead on baskets by Mark Martini and Milo Barnaby. The latter was still playing with his protective mask, although it had been modified by the shop teacher from that first model. Martini finished with 18 points, and the masked man Barnaby dropped 13 on the visitors, but Bessemer lost by double digits again, 63-48.

Hard to believe, but it only got worse from there. Iron River beat the Speedboys 78-54, and the Maple Tigers drubbed them by 34 points, 84-50. The Ontonagon Polar Bears handed the Speedboys their 30th straight loss. And if they had not suffered enough already, the flu bug struck the team.

Rick Syrjala, George Sabol, and Mike Betlewski were out ill for the last home game of the year against the Stambaugh Hilltoppers, leaving the team with five starters and one substitute on the bench, Bill Joki. Just six players.

Despite being shorthanded, the Speedboys gave one of their best efforts of the season. They held the Hilltoppers to 27 points in the first half, but when Barnaby picked up his fourth foul in the third quarter, Coach Bonk panicked. He motioned for Coach Gregas to come to the end of the bench, then asked him to go find a junior varsity player to suit up. Gregas left the bench and walked over to the student section.

Like the hand of God, Gregas pointed his finger into the stands at three junior varsity players seated at the top of the bleachers. All three players pointed to himself.

"Do you want me?" each player said. "Me?"

It was hard to know who he wanted when the coach pointed in their general direction, and they couldn't hear his request over the crowd.

Frustrated, Gregas enunciated in three syllables.

"Draz-kow-ski."

He finally got his man and waved for Gerry Drazkowski to come down to the court. Drazkowski worked his way through the student body and arrived at Gregas' side.

"Go suit up," Gregas said. "We're running out of players."

The player appeared stunned, but he did what he was asked and ran to the locker room to change. When he emerged from the tunnel in his junior varsity uniform, he received a standing ovation from the student section. After all, he was our local Clark Kent, who had been summoned from the crowd to become Superman and put an end to this losing streak.

When he entered the game, the Speedboys were trailing the Hilltoppers 34-28. Martini missed a shot; Drazkowski grabbed the rebound and put the ball off the glass and into the basket. The Bessemer student section went crazy. Superman to the rescue.

The fourth quarter began with a 37-30 lead for Stambaugh. The Speedboys had never played for this many minutes with so few substitutes, and the heaviness in their legs started to show. Lazy reaches for the ball and over-the-back fouls sent the visitors to the free throw line too often and the Hilltoppers pulled away.

The final score was 56-41, an expected outcome and another loss for the lowly Speedboys. Their 31st loss in a row. Even Superman couldn't save this team tonight.

CHAPTER 42

Maybe I Should Have Played Elsewhere

Every small town in America had a special little café to call their own. The Tip Top Café was the favorite in Bessemer. Above its entry hung a large neon sign in the shape of an ice cream cone to attract both residents and visitors. Coffee, cherry coke and ice cream were all in high demand.

For most young kids, it was the one-stop shop for candy. As children went through the front door, they were tempted with a variety of delicious treats in the front display case. Chocolate bars of all brands, long ropes of red licorice and stubby black licorice too.

There were penny candy machines on top of the glass counter. For one cent, you got red cinnamon candies or two small gum balls. If you twisted the handle just right and luck was with you, three gum balls would roll out of the dispenser.

As my brother John and I arrived at the front counter, our buddy, Jim Rooni, had his face pressed against the glass display case looking deeply into the vast array of candy selections. When he looked up to the waitress, he said, "Valomilk bar, please."

Jim's face lit up with a big, wide smile as the waitress reached inside and grabbed his exotic choice. Apparently, Rooni was the number one consumer of this marshmallow treat. Jim handed over his ten cents, eagerly grasped his treat and ran out the door.

The Tip Top had a horseshoe counter that ran halfway through the café. The floor was covered with black and white tiles. It was always clean and waxed. Customers, mostly local business folks on their coffee break, were sitting on the round red stools at the counter: Ed Sendek, Ward Sliva, Don Strelcheck, two gray-haired ladies from

Ben Franklin, and Joe Maccani, the big brother of our friend Tommy, sitting with his banker father Isadore. Joe was sipping a Cherry Coke and devouring a hot pasty, his father enjoying a bowl of chicken soup as he chatted with some of the locals.

John and I had a nice conversation with our neighbor, Leone LeClaire, who was on her break from General Insurance and enjoying a hot cup of afternoon coffee. She held a special place in our lives, often keeping a watchful eye over us, akin to a second mother.

"Hello boys." Leone said.

She was always so proper and delightful. Perfect make-up. Fresh lipstick. Pearls around her neck. She held the cup just right, blowing slightly across the top to cool it and then sipped delicately. As she drew her coffee to her mouth, you would have thought it was a television commercial for Folgers. The perfect model pose. Then she quietly placed the cup back on the saucer.

We found a table in the back. There was a small partition that separated the rear tables from the front lunch bar. Six tables with red and white tablecloths. In the center of each table were napkins, salt and pepper shakers, and squeeze bottles of ketchup and mustard. When we sat down, the waitress walked immediately to our table.

"What'll it be fellas?" she asked.

"We're gonna have malts," John said.

"Ok," she said. "What flavor?"

"Strawberry, vanilla," we said at the same time.

The waitress wrote our order down on a small green pad. Tore it out, walked over to the prep counter and clipped it to a stainless-steel wheel with other orders.

As we waited for our malts, I looked up and noticed Speedboys basketball player Bill Ryan sitting at the next table. He was drinking a Coke through a straw and had a juicy hamburger and fries on his plate. He reached for the ketchup and squeezed a small circle of the condiment on his plate. Then he took his time, dipping and eating his hot french fries.

To my surprise, Milo Barnaby walked into view from the lunch counter towards Ryan's table. Ryan motioned for Milo to sit. My brother and I could easily hear their conversation.

"How's the ankle, Billy?" Milo asked.

"Still swollen." Ryan replied. He pulled his leg from under the table to show Milo the puffy sock and ace bandage that covered the injury.

"Even if it heals soon, I'm not coming back," Ryan said.

"But we sure could use you," Milo replied. "Coach Bonk isn't listening to us much. I asked him last week if we could work on an out-of-bounds play. He told me to just get open. I'm not sure he knows any plays."

Ryan dipped a french fry in ketchup and then looked up at Milo.

"He's a center," replied Ryan. "He was a very good center. But, come on, a center on a team doesn't understand how to run an offense. When you play guard, you see the whole floor. You see the movement of the offense and the defense. You learn their tendencies and how to break them down."

Ryan paused.

"Bonk is 6'6"," he continued. "My guess is he was always the tallest kid on his team and always played center. You don't see the game the same way if you spend your whole career standing still with your back to the basket."

Milo nodded.

"I never try to make waves," Milo said, "so when Coach asked me to play center against Iron River, I did it."

"What?" Ryan asked. "Well, I'm sure he taught you a thing or two about that."

Ryan and Milo both laughed.

"What's the streak now?" Ryan asked.

"The newspapers say it's 31 straight losses back to 1963," Milo said. "But you know, Bill, I just love to play basketball. Here or anywhere."

"I do too," Ryan replied. "I don't regret giving my all on the court. I got a swollen ankle to prove it. But I sometimes think that if I had to do it all over again, I would have asked my parents if I could attend high school at St. Ambrose in Ironwood instead of Bessemer High."

Milo seemed surprised. "Really?" he asked.

"I would have been playing on a competitive team at St. Ambrose and playing great schools like Mass and Ewen. It would have been a tough league."

Ryan paused and dipped another french fry in the ketchup and then kept talking, pointing with his french fry to emphasize his story.

"I know I could have started and played three years for the Ramblers. I would have played with Tziani and Stano. Really great players. We would have won more games than we lost. Not like here. It's not the way I wanted to close out my career on the hardwoods. But, as I said, no regrets."

Milo looked like he had swallowed a canary.

"Coach Daniels from Wakefield saw me last April," Milo said, "when I was a sophomore. He asked if I had ever considered changing schools and playing for the Cardinals. I only lived a couple blocks from the Ramsay bus stop that went to Wakefield."

"Wow, did you consider it?" asked Ryan.

"Well, I talked to my mom as she was a Wakefield graduate," Milo continued. "And I knew that my Uncle Nick was a big basketball star in Wakefield. It was pretty tempting to have the opportunity to play with Jim Franck and Al Inkala and the other young guys. But, in the end, my girlfriend Mary Lee would still be in Bessemer, and all my friends were here too, so no, I never considered it for long. Even with this losing streak, I still feel something good is gonna happen. It's got to, right?"

Milo pushed his chair back and got up from the table.

"I guess I'll see you Monday at school, Bill."

"Yup, I'll be hobbling around there," said Ryan. "See ya."

As Milo walked away, I could see the waitress pulling the aluminum container from the Hamilton Beach mixer. Our malts were on the way. She brought two seven-inch-tall, ribbed fountain glasses to our table with straws still in their paper sleeves.

She poured the vanilla malt into John's glass and then set the silver container next to it. She did the same with my strawberry malt. Even when she filled our glass to the top there was still a lot more in the container. We were going to have full bellies heading home.

"That'll be 35 cents each," she said, placing the green receipt on our table. "Pay me when you're ready."

She glanced over at Bill Ryan's table. He had left while we were being served. She cleared and cleaned the table and pocketed the dime tip.

I tore the paper off the edge of my straw, pointed it towards my brother and blew hard into the straw. The paper sleeve flew off like a bullet from a gun, whizzing past John's face.

As it flew through the air, Ed Strahs, the owner and short order cook, was coming out of the back. The paper sleeve fluttered and floated and swooned until it landed right between Ed's big shoes. He gave me that look. The look that said I had better make the next move. He fiddled with the wet towel in his hand, grinding his teeth and staring right through me.

"You gonna pick that up?" the owner said.

He didn't have to ask twice.

CHAPTER 43

After losing to Ironwood 75-41 two days earlier, the trip to Superior for the last game of the season seemed like a relief, the kind you get from pulling an aching tooth. It's not what you might prefer, but thankfully the pain will be over soon.

All season, Coach Bonk had been reminded weekly by the *Ironwood Daily Globe* of the struggles of his bottom-ranked basketball team. A story couldn't be penned without mentioning the losing streak. It had become the paper's obsession to put in bold headlines the number of games lost in a row. And that number was now 32, dating back three seasons. Their last win was over Wakefield in the district tournament on March 6, 1963.

Bessemer and Superior East both had perfect records, so to speak. Charles Erickson, in his third year as head coach at Superior East, had his team atop the Michigan-Wisconsin Conference with an 11-0 record. Bonk's Speedboys were 0-11 in conference play, and 0-15 overall.

The game was played at Gates Gymnasium on the campus of Superior State, where Bonk played his college ball. The game, like the season, was a story of two teams going in different directions.

Superior East would start three All-Conference players in Tom McCauley, Bob Peck and Lanny Haglund; players that would have college recruiters calling them day and night. Bessemer would place not a single player on the All-Conference team, and the only call a senior would receive was from their military draft board.

From the opening tip to the end of the first half, Superior East put on a suffocating full court press. The Speedboys tried their "stall ball" game early, but turnovers allowed East to build a 36-12 lead after the first quarter.

When sophomore Don Barbacovi tried to inbound the ball after each Superior East basket, the 5'6" guard was often unsuccessful. A five-second violation was called on the young player three times. Barbacovi finally screamed at the referee that Superior East's center was stepping over the end line and not allowing him to get the ball in.

Bonk, sensing that Barbacovi was frazzled, sent in Don Johnson to replace him. Barbacovi was hopping mad as he walked off the court. The Speedboy guard wanted to spew a tirade of expletives but wisely chose not to at this point in his career.

Just before halftime, Mark Martini's career for the Speedboys came to an abrupt end. After receiving a cheap shot elbow from an East player under the basket, he suffered a severe eye injury, one that would knock him out of both this game and likely the district tournament the following week.

At the end of the first half, the score was 52-24 and Bonk had reached his boiling point. He marched over to the Superior East bench and gave Coach Erickson a piece of his mind.

"Charlie," Bonk screamed, "if you don't pull off that full court press, I'm taking my team home right now."

The East coach was taken aback.

"You want me to stop competing?" he said.

"I've got a bunch of sophomores out there trying to learn this game. Your team is physical and chippy. You took out my best player with a cheap shot to the head. Take off the press. Let's have a competitive game."

Coach Erickson chuckled. "John, I've never had any coach tell me to let up. But if that's what you want."

"If your goal is to embarrass our young team, then I guess that's your prerogative. But if you want to show sportsmanship, well..."

Bonk didn't finish his thought and stormed off the court.

He paced and shouted in the locker room. His players had never seen him this worked up and they tried to calm him down. The coach finally sat down and put his head in hands and raked his fingers through his hair.

"Sorry, boys," Bonk said. "I don't think their coach plays fair and I let my emotions get to me. Let's just go out there and play the best we can."

Superior East did stop pressing in the second half, but the misery continued for the Speedboys. Superior East made shot after shot. When the visiting Speedboys missed a basket, it was a fast break the other way. The bigger, faster and more experienced East team made easy layups and ran up the score.

By the end of the third quarter, the home team could smell the century mark. Midway through the fourth quarter, when Bob Peck hit a shot to reach 90 points, the local Superior East fans started to chant, "We want a hundred! We want a hundred!"

When the score hit 96-44, the Superior East fans got louder and louder. Soon enough, the wish of the hometown team came true. Bruce Pukema hit a free throw that put Superior East at 100.

The small contingent of faithful Bessemer fans that had made the trip didn't let the Superior East fans get under their skin. The same sense of humor that helped generations of folks endure long snowy winters certainly helped their basketball fans get through back-to-back winless seasons. They chanted back.

"We want fifty! We want fifty!"

The final score was 104-46.

The scoreboard told one story, while the sweat pouring off the backs of the boys in blue-and-gold told another. Even when facing an opponent that would give a good college team a run for their money, the Speedboys never stopped trying.

Though Bonk was angry that Superior East had run up the score, he was also proud of his team. He was satisfied that the Speedboys represented Bessemer the best they could and gave everything they had for their teammates, and for their town.

CHAPTER 44

Where There's a Will, There's a Way

The janitor at St. Sebastian School was a mountain of a man named Andy Ciesielczyk. His janitor's closet, located between two water fountains as you entered the school, was his office. We all called him by his first name, Andy. God help us if we had to pronounce his last name or worse yet, had to spell it.

"Good morning, Andy," we would say as we arrived.

"Morning, kids," he would reply, never looking up from the item he was fixing or cleaning.

Andy took great pride in his work both at the school and at church. Whatever was needed, he would do it, even if it meant working long hours and late nights. He ran his push mop through the halls constantly. With 190 students in the building, it created a lot of dirt, dust and scuff marks, but he said he loved his job. He had a sense of purpose.

Most of all Andy loved basketball. His son Allan had been a very good player at St. Sebastian and had won a grade school championship. But his son Brian, whose nickname was Salty, was a budding superstar.

"Andy, are you going to watch Salty in the St. Mary's tournament in Hurley this weekend?" I asked him one morning as he sat on a folding chair, attaching a new cotton yarn mop to the handle. He told us he had only four mops to make it through the entire school year, as the church budget was even tighter than that of the Bessemer Public School.

"I wish I could," he said. "But I've got to wax the floors in the sixth and seventh grade classroom this weekend. Plus, with three masses on Sunday, it doesn't let me get away to watch him."

Andy, like most men in Bessemer, sacrificed a lot. They had to work to provide for their families and that meant missing out on big occasions like watching a son play basketball. But Andy never complained.

"My guess is the boys will bring home a championship trophy," Andy said. "Bill Farrow has had a very good year, along with my boy. And the others are strong players, too, even the B team players."

The grade school tournament over the weekend at the J.E. Murphy gym in Hurley didn't disappoint. Andy's son Salty was the big star, scoring 45 points in the three games. Most of his shots came from the corners, where he was deadly accurate. There wasn't anything a team could do to stop him.

Just as we expected, the St. Sebastian Knights A team beat Tomahawk and Saxon to get to the championship game against the St. Mary's Saints.

In the championship game, St. Mary's strategy was to let Salty take all the shots he wanted and focus instead on shutting down the other players. Their plan worked. Led by Dave Madenoff, Greg Loreti and Mickey Grandelis, St. Mary's beat the St. Sebastian Knights 29-25 to win the championship trophy. Salty scored 16 of the Knights' 25 points in the losing effort.

The St. Sebastian Knights B team beat St. Mary's Saints B team in the championship game, however, to win the trophy. My brother John and his teammates all brought home a medallion to signify the championship.

On Monday morning, I got to St. Sebastian School a bit early. I wanted to talk to Andy as soon as I arrived. I found him outside his office in a heated discussion with Father Franczek, the senior pastor. I detoured to the nearby boy's bathroom entry, where I could hear their voices, loud and clear. The conversation was not about the loss in the basketball tournament.

"Did you read the label?" Fr. Franczek asked.

"I've been putting down floor wax for years, Father" Andy replied. "I have never had a problem."

"Then why did it yellow?" asked the Pastor.

"Maybe it was a bad batch."

"Well, what are we going to do about it?"

"We'll have to buy stripper and then sand it off."

"How much will that cost?"

"Probably $40 dollars or so."

"Forty dollars?" Franczek replied. "We can't afford that."

"What do you want me to do, scrape it off by hand?"

"I want you to get it done for $10."

I walked out of the bathroom past the two combatants and kept listening as I made my way down the hall.

"I'll see what I can do, Father," said Andy, "but that wax is on there to stay."

Fr. Franczek said he would come up with a solution that wouldn't cost anything, then walked out the door.

On Tuesday morning when my brother John and his classmates entered their sixth and seventh grade classroom, they were asked to step on a sheet of 60-grit sandpaper that was on the floor. Sister Charlene outlined their shoes on the back side of the sandpaper, cut it and then handed the shoe-sized sandpaper back to each student.

As John explained it, when all the students were seated at their desks, Sister Charlene asked them to take out their two pieces of sandpaper. "Now, children," she said. "Place the sandpaper abrasive side down on the floor, then put your shoes on top of the sandpaper."

The children did as they were instructed.

"On my count, I want you to shuffle your feet back and forth under your desk. Ready? One, two, three, shuffle."

The scraping sound was rhythmic. The boys tried to go faster and faster while the girls kept sanding in time.

"Ok, stop!" announced Sister Charlene.

All the students stopped and started to giggle. It was the first time they had been asked to purposely damage school property.

"Now, pick up the sandpaper," said Sister Charlene.

The children did so and listened for the next step.

"Now, everyone lift up your desk and move to your left on my count. One, two, three, lift and move."

Then she instructed the children to scrape again in this new location.

The students did this once in the morning and once in the afternoon each school day for the entire week. They were successful in removing not only the new layer of yellowed wax, but all previous floor coatings.

Father Franczek came by with Andy to examine the results of the "Franczek Plan." Both were quite impressed. By the end of the week, Andy would have the floor ready for a weekend of waxing.

CHAPTER 45

Were We Ever Good?

In the Class C District Tournament, the fortunes of the Bessemer Speedboys did not improve. The team lost 79-41 to the Wakefield Cardinals in the first round. Captain Mark Martini did not play due to the eye injury he suffered in the blowout loss to Superior East the week before. The season came to an end for the Speedboys, but not their losing streak which now stood at 34 straight games.

Coach John Bonk closed out a second straight season without a victory as Bessemer's varsity basketball coach.

After I read the game summary in the *Ironwood Daily Globe*, I folded up the sports section and passed it to my dad.

"Were we ever good, Dad?"

"What are you talking about?" Dad asked as he reached for his pack of cigarettes.

"The Speedboys basketball team."

He held a match to the tip of a cigarette, puffed twice, then shook the match and placed it in the large ash tray next to his armchair.

"Good?" he asked incredulously. "We had *great* basketball teams in Bessemer. You're just too young to remember."

"You won a championship in 1947," I said, "but did Bessemer ever win again?"

"Yes!" he said. "The next damn year! That '48 team won the conference, the district and the U.P. Championship. Dave Webber, Windy Kangas, Studge Barron, Skwor — a great bunch of athletes. They were the first team from Bessemer to go downstate to play the city schools in the state tourney. Lost in the semifinals to the eventual champion. I was in the Army and stationed in Japan, but Uncle Bruno sent me clippings."

The ash on his cigarette was getting long. He tapped it in the ash tray, took another drag, then blew smoke rings into the air as he rested his head on the back of the chair and thought for a moment.

"There were other great teams," he said. "Did you ever see that 6'7" man shopping in Super Valu?"

I shrugged my shoulders.

"That was Jim Beissel," Dad said. "A three-year starter. He re-wrote the scoring records in Bessemer. Windy Kangas from our team held the record, but it was no match for this guy. Beissel scored over 350 points his senior year. He was impossible to stop."

Dad paused to think for a minute and then continued. "Jim's teams were district champions back-to-back in 1952 and '53. I think that was Coach Pete Fusi's first year in Bessemer. When I got back from Japan, the A.D. Johnston gym was the place to be on Friday nights. We had to get there early. Your Aunt Rosie was in high school then. She could tell you more."

"So that was it?" I asked. "1947, 1948, 1952 and 1953. That's over 10 years ago and I wasn't born yet."

Dad pulled the pack of cigarettes from his pocket. He was getting agitated. Not at me, but at the idea that kids like me had no idea that Bessemer was ever any good in basketball. This losing streak had not done the town much good. He pounded the pack once on his hand, and a single *Tareyton* popped to the top.

"Listen," Dad said, "with Pete Fusi at the helm, the Speedboys were always competitive. Even when his athletes were better at foot-ball or baseball than basketball, he knew how to coach them, regard-less of the sport. He taught teamwork."

Dad drew the cigarette from the pack, slipped it into his mouth, and tilted his head down to light it. Then back went his head and out came the first puff.

"Do you know the name Jim Corgiat?" he asked.

"You mean Jerry Corgiat?" I asked. "I saw Jerry play football for Bessemer this past fall."

"No, I mean his older brother, Jimmy," Dad said. "He may have been the greatest all-around athlete to ever play for the Bessemer Speedboys. Had a major league baseball tryout with the Milwaukee Braves. I think he's the only guy I ever saw hit a baseball out of Massie Field and into the Little League field. Anyway, he led Bessemer to the District title in 1956."

Dad took a long drag. Then he got his thoughts together before exhaling.

"If I remember right, back in 1957, Speedboys were down by a point in the district semifinals against Ontonagon, and it was Corgiat who hit the winning shot as time ran out to send the Speedboys to the title game."

He thought again.

"Yeah, yeah that's right," he said convincingly. "I remember his teammates carrying him off the court after that shot. They beat L'Anse the next night to win the District trophy."

Dad leaned back in his chair, all smiles, the memories of Bessemer's better years replaying in his mind. I wanted to press him for more details, but decided against it for fear I'd get him more agitated about the current state of basketball in Bessemer and would have to breathe smoke from a third cigarette. Whenever he got worked up, it was best to let him read his newspaper and smoke his pack.

"The fans still come to the gyms on Friday night, but there's a big difference between this team and the old ones."

"What's that?" I asked.

Dad turned his head and looked at me square in the eyes.

"Back when we were winning, we played like a team."

CHAPTER 46

Coach John Bonk unknotted his tie as he looked down at a note pad on his desk. He had written "Letter Winners" at the top in pencil. He raised his hand to his brow and rubbed his forehead. Then he put pencil to paper and wrote down the names of ten players who would receive letters at the sports banquet in April. Mark Martini, Don Johnson, and George Sabol were all seniors who had suffered through two miserable seasons. They would get a letter. Milo Barnaby, Mike Betlewski, and Bob Abelman were juniors, and a letter would encourage them to come out next year. But what about the underclassmen?

Rick Syrjala was on the varsity all year and deserved a letter. So did Jim Milakovich, Bill Joki and Don Barbacovi, who all got called up from the junior varsity mid-season and gave the team important minutes from January on. Bonk knew that Principal John Sartoris would frown on handing out so many letters to players on another winless team. But he was less afraid of Sartoris this year, and these young men were the future of Speedboys basketball. He looked at the ten names he had written. Letters for them all.

Bonk put his pencil down, sat back in his chair and gave a sigh of relief.

Then, his office phone rang.

Just as he picked it up, Jim Milakovich poked his head into the office and asked if it would be okay for him to shoot some baskets. Bonk covered the phone's mouthpiece with his hand.

"Sure, Jim, go ahead and shoot anytime you want," Bonk said.

"Thanks," Jim said. "Hey, can we do this every day after school?"

Bonk smiled, waved Jim to the gymnasium and then put the phone to his ear.

"Hello, this is John Bonk."

"John, it's Howie."

Howie Anderson was a good friend of Bonk's from his playing days. He was also the coach at Drummond High School in Wisconsin, their alma mater.

"Hi, Howie, how are you?"

"I should ask how *you* are, John," Anderson said.

"Well, Coach," said Bonk. "I thought our team would start to gel eventually. That we would win a game or two, but it didn't happen. I feel so bad for the boys."

"John, it takes many years to be a good coach, just like it takes many years to be a good teacher. You teach, you learn. You coach, you learn."

Bonk took off his glasses, tossed them on his desk, and rubbed his eyes with his left hand.

He was 24 years old. As a basketball player, he had always been a winner, and yet in two years as varsity basketball coach, he was 0-33. He had never quit anything in his life, but he knew that he was letting down the players and the entire town of Bessemer, a town that had been good to him and his wife, Alice, since they first arrived.

But what would he do if he resigned? Stay on as the junior high science teacher and let someone else try to figure out a winning formula?

"John, the reason I called," Anderson said, "is that I'm going to leave Drummond to take a different job, and I want you to replace me as coach."

Bonk was stunned.

"But you're doing so great there, Howie," Bonk replied. "Winning championships, going to the State Tournament. And you want *me* to replace you as coach? You can't be serious. I'm winless as a coach."

"You'll win in Drummond," Anderson said. "We have a great group of athletes on this team and more talent on the way. Every boy in southern Bayfield County wants to be a Drummond Lumberjack. They come to the gym to shoot baskets nearly every day of the year. Summer, winter, spring, fall. Rain or snow or sun, doesn't matter. They're in the gym."

From his coach's office near the gym, Bonk could hear the muffled, rhythmic sound of a lone basketball bouncing on hardwood, as Milakovich worked on his ball-handling skills.

It gave him pause.

Maybe all the work Bonk had put into developing his players' skills and attitudes would pay off next year. Or maybe the deck was stacked against him in Bessemer, and would be until the padlocks came off the gym doors for good.

Bonk was torn between finishing what he had started in Bessemer or returning home. As he spoke, he became emotional. His voice quivered.

"Howie, I like these kids," Bonk said. "I want to win so badly for them. Not for me. For them. I just don't want to quit on them. They never quit on me."

"You're still young," Anderson replied. "You have a long career ahead of you with many different coaching opportunities. Your hometown needs you. Please consider coming home."

Bonk took a handkerchief from his shirt pocket and wiped the tears from his eyes.

"I'll sleep on it, Howie," he said. "I will just have to sleep on it."

Third Quarter
1965-66

CHAPTER 47

By June 15, the A.D. Johnston High School graduating class of 1965 had already walked with pomp and circumstance and accepted their diplomas. Among the graduates was Mark Martini, who would head off to Northern Michigan University to study education and play college football. Bruce Richardson would attend Michigan State and contemplate walking on for coach Duffy Daugherty's Spartans. And Gary Niemi? He was off to Michigan Tech on a scholarship but planned to play tennis all summer long with his good buddy, George Sabol. Bill Ryan had some business ideas and headed to Ferris State to get his degree.

If these boys didn't attend college, it was a sure bet that Uncle Sam would come calling. The Vietnam conflict was heating up. President Lyndon Johnson was determined to fight communism wherever it surfaced, even in the jungles of Southeast Asia.

In Bessemer, the grass was green, the brook trout were biting in Powdermill Creek, and there was a collective sigh of relief that warm, sunny days would improve everyone's mood.

The Cubs were at the top of the standings in the Bessemer Little League and likely to stay there all season. Boys were building treehouses in the woods behind Tourist Park and girls were learning to twirl the baton so they could march with the baton and drum corps.

The locals had long forgotten about the area's miserably cold winter and the Speedboys' losing streak. At least for now. They picnicked at Black River Harbor on the shore of Lake Superior or floated on inner tubes on Lake Gogebic. Summertime was here. How long could they make it last?

The Bessemer Board of Education met in a special session on June 15 to select a new Speedboys varsity basketball coach. John Bonk submitted his resignation in May, and had already moved back to Grand View, Wisconsin to prepare for teaching and coaching at Drummond High School.

The applications of the two finalists for the coaching position were presented to each member of the school board. One candidate was Carl Gregas, the current junior varsity basketball coach and high school English teacher.

Gregas, a native of Shenandoah, Pennsylvania, was a graduate of Wisconsin State College of Superior. He played varsity football for Superior State. Before college he served three years in the U.S. Navy. He accepted his teaching position in Bessemer in 1963 because the school was the only one that offered him the duo role to teach and coach.

The members of the school board were very familiar with Gregas and thought highly of him not only as a teacher, but also as a member of the community. His basketball resume was thin, having only coached the junior varsity, but he had won a few games in that role. Something in short supply in this town.

The second candidate was Ransom English from Evanston, Illinois. He was the brother of Jack English, who owned the Indianhead Ski Resort in Wakefield. His resume was quite impressive. A former marine, "Rance" English had a bachelor's degree from Missouri Valley College. Besides his fifteen years of teaching at the high school level, he coached basketball, football and wrestling. According to the credentials he offered to the board, he had developed several championship teams during his coaching career.

Winning coach? Championships? Those words glowed on the page. It was exactly what this school board was hoping to find in a candidate.

Superintendent Walter Newman reminded the board that there was only a basketball vacancy at the high school, not a teaching vacancy. The teaching vacancies were at Washington School in sixth grade and a general science teaching job.

After much discussion, a motion was made by board trustee Robert Hellman.

"I make a motion that we offer the head basketball coaching job to Ransom J. English," Hellman said.

"I second that motion," said Mario Re.

Elmer Erickson then voted in favor of hiring English. Dante Pricco, Paul Steiger and Antone Wysoski voted against hiring English as they favored Gregas. Paul Hoeft was absent, so the motion was defeated due to the 3-3 tie vote.

Dante Pricco, always the peacemaker, offered a plan to allow the board to hire the new basketball coach and still get English into the school system.

"If we hire Carl Gregas to be our new varsity basketball coach," Pricco explained, "it'll create a vacancy for a junior varsity basketball coach. English could fill that position. I make a motion that we hire Carl Gregas as varsity basketball coach and English as JV coach and sixth grade teacher."

Wysoski, Steiger, Re and Pricco voted yes. Hellman and Erickson voted no.

The school board President hit his gavel. "On a vote of four in favor and two against, it is approved to offer the varsity basketball coaching position to Carl Gregas, effective with the start of the school year."

The next day, Superintendent Newman stopped by Carl Gregas' classroom. Gregas was teaching summer school to the unfortunate few who didn't excel during the school year and needed to meet the criteria to advance to the next grade level.

"Congratulations, Carl," Newman said. "You're the new Speedboys varsity basketball coach."

Gregas was not surprised. He had assumed all along that he would be selected as the next coach. He had no idea that some on the board were leaning towards an out-of-towner.

"What will we do about the JV coaching position?" Gregas asked.

"Well, the board is planning to offer it, as well as the sixth-grade teaching position, to a guy from Evanston, Illinois," Newman said. "He's an experienced coach in football and basketball. Won some championships, too. Ransom English is his name."

CHAPTER 48

John The Tailor

My dad and Uncle Bruno cupped their hands around their eyes as they peered through the window of John the Tailor's garage, which was connected to the dry-cleaning business. Uncle Bruno had received a tip at Hunter's Inn that there was an old panel truck in disrepair that John Cychosz, affectionately known as "John the Tailor," might be willing to sell cheap.

Few people in Bessemer had two cars in the family. You might have one family car and an old jalopy to drive to work or go to the camp, but two *new* cars were out of the question. Thus, folks like my uncle and my dad would try to find an old vehicle to resuscitate. It appeared they found one today.

"Got two flat tires, Bru," Dad whispered to his brother as he looked through the window.

"How's the rust?" Bruno asked.

"Body looks to be in good shape," Dad said. "I think we make John an offer."

John Cychosz had once owned the house our family lived in. Dad told my brothers and me that the house once had a fire in the attic. John the Tailor bought it and fixed it up and then rented it to our cousin Ray Barbacovi and his family prior to my parents purchasing it in December 1955. Cychosz seldom sold what he owned unless he knew and trusted you.

Yet, here was Uncle Bruno and Dad acting like a couple of burglars casing the joint. Bruno lifted me up, so I could look inside, too. All I saw was the back end of the vehicle.

"Let's offer him $100," said Dad.

"Nah," replied Bruno. "It needs too much work. Let's say $75."

"Ok, Putto," Dad said. "You're the banker."

Bruno and Dad went around to the front of the store and walked in. The dry-cleaning establishment smelled like you were standing next to a dryer vent. Behind the counter was Donna Mae, a very nice lady and a classmate of my dad's. She wore heavy red lipstick and a light cotton dress.

"Is John around?" Dad asked.

"No, he went to Ironwood, but should be back shortly," she answered.

"Ok, well," Dad said, "we were wondering if he would sell that broken-down panel truck he has in the back. Can you have him call me?"

"Sure, Johnny," Donna said.

"Tell him we're willing to pay top dollar," Bruno laughed.

Uncle Bruno never married and lived on East Sellar Street with his mother, our Nonie, saving all his money. When the purchase of a new vehicle, home, cottage or other similar expense was contemplated by any of his relatives, Bruno was the banker who offered no-interest loans. Many people in Bessemer had someone like Uncle Bruno in their family. It's how they got by, especially when the mines weren't running at capacity.

Guglie's barbershop was abuzz with the announcement that Carl Gregas had been hired as head basketball coach.

"Gregas gets his hair cut here," Guglie said. "The old coach, Bonk, went to a barber in Grand View, Wisconsin. I didn't lose any money when he left town."

The men waiting laughed at Guglie's joke.

"Last I heard from the coach, our Speedboys had lost 33 straight," Guglie said. "But then who's counting."

More laughter.

An old iron ore miner sitting in a waiting chair piped up.

"When I was going to school at Three Rivers back in the 1930s," he said, "we had a losing streak of 54 games in row. It was a state record. My entire high school life I never saw our basketball team win a game until we beat Centerville in 1933. The score was something like 15-14. Anyway, the Speedboys are nowhere near that record so you guys can sleep easy."

Isabelle Gheller got Johnny Pel's attention in the butcher shop at Super Valu. "Johnny, it looks like John the Tailor wants to see you," Gheller said.

Johnny looked up and saw through the window the 80-year-old man with a top hat standing in front of the meat counter. He waved for Johnny to come out.

"Hello," John Cychosz said. "I understand you or Bruno want to buy that old truck of mine."

"Yes, I want to buy it," Johnny said. "Looks like it needs some new tires. Any other issues?"

"Well, it hasn't run in a few years," Cychosz replied. "So, it probably needs a new battery and a front-end alignment. I think you can patch the inner tubes in the tires."

"Ok, how much do you want for it?"

"Well, considering it's you and Bruno, I would say $75."

"Sold," Johnny said quickly.

"But you need to repaint it, because I don't want my store's name on the side."

"No problem," Johnny said. "Bruno likes to paint vehicles."

"Swing by the cleaners tomorrow," Cychosz said. "I'll sign over the title to you. Just remember, these trucks are more expensive to title and license than a car."

Johnny Pel froze for a minute. He had never owned a truck, so he had no idea it was more expensive to license. That could blow the whole deal.

CHAPTER 49

Dog Days of Summer

The dog days of the summer of '65 were settling in. Temperatures and humidity were high. The Ramsay Park swimming hole and picnic area were at full capacity. The Cubs secured the Little League title, much to the disappointment of the Yankees. Coach Jack White's Bessemer Speedboys football team started practice at E.J. Oas field with sights on a M-W conference title. The circular from Ben Franklin announced it was back to school time. And my mother broke the news to the family that she was expecting another baby in March. Her sixth child. Mom wanted a girl. Dad wanted another boy.

"Six boys?" Mom said, "people will think I'm crazy."

My brother John and I had earned $40 each by cutting grass all summer for elderly widows who lived on their late husbands' Social Security and wanted to stay as long as possible in their homes. We charged $2 per mow and we supplied our own gas, which cost us thirty-two cents a gallon. A lot of boys in Bessemer made money the same way. It was hard work.

The widows didn't want us to cut more than twice a month. This made it quite difficult after a week of rain to push our mower through the six-inch-high grass, but my mother said to never question the customers' authority. John and I would cut the grass, leave and never ask for the money after the mow. It would come in due time.

We were kept on a schedule by Mom, who had a close eye on our customers' schedules as well. We did not question *her* authority either. Mom would tell us when to collect.

"Mrs. Tobin is home now," or "Don't bother Mrs. Tobin, as she's having coffee with her daughter," or "Mrs. Tobin got her Social Security check yesterday, so go over and collect your money for mowing."

Mom also determined how we would *spend* our hard-earned money. When we had collected from the sweet ladies of the neighborhood, Mom would want to know how much money we had in our sock drawer.

"Do you have $35 yet?" she'd asked.

"Yeah, I think so," I replied. "Why?"

"Well, get down to General Insurance and see Leone LeClaire to get your season pass for the ski hill," she said. "It's $35 this year and you can ski either Big Powderhorn Mountain or Indianhead Mountain."

Yes ma'am.

On a Saturday in August, news came that Uncle Bruno had the panel truck running, with two new tires on the back and a new battery and alternator installed. He had sprayed the truck a Spartan green. Not his favorite color, but the paint was on clearance at Gambles.

Dad took the title papers that John the Tailor had signed over to him and headed down to the General Insurance Office to get the truck transferred to his name and get some new license plates.

"Tommy, go with your dad to General Insurance," Mom said pointing at me with a dish towel in her hand. "You can get your season ski pass while you're there."

Another appointment scheduled for me, and another one checked off Mom's list.

We arrived at the perfect time. No one else was in line for titles and registrations.

"Hi Johnny," said Roy Malmberg, the owner of General Insurance and the branch manager for the Secretary of State Office. "What can I do for you today?"

"Roy, I got a car out here to title and get plates," Dad said.

He was hoping to not bring attention to the fact that it was a panel truck.

"Let's take a look," Roy said, much to my father's dismay.

When we went outside, Malmberg took one look at the vehicle and Dad knew the jig was up.

"Johnny, you got a truck here, not a car."

"Oh, but I'm gonna use it as a station wagon," Dad replied. "Just back and forth to work. No hauling."

Roy opened the back of the truck and looked inside. The bar that held the dry cleaning on hangers was still installed.

"Hey, is this John the Tailor's truck?" Roy asked.

"It was," Dad said. "Hasn't been used in years. It was decommissioned."

"Well, John, there is no way I can license this as a car. It has no windows on the sides and there aren't any seats in the back for passengers. Sorry, you'll need to tag it as a truck."

Dad contemplated the response from Mr. Malmberg before answering.

"Tell you what, Roy," he said. "I'm not gonna license it today. I'll be back in a week and we'll take care of it then."

Malmberg was a bit confused but just shrugged his shoulders and went back to his office.

Dad and I left without the plates and without my ski pass. We walked across the street to Gambles.

"Hi, Don," Dad said to Donald Strelcheck, the owner. "Do you have two small windows, maybe 24"x20" and some sheet metal screws and caulking?"

"What are you up to this time, Johnny?" Don asked.

"Oh, Bruno and I just made a new purchase, and we want to do some remodeling."

"It's your lucky day," Don said. "Got it all right here. I was planning to put these in the sidewalk sale next week, but they're all yours now."

After the purchase, we jumped back into the panel truck and headed towards home. On the way, Dad turned into the alley behind Uncle Bruno's house. We found Bruno changing the oil on his lawn mower in his single-car garage.

"Bruno," Dad yelled. "Do you still have those old seats you took out of the jalopy?"

"Yeah, they're right over here," Bruno replied.

In the corner of the garage were two car seats that Bruno had pulled out of an old vehicle before selling it for parts. For some reason, he had thought he could get a lot of money for the seats. Yet, they sat in the garage all these years.

"Good, I need them and your help," Dad said.

The two of them started to talk about converting the truck to a station wagon. I was uninterested, so I walked home.

"Did you get your ski pass?" Mom asked as I walked into the house.

"No," I replied. "Dad couldn't get his car licensed yet, so he didn't give me time to buy the pass."

Mom added the ski pass back to her checklist of jobs to be done.

A week later, Dad and I made a second trip to General Insurance.

"Hi, Johnny," Roy Malmberg said. "You're back, hey?"

"Yes," Dad replied. "I got a station wagon to license."

Roy raised an eyebrow.

"What?" he said. "You bought a station wagon and got rid of that old panel truck?"

Dad didn't say a thing. He and Roy walked outside. Roy gasped when he saw the vehicle.

"You're kidding me, Johnny."

"No," Dad said. "It has windows on the side and back seats for passengers. Just like you said a station wagon has to have on it."

Dad whipped open the back doors.

Sure enough, he and Uncle Bruno had installed small windows on each side in the back of the vehicle. They also installed the old car seats. But rather than install them facing forward in the vehicle like most back seats, they installed them on each side in the back of the van, so passengers faced each other.

Malmberg was astonished. But he had in fact described a station wagon to my dad on the last visit, and so a station wagon is what he got.

Malmberg just shook his head and started walking back to the building.

"Okay, Johnny," Malmberg said. "Let's go license this *station wagon*."

Dad smiled wide, then dropped his cigarette on the sidewalk and put it out with his shoe.

"That will be $9, John," Roy said.

Dad handed over the cash. He had saved $5 by making the conversion. It was a proud day for Johnny Pel.

While Dad was settling up, I walked over to Leone LeClaire.

"Hi, Mrs. LeClaire," I said. "May I buy a season pass for skiing?"

"Sure, Tommy," she replied. "With this pass you can ski both Big Powderhorn Mountain or Indianhead Mountain."

"Great." I replied.

"He won't be skiing Indianhead," Dad said as he walked up behind me. "I'm not giving those stumblebums any business."

"Oh," replied Leone, a bit surprised. "Well, it is still $35."

Chapter 50

New Speedboys basketball coach Carl Gregas "expressed a bright outlook" to the readers of the *Ironwood Daily Globe* in the November 23, 1965 edition.

In the season opener, Gregas would put six letterman and six hopefuls in Speedboy blue and gold against the Hurley Midgets. If they were ever to break the 34-game losing streak, beating the young Hurley team would be their best chance in a very long time. The Midgets were rebuilding and would have been in the cellar last year if not for the winless Speedboys.

"We don't have a lot of height, but the determination is remarkable," Gregas told the *Globe*. "These boys are ready to plunge into the season with a will to win."

For Coach Gregas, lack of height was the same problem Coach Bonk had professed in the past two seasons. You can coach players to be more aggressive, but you can't coach them to get taller.

Senior Milo Barnaby and juniors Jim Milakovich, Don Barbacovi, and Rick Syrjala played significant minutes last season for the Speedboys, and no fan would doubt their determination or drive. They played hard every game.

Gregas stayed positive in the interview and stressed that a few freshmen got experience on the B squad last season, including 6'0" Mark Borseth and 6'3" Dennis "Eggy" Forslund.

"He's pretty raw," Gregas said of Forslund. "What he lacked in honed talent, he made up for in height. He'll only get better."

Gregas expected Forslund to be a real factor for the Speedboys later in the season.

Rounding out this enthusiastic bunch of cagers were lettermen Bob Abelman and Mike Betlewski. Others vying for their opportunity were Paul Carpenedo, Bob Martin, Tom Juntunen, Richard Schwartz, and Louis Menara.

The paper didn't mention coach Rance English or his junior varsity players in the article, something not lost on the JV coach. Slighted or not, English felt that with his new offense and his gifted players they would rack up wins for Bessemer; a commodity sorely missed in this town.

WJMS-AM could have picked any game to broadcast on Tuesday night, but they chose the Speedboys versus the Midgets as the game of the week. Certainly, the Ironwood Red Devils and Ashland Oredockers game would have been more entertaining. Did the radio station smell a victory? Would this be the night that the losing streak became history?

The team boarded the bus for the 15-minute ride to Hurley. Both varsity and junior varsity players rode the same yellow bus. Each player was accounted for, except one.

"Okay, listen up. Is everyone here?" Gregas asked.

"No, Dicky isn't here yet," yelled a player from the back of the bus.

"Schwartz?" Gregas asked. "Schwartz is not here?"

"He has to walk all the way from Yale," another player commented.

Gregas turned and took a seat. He told the bus driver to head to Hurley. The team had rules and Schwartz knew the rules. He would be left behind.

In Hurley, former Bessemer Speedboys cheerleader, Jackie Burt, found a seat on the visitor's side of the court. She had graduated last May and was now attending Gogebic Community College in Ironwood. In all her games as a varsity cheerleader, she had never seen the Speedboys win a game. Not one.

Tonight, Jackie came to see the new squad of girls and cheer the boys to victory. Marcella Boline, Barbara Ippolite, Dorinda Lund, Mary Jane Berwald and Doris Mascotti made it through tryouts and were selected to be on this year's squad.

The cheerleaders had updated their fashion to modern-looking homemade jumpers with long sleeve white tops. The white socks and Keds were the only holdovers from the previous year. Gone was the big B across the front of the sweaters, replaced by a BHS sewn on the left hip. The skirt was just above the knee to meet the school dress code.

"Hey, Jackie," one of the girls called out. "What are you doing here? You're bad luck."

All the cheerleaders kept straight faces and then burst into laughter and ran up to where Jackie was sitting and gave her a big hug.

"I know," Jackie said, "I'm a jinx. I'm hoping tonight's the night. If it doesn't happen, then for sure I'm a jinx. I love your new outfits, girls. Hey, maybe those old uniforms were bad luck!"

All the girls laughed.

Back in Bessemer, Speedboy Richard "Dick" Schwartz had his thumb out. He was trying to hitch a ride from Bessemer to Hurley. The senior had just missed the team bus and was still in shock that they had left him behind. He felt like quitting the team at that moment, but he was too ticked off to do so. He darn well was going to get to that game and take his place on the team bench.

A car pulled off slowly to the side of the highway. The driver saw the young man with a duffle bag standing there. He leaned across the front seat and rolled down the passenger side window.

"Dick, is that you?" the driver asked. He was one of Dick's classmates, but didn't know him very well.

"Yeah!" Schwartz replied. "I missed the team bus. Can you drive me to Hurley?"

"Hop in!" said the driver.

Off they went, speeding twenty miles over the limit.

The mood in the visitor's locker room in Hurley was dead serious. Head coach Carl Gregas stood before his new Speedboys team. He could tell that they were nervous. They had not even stepped onto the court for warm-ups and they were already sweating. Milo Barnaby had the shakes. Jimmy Milakovich was wound tight, pounding a ball in his hands as he walked about, ready to explode out of the locker room door. Don Barbacovi, who had grown a couple of inches over the summer, was thinking about his role in the new offense instituted by his coach.

Gregas continued to search for the right words to calm down his boys. However, before he could speak, the door slammed against the wall and the junior varsity team bolted into the locker room. They had just been beaten in the last second of the preliminary game by the Midgets B team. They were letting everyone know they were ticked off.

Coach Rance English came in last. Walking straight up to Coach Gregas.

"Well, we never got 'em," English said.

"Got what, Rance?" Gregas asked.

"The warm-ups. We come to the coldest gym in the league and we have no warm-up jackets. My guys cramped up in the 4th quarter and we lost. When are we going to get our warm-ups, Carl?"

Exasperated, Gregas just looked at his assistant.

"Please, not now, Rance," he said.

English glanced at the varsity squad and read the room.

"Sorry. I'll talk to you about it later, Carl."

English walked away.

Gregas asked his team to listen up.

"Boys, you know how to play this game," he began. "This is one game on the schedule where you know you can compete. The one that you can win and get that monkey off your back. You don't have a losing streak this season. That's for the newspapers and record keepers to follow. It's a fresh start. Now, go out and play as you did when you were kids on the playground and have some fun. The rest will take care of itself."

Clearly inspired, the team jumped off the locker room benches and took to the court with an added spark in their step.

Unbeknownst to them, their 10th man, the hitchhiker, had arrived at J.E. Murphy High School gymnasium.

"I'm telling you, I play for the Speedboys," Dick Schwartz said.

The gal sitting at a ticket table at the gym entrance did not believe him.

"I'm sorry, I don't know who you are," she said. "You need to pay 50 cents to get in."

"That's my name on the program right there," he said pointing to the program.

"Anyone could say that," she responded. "Fifty cents please."

Schwartz wasn't sure who to be angrier with, the ticket gal or his coach for leaving him behind. He was very upset.

"I'm not going to argue with you anymore," Schwartz said. "I'll be back at the end of the game to get my money back. Here's your 50 cents."

Schwartz placed two quarters on the table and didn't bother to take the ticket. He just ran into the visitors' locker room, dressed quickly, and ran onto the court. He fell in line for drills and acted as if nothing had happened. But underneath, he was seething.

When the Speedboys went back to the locker room prior to the opening tip, Gregas announced the starting line-up.

"Milakovich and Syrjala at forwards," Gregas said, "Barnaby and Barbacovi at the guards. Bob Abelman at center."

Then, turning to his late arriving player, Dick Schwartz, he said, "Glad you could make it, Richard."

Schwartz bit his tongue. It was the better part of valor.

"Richard, you can help this team," Gregas said. "But you need to follow the team rules. Now, because you missed the team bus, you are going to sit on the bench for a while. Do you understand?"

Schwartz looked at his coach and said through his clenched jaw, "Yes, sir."

Turning to the rest of the team, Gregas announced that if anyone missed the bus or broke another team rule, they too would sit on the bench.

"Everyone understand?" Gregas asked.

All acknowledged with a nod or a grunt.

From the opening tip the crowd saw that the Speedboys had come to play. Don Barbacovi hit a jumper just a few seconds into the game, and the visitors had an early lead. Then, Milakovich did the same. The first quarter was back and forth, but when the buzzer sounded, the Speedboys led 14-13.

Bob Abelman found himself getting significant minutes and finding the basket for a few points. However, the referees whistled him for two fouls early in the second quarter, so Gregas looked at his bench for a player to give Bobby a long breather. He saw Schwartz at the end with his head down. Most coaches might have let him sit for the entire game, but Gregas was different. The coach knew that any kid who would hitchhike to get to the game had something brewing inside. Gregas wanted to tap into it, whatever it was.

"Richard!" Gregas yelled.

Schwartz's head popped up and he looked at his coach.

"Check in for Abelman," Gregas said.

Gregas had lit the fuse and Schwartz exploded off the bench.

"Schwartz to forward," Gregas yelled to his team. "Syrjala to center."

The Dick Schwartz Show was about to begin.

The team moved the ball around the top of the key. Syrjala found Schwartz in the corner. Schwartz took one dribble and hit his first shot. The forward continued to bang the boards on both ends of the court. His aggressive play caught the Midgets by surprise. They were late for each rebound, fouling Schwartz multiple times over the next two quarters. He was happy to step to the charity stripe. Schwartz may have missed the bus, but he refused to miss his free throws, sinking thirteen over the second and third quarters.

When the third quarter ended, the Speedboys held a thin 44-42 lead, no small thanks to the hitchhiker and his 19 points.

Don Barbacovi looked over at the Hurley bench and saw his lifelong basketball nemesis, Gary Gotta. When Barbacovi played for the St. Sebastian Knights, Gotta played for St. Mary's Saints. Gotta was the go-to guy in crunch time. Tonight, he would be again.

When the fourth quarter began, Gotta sunk a shot from the corner to knot the game at 44 each, then he continued to make shot after shot.

With 4:43 left in the game, it was Hurley 60, Bessemer 50, and the Midgets cruised from there. The basketball was firmly lodged in the throats of the winless Speedboys.

When the final horn sounded, Hurley defeated Bessemer 70-64. Gary Gotta embraced his teammates and then his father, Marco, who walked onto the court from the stands. Father and son were elated that they had taken down another Bessemer team. Gotta's teammate, Herbert Perlberg, was the game's leading scorer with 22 points.

Dick Schwartz finished with 21 points, the most in a single game by a Speedboy in three seasons. Few would know of Schwartz's determination to get to the game or remember his remarkable performance on the court. All that most Bessemer basketball fans would remember is the blue and gold failed to win a game for the 35th straight time.

CHAPTER 51

Don't Needle Me

I t came as great news to St. Sebastian Church parishioners that final blueprints had been completed for the new auditorium that would be annexed to the St. Sebastian School. The church would call it a "multi-purpose room" that would feature a large kitchen for a hot lunch program and seating capacity for over 500. Church bazaars, bingo nights, choir concerts and much more could be held in this new facility.

For the students that attended St. Sebastian, they would call it a gymnasium and home to their beloved St. Sebastian Knights. The basketball team that was locked out of Washington School except for one practice per week and the occasional Sunday game would now control their own destiny. The Knights could practice every day with games and tournaments whenever they wished. They would even have their own electronic scoreboard.

Father Chester Franczek, pastor of the church, encouraged all parishioners to continue their "social and family parish spirit" to complete the new "multi-purpose room" by November 1966. In other words, keep sending money.

In the early 1960s, the best-known immunity against mumps, measles and chickenpox was to expose children to the disease, so they acquired it and had immunity for life. If one child in the family had chickenpox, it was likely all children would catch it. The same with measles and mumps. There was no widespread panic when a kid had one of the three most common childhood diseases. It was more about how long it would last.

But tuberculosis (TB) was different. Not the type of disease you wanted to spread. It could be deadly. At least that's what the local experts communicated.

It was tuberculosis skin testing day at St. Sebastian School and we lined up like lemmings on the cliff. You could hear the crying coming from the testing room down the hall. The biggest brute in fifth grade was no match for the nurse dressed in white, armed with a long needle.

Some children carried notes from their parents about which arm to administer the test. Others had notes requesting their child be spared the agony of the TB test altogether.

"Take the note to the nurse," Sister Superior would say, washing her hands of the matter.

It was a scene repeated annually in our school as the local health authorities tried to eradicate tuberculosis.

I never met a school age child with a positive test for TB. My father often told the story of his own father, Pietro, who was in the tuberculosis ward at Grand View Hospital in Ironwood for seven years in the 1940s.

"The damn mine said my Pa had TB," Dad said, "because they didn't want to pay for his medical bills or give my Ma any money after he died. The mine said they weren't responsible for his illness and death, because he had TB before he started working in the Tilden mine. I don't think there was any man in the ward that actually had TB. My Ma was powerless against these big mine companies. They were nothing but a bunch of finks."

On our way to the little lunchroom where the testing was being conducted, Jay Maccani grabbed a newspaper out of his locker as we passed by. Jay loved to read, mostly about sports. It was yesterday's *Globe* and he opened it to the sports section and read out loud.

"Coach Jim Daniels' Wakefield Cardinals trounced the Bessemer Speedboys 55-33 in their traditional battle at the Gogebic County Seat gymnasium Tuesday night."

"Yeah, that's quite a tradition," I said. "They win, we lose."

Jay continued to read.

"Inability to score with any consistency against a tough Cardinal defense, and failure to match the visitors in the rebound department, cost the Speedboys their 36th straight loss over a period beginning with the final game of the 1962-63 campaign."

As Jay was just starting to read that the B team lost as well, the paper was ripped from his hands by Sister Mariella.

"You kids should not be reading in line," she said as she peered through her thick glasses at the offending child.

She carefully folded the paper and placed it under her arm and walked to her office. She now had something to read with her second cup of coffee.

As we closed in on the room where the pain was being inflicted, student after student came out with one arm held straight in front of them, palm up. A small, clear bubble was apparent on the inside forearm. Some girls had tears running down their cheeks while one of the older boys was bragging that he had the biggest bubble of all. But you could tell that his eyes had been watering, too.

My classmate, Scotty, was next in line to receive his skin test. I was right behind him. He handed the nurse a note from his mother that requested a right arm puncture and not a left. It went off without a tear.

Then it was my turn. I placed my left arm on the table and she swabbed my inner forearm with a cotton ball soaked with rubbing alcohol. She took out her needle and drew some type of liquid from a little glass bottle. One kid told us in line that it was actually the TB virus, while my mother had told me it was just saline water.

The contents of the syringe didn't bother me, it was the needle itself that I feared. The needle was inserted slightly under my skin. It stung and burned a bit as she pushed on the plunger. A small bubble began to appear and then she removed the needle.

"That's it," the nurse said. "In two days, we'll come back and check. If it's red and hard and bigger than this bump, we'll do another test. If it looks like this, you are good until next year."

It would be a couple of sleepless nights for me.

CHAPTER 52

Junior varsity coach Rance English had coached two games in the 1965-66 season and lost them both in the last seconds. He was upset, but not about the losses. It was that no one was listening to him. Not the Superintendent, not the athletic director, not the varsity basketball coach.

English was ticked off because his team did not have warm-up jackets. Rance had requested them multiple times, but to no avail. His frustration had been building and the dam was about to burst at today's practice.

"Carl, I have asked since the first practice, where are my warm-up jackets?"

"Rance, I told you, that's not my decision," Gregas said. "You need to discuss it with Jack White. He's the athletic director and controls the purse strings."

"Can't we get last year's warm-up jackets from the varsity?" English asked.

"We're still wearing them," Gregas responded.

"You're putting my team at risk," English snapped back. "We need to keep their muscles warm. Otherwise they'll tighten up, and the boys could pull or tear a muscle. If that happens, it's on you and Jack."

Gregas crossed his arms and took a deep breath.

"I understand what you're saying, Rance," Gregas said. "But I don't have any say in the matter. It's a budget issue. If you don't like Jack's answer, then go ask Superintendent Newman."

With that, Gregas walked to his office to gather his things and head home. He had enough problems trying to win a game, let alone worry about Rance's issue.

Before Gregas was able to leave, there was a knock at his office door. He looked up to see senior Bob Abelman standing there.

"Hi Bobby," Gregas said. "What's up?"

Abelman's face said it all. He wouldn't be delivering good news.

"Coach, I've decided to leave the team," Abelman said.

"Why, Bob?" asked Gregas.

"Well, you got a lot of young guys you want to play," Abelman said. "Heck, you had twelve guys plus me on the bench against Wakefield on Tuesday. There's strength in numbers for sure, but it also means spreading out the minutes and, well, there's just not enough playing time for all of us. You're building for the future, Coach, and I have to figure out my future, too."

Gregas listened intently as Abelman continued to explain his reasoning.

"I plan to go to Northern Michigan next year, and I need to work to save some money for college. My father really wants me to be at the store, especially now during the holidays. I just think it would be best if I left the team."

Gregas sat forward in his chair, pulled the whistle from around his neck and placed it on the desk in front of him.

"Well, Bob, I'm sorry you want to leave," Gregas said. "I still think you can really help our team this year."

But there was no changing the player's mind. Abelman shook his coach's hand and walked out of the basketball locker room for the last time.

CHAPTER 53

Ready to Meet My Maker

The telephone rang at 4 p.m. Mom answered and then hung up the phone quickly. She ran to the window in the living room. Then to the window in the dining room, her hand over her mouth. Suddenly, cousin Ray Barbacovi's station wagon pulled up. Ray and uncle Art Stancher jumped out and ran quickly to open the back door of the Ford. Our mom held open the front door, frantically yelling to our two relatives to hurry.

"Bring him in here!"

As we watched, they pulled Dad out of the back seat. He was groggy and could barely stand. He looked as if he were drunk. He had his arms around the necks of both Ray and Art as they steadied him to walk. Suddenly, his legs gave way and they dragged him into the house, his legs limp beneath his waist.

Ray and Art placed Dad on the sofa. Mom ran to him with a glass of orange juice and put it to his lips.

"John, John?" Mom cried. "Drink this!"

The orange juice just ran down the sides of Dad's mouth.

My brothers and I had no idea what was going on. Uncle Art looked at us without a smile, which was so very rare for him. He kicked at the carpet in disgust.

"Get him to the Divine Infant Hospital," Mom yelled as she pointed to the front door.

"Shouldn't we call an ambulance, Mary Lou?" Ray asked.

"We don't have time to wait and we can't afford $150," Mom shouted. "Go, go!"

Art and Ray quickly moved to the sofa and hoisted Dad up, Ray holding Dad under his arms and Art holding his legs. They carried him out the front door and placed him in the back seat of the station wagon. Mom crawled in with him.

My four brothers and I lined up along the window ledge and watched as they drove off. We had no explanation for what we had just seen. We knew that dad was in bad shape, but unsure why.

Soon, I saw our 67-year-old grandmother Alma, walking quickly towards our house. She had her apron on over her dress, her winter coat resting on her shoulders. Seldom had we seen her so determined to get anywhere.

When she arrived, she started talking in Italian. Fast. She kept repeating the word "diabete, diabete." She would cry and rub her hands and then she would get mad and push a chair.

"Tuo padre e malato, tuo padre e malato," Nonie said.

I had no idea what she was saying, but she was nodding like it all was going to be alright.

My Nonie had been in this country since 1920, but she preferred to speak in her native Italian and add a few English words when necessary.

Kids were on a need-to-know basis in our family, so my brothers and I would not have answers about Dad's condition for a day or so. I just watched Nonie making supper and crying and setting the table and crying. She would raise her polenta spoon and wave it at the ceiling as if she was crying out to God to do something.

"Perche!" she cried. "Perche!"

My father would return home from the hospital three days after the incident. I heard my mother tell every relative on the phone the same story.

"Johnny had an insulin reaction while working at Super Valu," Mom told the person on the other end of the phone line. "Art and Ray did what they had to do to get him to the hospital. He's home now and in good spirits."

She crossed out each name on her call list after she spoke to them. One by one she made the call. Everything was under control again in Mom's world.

Dad was sitting in the living room. Big smile on his face.

"Tommy, let's go for a walk," he said.

I was hesitant.

"Ah, I really can't," I replied. "I got homework and stuff."

Of course, I didn't have homework. But no kid wants to go for walk with a parent unless there's a specific reason, like you want a new bike or something. This walk had a good chance of turning into a lecture or an unexpected new task.

"Come on," he said. "I need some fresh air. Doctor's orders."

Dad smiled. I relented.

We put on our winter ensemble, walked slowly down the steps to the driveway, then made our way to Sellar street.

"It's a beautiful day," Dad said.

I just nodded and kept walking with him. He was seldom this much at peace.

"I had a lot of time to think in the hospital," he said. "Life is way too short. I can't take things so seriously. I almost died, but now I have a new lease on life."

"What?" I said quickly. "Died?"

"I'm fine now. Just needed an adjustment to my insulin and my diet."

My anxiety was rising. My father was 36 years old and talking about death. Our neighbor, Mr. LeClaire, had died at 37. It was suddenly very real.

"I'm ready to meet my maker when God is ready for me," Dad said. "But it's not going to be this week or this year. We have a lot of living to do as a family, right Tommy?"

Such a heavy question to lay upon a ten year old. Yet Dad was smiling, and I could see in his face that his words were sincere.

We walked side by side, talking about hunting, fishing and little league baseball. He talked about taking a family vacation around Lake Superior next summer. We would camp along the way and see the Mackinac Bridge and go up into Canada.

It was a good moment. A boy and his father just walking and talking. A cherished few minutes framed in my mind forever.

CHAPTER 54

On The Radio

"Can I use the transistor radio?" I asked John. "I heard the Speedboys game will be on the radio." John and I had received the radio for Christmas. It had just one earpiece, so we had to share it.

"Yeah, you can use it," he replied. "I'm going up to Maripat's house to play 'Life.' Joanie and Holly are coming to play, too."

Seemed my brother was a girl magnet.

I retired to my room to listen to the game. I plugged the earphone into the little black transistor radio, dialed in WJMS and listened to Bob Olson, the play-by-play man, deliver his pregame comments on the Bessemer vs. Ontonagon game.

"The Bessemer Speedboys are 0–3 on the season. What has been the talk of the town is the long, nearly three-year losing skid. The Speedboys have lost 37 straight games dating back to March 1963. Ontonagon is coming off a win last night against Calumet, so they may be a bit tired for this one, giving a small edge to the winless Speedboys."

Bob Olson was the very best at setting the scene on the radio. And providing hope.

The Speedboys' 37th loss at the hands of the Maple Tigers a week ago had been a winnable game, but they were outplayed in the final minutes. Foul trouble, poor shot selection, the ball of nerves in their throats; it was same thing every fourth quarter of every game. Milo Barnaby had 23 points, and Rick Syrjala and Jim Milakovich each scored in double figures, but their contributions were not enough. The final score: Maple 67, Bessemer 57.

"Starting for the Speedboys tonight," said Olson, *"are #11 Rick Syrjala at center, Milo Barnaby #13 at guard, Don Barbacovi #41 at*

the other guard. Jim Milakovich #45 will play forward and at the other forward, in his first start, sophomore #51 Dennis Forslund. Coach Carl Gregas will routinely go to his bench, so we expect to see sophomore Mark Borseth get some minutes."

As Bob Olson described it, the first quarter was a back-and-forth battle. The Speedboys matched the Polar Bears basket for basket. Barnaby and Barbacovi got plenty of opportunities off screens to score and made the best of it. Forslund picked up some early fouls and was quickly on the bench. Borseth did a fine job filling in, according to Olson. At the end of the first quarter, the Speedboys trailed by one, 17-16.

The second quarter was better for the host club. The Polar Bears found their legs. Led by Chuck Tandlund and Bill Marks, they ran off to a 41-32 halftime lead.

Mark Borseth got the nod to start the third period for the Speedboys. During the halftime break, Bob Olson sang his praises.

"Borseth is new to the Speedboys five," he said. "His aggressive play under the basket and keen position on rebounds has been paying big dividends. Borseth has seven points and seven rebounds. Nice new addition for the visitors."

With Borseth and Forslund, both sophomores, adding some scoring punch, and with Don Barbacovi having his best game of the year, the Speedboys were making a push to win their first game in three seasons. Throughout the third quarter, they steadily cut into Ontonagon's lead.

"That's the end of the third quarter with the Polar Bears leading 54-51. We'll be right back with the final stanza after these messages from our local sponsors."

"Come on, Speedboys!" I yelled, trying to channel energy through the radio to our local lads.

The fourth quarter was back and forth. Ontonagon was trying to put the game away but the spunky boys from Bessemer refused to yield.

With a minute and half remaining in the game, the Speedboys made their move for the win, one that could be their first in three seasons.

"The Speedboys inbound the ball and Barbacovi brings it up court. 1:28 to go in the fourth quarter. The Polar Bears lead Bessemer 60-58. Barbacovi feeds inside to Mark Borseth who turns and goes up for the layup and banks it in! And he is fouled by Tandlund. Borseth has a chance for a three-point play."

I started to bite my nails. The game was getting so intense I wanted to turn off the radio, but I didn't want to miss history in the making.

"Borseth takes his time at the line. Dribbles two times, pauses and puts up the free throw. And it's good! Speedboys lead 61-60."

"They're going to do it!" I shouted.

I wanted to share this moment in history with someone. John was gone, my dad was watching Gunsmoke, and Mom was putting little Pete to bed. Petey had the *croup*, so she was taking her time getting the vaporizer running to help him breathe and sleep.

I yelled to my brother Paul to come into my room. He was doing his homework in the middle room.

"What's up?" Paul said.

"Speedboys may get a win," I said, "they just took the lead."

I pulled the earpiece out of the transistor radio so both of us could listen to the game.

The lead went back and forth throughout the final quarter, with neither team able to mount a scoring run.

"Defense has been the name of the game here in the fourth quarter," Bob Olson reported. *"Both teams smothering the other. There is less than a minute to go in this one. Speedboys up by one."*

Paul and I grabbed hands and started jumping up and down on the bed.

"What are you two doing in there?" Mom asked. "Quit that jumping. I'm trying to get Peter down."

The fun police had arrived but thankfully she left quickly. We sat down and listened. Bob Olson painted the picture perfectly.

"Marks drives the lane for Ontonagon and lays it in. There's a whistle and a foul called on Borseth. That's his fifth foul. He's done for the night. Tough break for the Speedboys."

We threw our hands in the air. We couldn't believe it.

"*Marks hits the free throw, and the Polar Bears now lead. Speedboys take it out of bounds. They try a long pass. The ball is stolen at mid-court by Hoffman. He drives the lane and he scores and is fouled by Barbacovi. Now Don Barbacovi has his fifth foul. Just like that, two big scorers, Borseth with 11 and Barbacovi with 15, are done for the night with 5 fouls each. The Speedboys can't buy a break.*"

A few seconds later, Olson reported that Syrjala committed his fifth foul, placing three of the Speedboys' top six players on the bench collecting splinters. The Polar Bears converted on all their free throws down the stretch and outscored Bessemer 17-12 in the fourth quarter.

As the final seconds ticked off the game clock, Paul and I sat on twin beds looking at each other in silence. Our disappointment needed no words. We truly believed in this team and just couldn't figure out why they couldn't win a game.

"*What a gallant effort by the Speedboys. The three Bs, Borseth, Barbacovi and Barnaby, all scored in double figures tonight. But the difference in the game was Bill Marks. He scored 27 points for the Polar Bears. Ontonagon hit on 21 of 28 at the charity stripe while the Speedboys were only 13 of 25. The Speedboys featured five underclassman and one senior. That young talent kept them in the game until the very end. The losing streak has now hit 38. Next up for the Speedboys are the undefeated Ironwood Red Devils. That will be a tough one. This is Bob Olson saying good night from Ontonagon, where the Polar Bears defeated the Speedboys 71-63.*"

CHAPTER 55

Penny For Your Thoughts

Cartoons were broadcast on television every Saturday at 7:00 a.m. The cavalcade of great animated characters continued all morning, interrupted often by commercials for sugary cereals that would never grace the breakfast table in our house.

We would turn the channel every half hour to see what we were missing on the other station. Cartoons were carried on both CBS and NBC, but now and then an old western would break the flow. We had to determine whether it was black and white animation that kept our attention or an old fashioned shoot'em up western.

The mail was delivered at 11:30 each morning. The mailman was very prompt. On Saturday mornings, we would hear the metal flap on the mailbox open and the sound of paper being stuffed in. Newspapers or magazines were hung on the hooks below the box. Checking the mail was like opening a box of Cracker Jacks. You never knew what prize was inside.

On this Saturday my brother Paul, who was just tall enough to reach in the mailbox to pull out the letters, found a large envelope addressed to me.

"Mr. Tom Bellasaro," Paul said.

He laughed at the bad spelling of our last name.

"Just give me the package," I said.

The envelope was a response from a company that ran special offers on the back of comic books. I shook it and could hear jingling inside. I was excited but scared at the same time; I had gone against the explicit instructions of my parents. They had told me many times that the offers in comic books were not real. Just a way to steal money from unsuspecting children. Like the time I wanted to buy the X-Ray vision spectacles for $1 so I could see the bones in my hands. My dad immediately said not to fall for it.

With Paul eagerly sitting next to me, I tore open the package.

"I paid 50 cents for this," I said.

Two coins fell out. Both were pennies.

"You bought two pennies for fifty cents?" Paul asked. "What a gyp!"

However, my brother didn't know the real secret behind these two coins.

"Yes, but these are not two ordinary pennies," I said. "These are one-of-a-kind."

Paul picked one up and looked at it, first on the front and then the back.

"I don't see anything that would make them special," Paul said.

He flipped the penny back to me.

"Look at President Lincoln," I said. I held the penny in front of his eyes. "Notice anything?"

Paul looked intently. Finally, he shrugged his shoulders. "No."

I put the two pennies in the palm of my hand and pointed to each. "President Lincoln," I said, "is smoking a cigar in this one and a pipe in that one."

"You mean he doesn't normally smoke a cigar or pipe?" Paul asked.

Actually, a good question from the little guy.

"No. That's why they're special," I said. "I plan to play a trick on my friends or maybe Sister Camille at school."

Just then, we heard Dad come through the back door. It was 11:45 and he was home for noon dinner. We heard the crackle of a grocery bag as he set it down on the counter by the sink. He washed his hands as he normally did and got ready to eat. Dad was feeling better since his diabetes episode.

"Tom, why don't you fool Dad with the pennies," Paul said. He started giggling at his great idea.

"Okay. I'll do it."

We started tickling each other, trying to contain our excitement.

We both knew what was about to happen, but Dad did not. Of course, there was always a chance our plan could backfire.

We hurried into the kitchen and took our seats at the table. Dad was positioned at the front of the table with his chair close to the phone. He could just lean over and reach the phone should an important call come in from Super Valu, like a freezer wasn't cooling.

Dad was as serious as always at the table and did not appear to be ready for a conversation.

Paul gave me a poke. "Go ahead," he whispered.

I cleared my throat. "Hey, Dad," I started, knowing this conversation might end before it started.

He looked at me. "What?"

"I wanted to give you the two pennies I owe you from the last time we played cards."

My dad looked at me as I held out the pennies in the palm of my hand.

"Keep'em," he said.

"But Dad, these are two very special pennies," I said.

Paul started to snicker as my dad reached for the pennies.

Dad looked them over. He suddenly popped back in his chair as he noticed the addition to each coin. It was at that moment that I was reminded that you should just play jokes on your friends and not your father.

"What the hell?" he exclaimed. "You defaced American currency? You could go to jail. Heck, I could go to jail."

My father was beside himself.

"No, no, Dad," I said. "It's a joke. I got them from an offer in a comic book."

But it was too late. He was hopping mad.

"It's no joke," he shouted, "when you scratch a coin to put a cigar in the mouth of our 16th President of the United States. Oh, my god, look at this one. He's smoking a pipe. How many times have I told you not to trust anything you see in those damn comic books? What if these coins got into circulation? It would be a crime."

Paul went quiet and started eating. He acted as if he had never heard about the pennies.

Mom couldn't help but chime in as well.

"I've told you a thousand times, mister," she said, "comic books are the worst influence on you kids. No more comic books for you, young man."

My father twirled his spaghetti with a curious look on his face. He was contemplating something.

"Tommy, give me one of those pennies," he said. "I'm gonna play a little joke on a cashier at the store. See if she notices anything when I go to pay with a penny."

"Do you want the cigar-smoking President Lincoln or the pipe-smoking Lincoln," I asked.

"Just give me both," he said. He flashed a small smirk as he thought of the reaction of his favorite cashier at Super Valu.

The rest of the afternoon was spent outdoors where the air was crisp like a typical December day. By mid-afternoon, we had completed a snow and ice fort along Beecher Street. It was built in close proximity to the sledding youth. Should they choose to glide by, they would be met with a barrage of snowballs, ice chunks and verbal insults as they cascaded down the hill. We spent three hours building the fort for ten seconds of pleasure raining snowballs on unsuspecting sledders. It seemed well worth it.

When the paperboy delivered the *Ironwood Daily Globe* at 4:00, it was our cue to head to the house to warm up. Once inside, I placed my frozen wool socks onto the heat register. The coal-burning furnace was doing its job, blowing the most wonderful warmth through the duct work and into the room. I could hear the melted snow sizzle as it dropped from my socks and hit the inside of the heated vent.

At exactly 5:30, I heard my father come through the back door. Same time every day for supper. Mom had made macaroni and Dad brought the Italian bread.

Dad set his grocery bag next to the sink and began to wash his hands. I came up behind him as he reached for a towel.

"Hi, Dad," I said. "Can I have my pennies back?"

My father reached into his right pocket to pull out his coins.

He held a variety of coins in his hand. Quarters, nickels, dimes and pennies. He poked at the coins with his finger to find the right pennies. Suddenly pure panic came over his face. He reached into his other pants pocket and then put his hands to his shirt pocket to feel for a coin.

He suddenly blurted out, "Oh my god, I paid for the bread tonight with your Lincoln pennies."

His face turned red. He rubbed his hands on his temples.

"I just put Lincoln smoking a cigar and a pipe into circulation."

He sat down heavily in his chair. He was distraught.

Mom stood across the kitchen from him and shot her husband the most disgusted look.

"Serves you right, Mr. Funny Guy," she said. "Well, the joke's on you."

CHAPTER 56

Always Expect the Unexpected

When Rance English moved to Bessemer he bought an old farmhouse on the east end of town, complete with barn. English had thoughts of raising a dairy cow and chickens to keep his wife and boys busy while he taught school and coached basketball. He thought about running for city office and writing articles for the local paper to get his opinions in print on a variety of subjects. He had a lot on his mind. Not the least of which was a nagging issue with the Bessemer athletic director, Jack White.

Among English's many passions was the game of chess. A game he loved so much that he taught it to his students at Washington School. He was a master chess player. He beat all comers and used this prowess in day-to-day situations. He calculated his every move. Today, he would make his biggest move since taking over coaching duties with the Bessemer junior varsity basketball team.

"Carl, is my team getting those warm-ups jackets or not?" he asked coach Carl Gregas before practice.

Gregas had the same old answer.

"I'm trying to get my team ready to play Ironwood," Gregas replied. "I can't worry about your warm-ups."

English abruptly turned and walked away, not saying a word. The ball was now in his court.

Gregas considered the undefeated Ironwood Red Devils team a dominant force in the Michigan-Wisconsin Conference. When he looked at his 1965-66 schedule before the season, he could see all the potential losses ahead. He had drawn circles around Hurley, Maple and Ashland. Those were winnable games for his young team. The rest of the schedule would take a miracle from God or an outbreak of influenza in the opponent's locker room to change the predictable outcome. He prayed for the miracle.

It was Thursday night intramurals at Washington School and the basketballs were flying around the gym. The boys were now good friends and teammates.

One of the new kids in town was Eric English, but everyone called him Ric. He had moved to Bessemer this year when his father accepted the teaching and coaching job in the Bessemer School District. It was good to have a family move into town versus moving out. The mine closings reduced the Bessemer population by the hundreds.

Ric was a natural at basketball and it was obvious he had been taught the fundamentals by his father. But mostly, he just loved to play the game.

"Do you follow the NBA much?" I asked Ric.

"Yeah, sure," he replied, "Oscar Robertson of the Cincinnati Royals is my favorite player."

"The Big O," I said. "So, you must be a Cincinnati Reds baseball fan too?"

"I was, but then the Reds traded my favorite player Frank Robinson to the Orioles, so now I'm a Baltimore fan."

"Well maybe they'll trade the Big O to the Baltimore Bullets and you can be a one-town fan."

Ric smiled and dribbled to the basket, laid in a perfect bank shot and I grabbed the rebound. He started to guard me as I dribbled towards the basket and as I went up for my shot, he blocked it. No foul, just a perfect block.

Harry Rizzie, our intramural coach, had taught us to stop any easy layups by blocking or fouling the opposing player. Make the player shoot from the free throw line where his luck would be less than 50%, Rizzie would tell us. Ric had been listening.

"Boys, bring it in," Rizzie yelled to all the boys on the court.

Rizzie took a set shot from half court and it swished through the net. We all applauded our instructor.

"You boys are looking great," Rizzie said. "However, your passing stinks. The biggest issue is not the guy throwing the ball to you. The biggest issue is YOU. You aren't ready when it's tossed your way. Boys, you have to always expect a pass. Don't wait for it to get to you. Move toward the ball. Fight your way in front of a defender. Always expect the ball, got that?"

We all nodded our heads.

"Okay, let's try that out."

Rizzie had five players on defense and selected four boys, including me, to be on his team as he dribbled it up. As he crossed the timeline, he faked a pass to his left and then threw it to his right. Right to me. I wasn't expecting it, and it hit me square in the face. The basketball stung like being slapped with a wet towel. I tried hard not to cry and covered my face with my hands.

"Pelissero," Rizzie shouted, "what did I tell you? Always expect the ball. Are you okay?"

I removed my hands from the front of my face. My eyes welled with tears. I just looked straight ahead, refusing to cry.

"Oh, you're okay," Rizzie said. "Look at that. You got the *Wilson* logo branded on your forehead."

Everyone laughed, including me, though tears still filled my eyes. Coach Rizzie had a way of taking a bad situation and making it seem better.

"Let's bring it in here," Rizzie said. "I got some good news."

We surrounded him at center court.

"You boys have been working really hard, and Jack White and I want to get you some big-time experience. I'm going to have some of you play before a Speedboys' game, probably the Iron River game next week. Then, we'll get the rest of you boys out on the high school court for a tournament a week after that."

We all cheered. Coach Rizzie dismissed us for the night. But all we could talk about on the way home was how exciting it would be to play on the same court as our beloved Speedboys.

CHAPTER 57

When Friday night rolled around, junior varsity coach Rance English made his big move. Actually, it was more of a statement, since only the small crowd that had gathered early for the JV game would see it, but it would make an impact on the basketball program.

While the varsity had lost every game since March 1963, the junior varsity found solace in the occasional victory. They found out that English could coach and deliver on his promise to win a game or two.

But this night wouldn't be remembered for the victory that Coach English engineered in beating Ironwood's JV team 38-37. No, it would be remembered for the pre-game drills.

As the Bessemer JV team came onto the court prior to the game, coach English's plan was on full display. If the school would not give them warm-ups, then the team would bring their own. Rance English's players ran through their layup drills in their thermal underwear and pajamas.

Athletic Director Jack White, standing in the upper bleachers, looked down on the court and couldn't believe his eyes. He pointed and shouted to Coach English, but the sound of the bouncing balls drowned out his verbal scolding. White ran down a flight of stairs and stormed to coach Carl Gregas' office.

"Do you see what your coach is pulling out there?" White screamed.

Gregas was both startled and confused. "No, what are you talking about, Jack?"

"He's got his team out there in their pajamas!" White yelled.

Gregas didn't know anything about it.

"I'm sorry, Jack, but I don't control Rance," Gregas said. "He must be ticked off about those warm-ups not being provided to his team. He warned us to do something."

"They're the B team, Carl," said White. "We don't have the money in the budget for warm-ups. Do you want me to buy warm-ups for the freshman team at Washington, too?"

"Well, actually they have warm-ups," Gregas responded.

"Do something about this," White shouted as he stormed out of the coach's office.

Gregas quickly ran out of the tunnel and across the court to talk to his assistant. As he looked at the boys, in their various warm-up attire, he was caught between scolding Rance and having a good laugh.

"Okay, Rance," he said. "You made your point. We'll work something out. Now, get the boys back in the locker room and take off those *warm-ups*."

The students in attendance cheered as the "long john squad" exited the floor.

English, the chess master, had made his final move. Checkmate.

The Ironwood Red Devil varsity team was 5-0 and held sole possession of first place in the M-W Conference. Whatever plan coach Gregas had drawn up on paper worked for about four minutes of the first quarter, as Jim Milakovich and Don Barbacovi gave the Speedboys an early 7-6 lead.

However, Gene Farrell, the Red Devils' head coach, could feel the local crowd cheering the boys on to an upset, so he turned up the heat. He put on the full court press and the game changed; the floor tilted instantly and decisively towards Ironwood.

When your team can't get the ball across the timeline, you are in for a long night. This was a very long night for the Speedboys. One minute it was 7-6 Bessemer, and a few minutes later it was 36-9 Ironwood. Red Devils Ben Finco, Tom Carli, Marty Murto, Guy Kangas, Art Pertile, and Louie Vlasich all found the basket for double figures to bury the Speedboys with their 39th consecutive loss. Ironwood 86, Bessemer 32.

Far away from the game, under a single streetlight, a young boy dribbled in circles and shot at a basket nailed to a telephone pole. It was dark, cold and getting late, but he didn't mind. He was working at his craft. Dribbling, shooting, rebounding.

He imagined there were only five to go in the game and the ball was in his hands. He would use all his moves to get into position as the clock wound down, then take the final shot.

5-4-3-2-1…

As the final second clicked off the imaginary clock, he turned square with the basket and allowed the ball to roll off his fingertips. The buzzer sounded as the ball was in the air. Then *swish*, through the net. He had won the game. He stood and admired his shot as the make-believe crowd roared their approval.

"Ric?" called his neighbor from her back door. "It's time for you to go home. It's getting late."

He tucked the basketball under his arm, waved to her, and quietly walked home. Silent except for the dribbling of the ball and the swirling wind whipping snow about his feet. The single streetlight lit his path home.

CHAPTER 58

The Vietnam war appeared on the front page of the *Ironwood Daily Globe* nearly every day. President Lyndon Johnson called it a "peace offensive" and not a war, however the bombing raids in Vietnam and Laos screamed it was not about peace. But it was seldom talked about in the local shops and cafés. The chatter in Bessemer was about the 80 inches of snow to date, the upcoming frigid temps of January, the influx of skiers, and the high school basketball team's struggles.

The Speedboys were about to lose their 40th game, and everyone in town knew it. The undefeated Panthers of Superior Cathedral would play host to the boys from Bessemer.

Superior Cathedral was new to the Michigan-Wisconsin Conference having replaced Superior East. East left the conference when they consolidated with Superior Central to form the new Superior Senior High School for the start of the 1965-66 school year. No previous competitor was sad to see the powerful Superior East team dissolved.

Superior Cathedral played their games at Superior State College. The gym would be half full. Panther fans would be there, but after 39 straight losses most Speedboy boosters wouldn't travel the 110 miles to Superior; some parents and maybe one pep bus, but that was it.

Coach Carl Gregas' job was to keep the game competitive and get game experience for his young cagers. He would accomplish the latter, not the former, in an 82-35 blowout loss.

It was another long, cold bus ride home to Bessemer on Highway 2. The boys got back to their unlit high school around midnight and then walked home in below-zero temps. They could sleep in on

Saturday morning, unless they had a job like Don Barbacovi did at Super Valu.

Don would be there at 8 a.m. to endure another day of chiding from good-hearted co-workers.

"So, what is that, Donny, the hundredth loss in a row?" they'd say.

Don took the ribbing in stride. The Speedboy guard knew that the team's best bet to break the losing streak was coming soon against Hurley, and he would laugh off the teasing and concentrate on the work at hand until then. He knew that one day the streak would be over and the fair-weather fans would eat their words.

Staff Sergeant Adrian Anglim was burning the midnight oil in his office under the north bleachers of A.D. Johnston gymnasium. His light was the only one on in the place.

The Junior ROTC office was close to the gun racks, the training manuals, and the training floor. His desk, supplied by the Army for the program, had faded from dark green to khaki brown after years of use.

Tonight, Anglim was grading one of the few written tests taken by his cadets; this one about first aid. Most tests were manual in nature: how to take apart and re-assemble an M-1 rifle, how to march in formation, how to salute, and how to shine your brass buckles and buttons. These tests were performed by high school cadets in front of their commanding officer. Few cadets failed; most excelled.

Behind Anglim was a silver footlocker, one that he would fill with his belongings if he was suddenly asked to deploy. He was still on active duty, but on permanent assignment to Bessemer High School. He had been in the military his whole life. Packing and moving to a new assignment was always a possibility. It didn't bother him, but he was always concerned about his family, as they bore the brunt of the change. New assignment, new home, new school, new friends. Military life was tough on everyone.

Anglim heard the sound of a basketball being dribbled in the gym outside his office. The sound grew louder as the dribbler got closer to his office door. Finally, the culprit poked his head in.

"Hi, Sarge," said Milo Barnaby. "Mind if I shoot a few baskets while you're here?"

"No problem, Milo," Anglim replied. "Just don't turn on those gym lights or the administration will be here in five minutes and my rear will be in a sling."

"Got ya, Sarge."

Barnaby dribbled and shot in the semi-darkness. There was just enough light emanating from Anglim's office that he could see the net and a slight glare off the glass backboard.

He played as if he had his eyes closed, and it helped him with his concentration. Barnaby got a feel for where to hit the backboard for the easy bank shot. He worked on his layups, left-handed and right, and took a few jump shots before deciding it was too difficult in the darkness. He sauntered back to Anglim's office.

"Thanks, Sarge," Barnaby said.

"No problem," Anglim said. "Hey, Milo, who do you play next?"

"We've got Iron River here on January 11th."

"Okay, good luck," said Anglim. "Say, what are the plans for next year after you graduate?"

"I got an academic scholarship to Northern Michigan," Barnaby said. "I'd like to be a teacher and maybe coach when I graduate from college. It would be nice to get a job in the U.P. or Wisconsin. You know, not too far from home."

"You'll do well, Milo, in whatever you decide to do."

"I also have an opportunity to go to Michigan Tech on a ROTC scholarship," Barnaby added. "They'll pay for my education and then I give them four years after graduation. I would start out as a Second Lieutenant."

Staff Sergeant Anglim looked down and rubbed his chin.

"Yes, I know the program," Anglim said. "Milo, as an Army career man, we would love to see you in our branch of the service. You have great leadership skills, and you would be the perfect soldier and officer."

"Thanks," Milo said with a wide smile.

Anglim paused and took a deep breath.

"Milo, now I'm going to talk to you like you're my son. Take the academic scholarship at Northern Michigan."

Barnaby looked at Anglim, curious.

"Why Sarge?"

"Son, you're going to come out of Michigan Tech through that ROTC program as an officer. With your leadership skills and your gung-ho attitude, the Army is going to send you right into the jungle in Vietnam. You won't last 30 days out there."

Anglim stood up from his desk, walked over and put his hand on Barnaby's shoulder.

"Milo, this conflict, this Vietnam War, is for career guys like me. We knew what we signed up for. It's not for guys like you. Sure, you appreciate that the Army is paying for your college education. Being a loyal guy, you want to pay the Army back with four years of service to your country. But this war in Southeast Asia is for me and the other grunts that signed our names on the dotted line and are willing to follow orders. I don't want you in Vietnam."

Anglim paused to let his message sink in. He went back to his desk, gathered his papers, then reached for the light switch.

"If in the end you've thought it through and want to take that scholarship from the Army, you'll have my full support. But please, take my advice and go to Northern."

CHAPTER 59

Playing in LaLa Land

The Iron River high school did not bring their JV basketball team to Bessemer with their varsity team on Friday night, so the fans got to enjoy an exhibition game between two grade school teams. The game featured a select group of fifth, sixth and seventh graders from the intramural program. Some of these boys would one day play for the Bessemer Speedboys, but not until the 1970s. That seemed light years away.

Rizzie's Raiders, coached by Harry Rizzie, faced off against *White's Blue Bombers*, coached by Athletic Director Jack White.

Sixth grader Kevin Borseth was high scorer for the Raiders. The Raiders stole the ball repeatedly from the hapless Blue Bombers. Without free throws, the Blue Bombers would have never scored. To get more boys in the game, a player came off the bench when a foul was called to shoot the free throw, then returned to the bench. Tommy Maccani was one of the designated free throw shooters for the Blue Bombers and made all three of his shots. The Blue Bombers lost 27-6.

In the varsity game, the Speedboys would not fare much better than the Blue Bombers had in the exhibition. Iron River exploded from the opening tip off, and the Speedboys did not have the speed or size to keep up with them. The local boys managed only three points in the second quarter. Three!

The Speedboys were figuratively and literally playing in *La La Land*. Dennis LaFountain and Jim LaRock contributed 14 and 13 points respectively for Iron River. Dane Dominici hit for 27 to lead all scorers. The trio blistered the Speedboys for 54 points, four more than the entire Bessemer team managed to score. When it was over, another loss was stacked on the streak.

My brother Paul and I ran all the way home from the game to catch Channel 3 sportscaster Marsh Nelson read the area basketball scores.

"Good evening, I'm Marsh Nelson, and this is KDHL-TV 3 sports," he said. *"There is still no joy in the Upper Peninsula of Michigan for the Bessemer Speedboys' faithful. They endured yet another loss, their 41st straight, at the hands of Iron River, 71–50. Next up for Bessemer are the Ashland Oredockers on Friday night. Good luck, Speedboys."*

Nelson failed to mention Rizzie's Raiders' win over White's Blue Bombers.

Guglie's barbershop was busy as ever on Saturday morning. Stan Servia, the owner of the Last East Inn, was sitting in the chair when my brother Paul and I arrived. He said hello as we walked in.

"Hey, boys," said Servia. "I heard your dad bowled a 300 game the other night. Is that true?"

"I think so," I said. "He was pretty excited when he got home, but I'm not sure."

My dad was very good at bowling. His name was in the paper often, sporting a high game of 250 or a 600 series. But 300? Not likely.

Paul and I took our seats until it was our turn.

Waiting for the chair to open was a guy whose White Pine shirt suggested he worked at the copper mine, and whose receding hairline telegraphed a quick clip and he'd be out the door. Next to him was a high school kid with bright red hair and freckles. His hair was thick and curly on top and trimmed tightly on the sides. A touch of Brylcreem gave his hair a sheen.

There was another man sitting in the old shoeshine chair in the back of the shop. The chair was set on a raised platform, four feet in the air, and the man's feet rested leisurely on the iron shoe holders in front of him. We couldn't tell who he was, as the newspaper he was reading covered his face. He seemed to be quite comfortable up there waiting for his turn.

"How's business, Stanley?" asked Guglie. "Must be good with all the skiers in town."

"Oh, we're packed every night at the bar," replied Servia.

"I'm happy to hear that," Guglie replied, "but I don't like those diesel buses running all night next to my shop. They wait for the skiers in Hunters Inn until the bar closes, but with the noise I can't sleep."

"Well, I'm happy and you're not," laughed Servia. "Just the way it goes in Bessemer."

Both men turned their conversation to the Speedboys.

"Well, Stanley, have you been getting to the basketball games?" Guglie asked Servia.

"Yes. I go to the Washington School gym some afternoons and even St. Sebastian games there on Sundays. The high school team, well, I have to pick and choose a bit because night games aren't good for me since I have to be at the bar. But yes, I've seen a few."

"What do you think of the new coach?" Guglie asked.

"Gregas?" asked Servia. "He's a good guy. Doing his best. But that league is just too tough for the talent he has now. When Salty Ciesielczyk gets there in a couple of years, things will improve."

Guglie did one final clip on Servia and then removed the barber's cape from his customer. Servia stood up, pulled his wallet, and paid for his haircut.

"Thanks, Guglie!" Servia said on his way out the door.

"Who's next?" Guglie shouted.

The man in the shoeshine chair folded his paper and stepped down from the chair. To my surprise, it was basketball coach Carl Gregas who had just listened to an entire conversation about him without making a peep.

"Were your ears burning, Carl?" asked Guglie.

"No, Guglie," replied Gregas, winking at me as he passed, "About what?"

CHAPTER 60

For the most part, the folks in Bessemer brushed off the headlines about anti-war protests that were printed in the *Ironwood Daily Globe*.

"Just a bunch of commies and long hair college students against the war," a veteran would say to another over coffee.

The young men of the area continued to enlist in the armed forces or sign up for the draft, and some even found their way to the jungles of Vietnam. It was just what you did. Just like your father. Just like your father's father. When you joined the service, you fought wherever the military told you to fight. Most people in Bessemer believed that American firepower would always win the day.

The boys who'd graduated high school, but who hadn't enlisted or been drafted, found that Friday night was a great night to unwind. Some drove their partially restored cars up and down Main Street hoping that some cute girl on the drug store corner would give them a wave. The over-21 crowd found their way to the White Birch, Hunter's Inn, Poor Joe's, Last East Inn, or other haunts. Those under the legal drinking age in Michigan might cross the Wisconsin border, where an 18 year old with a few coins in his pocket could drink beer at the Hamilton Club in Montreal.

But during the basketball season, many traveled to A.D. Johnston Gymnasium to watch their younger buddies try to win a basketball game.

For Don Barbacovi, his afternoons and nights were filled with homework and basketball. When he wasn't doing either of those, he was at Super Valu stocking shelves, bagging groceries and helping his dad, Ray, with the store's book work. Today's assignment was delivering groceries to some elderly residents who could no longer make it to the store to shop.

His first stop was a delivery to the Sisters of Notre Dame in their convent above St. Sebastian School. Sister Charlene and Sister Camille met him at the top of the long stairwell and kindly accepted his delivery. They told him to drop off the bill at the church office, which he promptly did.

Don made three more deliveries. One to a widow, one to a single guy who had been hurt years earlier in the mine and one to a family of four on welfare. They all politely thanked him for the delivery and closed the door. No one paid for the groceries, nor did they even offer a reason. Don was confused and torn as to what to do. He got back in his car and figured he would take it up with his father later.

On Friday night, January 14, the Ashland Oredockers wanted no part of being the first team to lose to the Bessemer Speedboys. The two teams had been battling each other in the Michigan-Wisconsin Conference since 1937. Back then Ashland was nicknamed the *Purgolders,* because their colors were purple and gold. The colors survived but not the nickname.

The Bessemer fans had packed the house and gave the varsity team a warm welcome when they came out of the tunnel for pre-game drills. The fans had just been entertained by a thrilling 45-43 win by the Rance English coached junior varsity team in the early game. English was showing the locals that there was talent in both players and coaching. The fans wanted more of the same from the varsity Speedboys.

The Speedboys surprised Ashland by opening the game in a full court press. The Oredockers had clearly not practiced breaking a press in preparation for this game, and they seemed rattled. They struggled to get the ball up the court, and when they did, they couldn't find the hoop.

Rick Syrjala and Jim Milakovich pulled down rebounds and fired sharp outlet passes to Milo Barnaby, Don Barbacovi, and Dick Schwartz. Bessemer's shooting was less than desired, though. Barbacovi got himself to the free throw line with drives in the lane, but his outside shot was non-existent in the opening stanza. Finally, with four minutes gone in the first period, Barbacovi sank a jump shot.

The local lads were starting to feel it. The crowd was starting to feel it. There was excitement like never before at any home game during this 41-game losing streak. The Speedboys were hanging tough with an above-average conference foe who had come to town thinking victory was a given. The first quarter ended with the score tied at 14.

The Speedboys opened the second quarter with a put-back shot by Syrjala and a fast break layup by Barnaby. Suddenly the Speedboys were up 18-14.

Fans in attendance saw how competitive the Speedboys had become. In each game, the boys developed their skills and started to play unselfish basketball. Coach Gregas had instituted a few new plays and rotations that were confusing to their opponent.

"Run the play," Gregas shouted. "Don't force it. Get it to the guy who is open. Follow your shot."

The Speedboys followed his advice. But midway through the second quarter their energy level was starting to wane. The full court press had taken a lot out of them. Gregas was forced to go to his bench. Mark Borseth, Eggy Forslund, Paul Carpenedo and Mike Betlewski gave the starters a breather.

The Speedboys called off their full court press once the Oredockers figured out a way to break it. Bessemer sat back in a 2-1-2 zone for a few minutes. This allowed Ashland to gain some momentum. When the Oredockers started to pull away, Gregas called a timeout and put his rested starters back in the game. The Speed Boys returned to the full court press.

Barbacovi scored on drives and drew fouls on Ashland's key players. Milakovich hit an outside shot just before the buzzer sounded. At the half, Ashland was up 36-32.

The Bessemer faithful cheered loudly as the Speedboys headed to the locker room. Fans patted the players on their backs as the team ran through the tunnel. The team was all smiles, except Jim Milakovich.

"Don't get complacent," the starting forward told his teammates in the locker room at halftime. "We lost our focus on the press when we got tired. We have to keep our energy level up."

His teammates agreed.

After the halftime break, the Oredockers still had no answer for

Bessemer's ferocious press. Steal after steal. Rebound after rebound. Basket after basket. The winless Speedboys were putting on a clinic for the visiting team. The Speedboys outscored Ashland 21-15 in the third quarter and took a 53-51 lead into the fourth.

Not one fan was heading to the exit. Word was spreading to the cafes and bars that the Speedboys were on the verge of breaking the streak. More fans poured in through the side doors. A few of them half in the bag.

Throughout the fourth quarter, the fouls for both teams began to pile up. Oredockers Ted Buetow fouled out midway through the period. Milakovich and Barnaby were both in foul trouble, but Gregas kept them on the court. The lead went back and forth over the final minutes.

With two minutes and 50 seconds to go in the game, Bessemer's Jim Milakovich hit a 15-foot jump shot to bring Bessemer within a point, 59-58. The shot rocked the house.

Bessemer fans were thrilled with this brand of high-energy, up-tempo basketball. The dream of pulling out of victory tonight was real. The Speedboys needed a couple of defensive stops and one big basket to pull this one out.

But there would be no stops.

Ashland scored with one minute to go and went up 61-58. Then the Oredockers stole the ball with 20 seconds left and Ashland star Ryan Hmielewski hit a jumper to make it 63-58. That shot iced the victory for the visitors. The Speedboys scored as the buzzer sounded but lost 63-60.

The 42nd consecutive loss for the Bessemer Speedboys was in the books. But for those fans who were there, it was the finest basketball game they had seen all year; maybe in the last three years. The fans had hope. This was the kind of fight they wanted to see in their high school team. An unselfish team. A team that was pulling in the same direction.

The losing streak had taken its toll on the team and the town. But the Bessemer fans saw something different tonight, and they were energized.

CHAPTER 61

Our Moment Had Come

Harry Rizzie blew the whistle to end the scrimmage between the skins and shirts. He asked us to take a seat in the Washington School bleachers.

We wiped our faces with our t-shirts to soak up the sweat. We had worked hard to make an impression on our instructor. As squirrelly as we were in the classroom all day, we were always attentive at our twice-a-week basketball practice.

"Boys, you've been playing hard for two months," Rizzie started, "and have improved dramatically."

We grunted in agreement.

"I've got good news," he said.

We sat forward to hear.

"You're going to play in a basketball tournament at A.D. Johnston gymnasium."

We cheered and whistled.

"It'll be a two-night tournament, with the championship game on the second night."

This was the most excited we had been since the grade school basketball program began. A tournament, in the big gym, with glass backboards, a scoreboard and fans. It was what we had dreamed of since we first attended a Speedboys basketball game.

"Okay, now listen up," Rizzie said. "Here are the teams, your captain and your coach. Pay attention, so you know what team you're on.

He opened his notebook and put his finger to the page.

"First, the Celtics." Rizzie said. "Your coach will be Milo Barnaby."

Holy cow! I thought to myself. One of Speedboys' players would be at the helm. How cool is that?

Rizzie continued. "The captain of the Celtics will be Jim Rooni. Players on the Celtics are Bob Obradovich, Ric English, Jay Maccani, Dave Webber, Mike Hoffner, Dave Ojala, Darren Silkworth, and Wayland Koski."

I could hardly contain myself. That was one team down. I was sure I'd be on the next team. Or could it be like Little League and not everyone is on a team? My anxiety was starting to build.

"Next team is the Lakers. Coach is Mark Borseth. Captain is Kevin Borseth. Players are Gordy Hill, Jimmy Joe Martell, Fran Re, Bruce Hensley, Paul Harley, Paul Erickson, Mike Ojala, Tommy Kangas and Mike Gustafson."

The Lakers cheered.

Geez, half of the teams selected, and I was still not picked. He wouldn't leave me off a team, would he? I was rubbing my legs to relieve the stress.

"The Royals. Captain Camelo Switzer. Coach Rick Syrjala. Players Bruce Sanger, Billy Walls, Greg Adams, Dave Betlewski, Art Boline, Greg Langdon, Dick Matazel and Billy Kravetz."

I was starting to turn red as it seemed my name wouldn't be announced. Only one team to go. Jeff Pricco and Joel Massie were talking to each other. They had not been picked either. Maybe they were getting nervous, too.

"Ok, the final team is the 76ers, to be coached by Jim Milakovich," Rizzie said.

I rocked back and forth with my hands over my mouth praying he would say my name.

"Captain of the 76ers is Dave Forslund. Players are Jeff Pricco, Joel Massie, Mike Berkowitz, Bill Nyman, Tommy Maccani, John Hellman, Denny Sliva, Charlie Kravetz, and Tom Pelissero."

I breathed a sigh of relief.

We all started to push and shove one another in excitement of the coming competition. A few starting ribbing each other on who was on the better team. It was all in good fun.

Rizzie raised his hand and told us to calm down.

"The games will be next Monday and Tuesday," he said. "The first game is at 6:30. The Lakers play the 76ers."

We all cheered again.

"Now hear me out," Rizzie continued. "No player is to be in that gym until 6 p.m. If I catch you shooting before 6:00, you'll not be allowed to play. Is that clear?"

Of course it was clear. Why would I screw up and lose a chance to play in a big-time game?

My stomach was doing flip flops. A real team. A real coach. And the coolest name for a team, the 76ers. The team of Wilt Chamberlain and Billy Cunningham. And now coached by my favorite Speedboy, Jim Milakovich. It could not get better than this.

Fourth Quarter
January 1966

CHAPTER 62

Just Like the Speedboys

"Do you have all your basketball stuff packed?" my mother asked. "We'll all be there tonight to watch you play. You boys are gonna die on that big floor tonight. Pace yourself."
"Yeah," I said.

I had already looked through my satchel three times. But that question triggered me to check again. Blue shorts, white socks, clean jock, Red Ball high top tenners, and a slightly stained white t-shirt. I headed out at 5:30, knowing that I couldn't step into the gym until 6 p.m.

My walk was brisk. I covered the half mile sooner than expected.

The temperature was in the low single digits as I stood outside the high school door. I wanted to walk into the gym, but I understood Harry Rizzie's instructions. Not before 6 p.m.

I looked at my watch and it was only 5:55. Certainly I could stand in the cold for another five minutes.

No other boys were waiting at the south side door of the gymnasium, which seemed odd to me. Maybe they were hanging on the north side door, as most lived over there. I was trying to convince myself I had not screwed up.

I could hear balls bouncing and shouts of young voices coming from inside the gym. Did Harry Rizzie say not before 6:00 or did he say not before 5:30? Now, I am in a tug of war with my memory. Why wasn't anyone else here?

Finally, my watch read 6:00. I pulled open the heavy metal door to the gym and the echo of balls bouncing and shots hitting off backboards filled my ears. I looked over the railing and saw the Lakers on the court. What the heck?

"Tommy Pel!" shouted a kid down below.

I saw my teammates already in their basketball attire standing in the tunnel but not yet on the floor.

"Hurry up!" Jeff Pricco yelled. He motioned for me to get down the steps, pronto.

I ran down to the floor as fast as I could. My jacket still zipped and my hat and mittens still on.

"Where have you been?" Pricco asked. "We've been waiting for you so we could get started."

"I thought Harry said we couldn't come into the gym until 6:00," I said.

"The gym floor! Not the building!" Red Forslund said. He rolled his eyes, dumbfounded that I couldn't figure that one out.

My teammates followed me to the locker room and kept yelling *hurry up, hurry up!* They wanted so badly to get on the court and shoot.

I've never dressed faster in my life. Coach Milakovich threw me an old, wool jersey, complete with moth holes. It was yellow with blue and white stripes on the side and Bessemer stitched on the front. It was a bit oversized, but to me it was perfect. It was number 14, the same number my dad wore in high school.

We ran out of the tunnel onto the gym just like the Speedboys. We were down at the far end of the court where the band usually sets up. Some of the Lakers were shooting there too, but our coach directed them back to their end of the gym.

Coach Milakovich had us line up for layup drills. We had no idea how to do a layup off a glass backboard. Each of our shots was too hard and the ball came flying off in all directions. There were a few of my teammates who couldn't get the ball high enough to the basket, even though the rim was at 10 feet just like the Washington School rims.

Mom was right, the big gym was exhausting, but exhilarating at the same time. It was wider and longer than the one at Washington school. But the big time meant the big gym, right?

Parents and interested parties, like the athletic director and diehard basketball fans, started to fill the stands on both sides of the gymnasium. We kept running our drills and couldn't help but look into the stands to see people that had come to watch our tournament.

Occasionally a parent or classmate would yell encouragement to one of our buddies on the court. It was so different to have people coming to watch us play. We were used to playing outdoors in the snow and cold without a fan anywhere in sight. But here we were watching young and old alike streaming in to sit and watch a bunch of ten-, eleven- and twelve-year-old kids put on a show.

The scoreboard buzzer sounded. It called us to the bench where coach Milakovich selected his starting five.

"Pricco, Massie, Forslund, Nyman, and Pelissero," he said. "You'll start."

I had waited my whole life for this moment; to be down on the court at A.D. Johnston gymnasium, playing basketball in front of the faithful Bessemer fans. Now suddenly, there I was, and the coach is pointing his finger at me, and saying "you're starting."

Could it get much better than this?

It could. Harry Rizzie picked up the microphone.

"Ladies and Gentlemen," Rizzie announced. "Welcome to our inaugural grade school basketball tournament! The young boys you will see tonight are participating in an intramural basketball program started two years ago by former Speedboys coach John Bonk. They have worked hard, two nights a week, to learn the fundamentals of the game. Tonight, they will show their progress. Basketball fans, let me introduce to you, your future Bessemer Speedboys."

The crowd cheered.

My heart was racing. My stomach was churning. But what a wonderful dream come true, for all of us.

Rizzie cleared his throat to announce the starting lineups.

"For the Lakers," Rizzie started, "coached by Mark Borseth. At center, captain Kevin Borseth."

Kevin ran onto the court, the fans cheering at that very moment just for him. Undoubtedly, he would have moments like this his entire life. He was that good an athlete. But for many of us this might be our finest hour.

Rizzie called the names of the rest of the Lakers team. Gordy Hill, Jim Martell, Fran Re, and Paul Harley. The crowd cheered for each and every player as they ran out to center court. The players stood nervously for a moment and then coach Mark Borseth waved for them to return to their bench.

Rizzie turned the page.

"For the 76ers," Rizzie announced, "coached by Jim Milakovich. At center, Dave 'Red' Forslund," Rizzie announced.

Red ran onto the court in front of the growing crowd that clapped and cheered. He was not sure where to go but finally stopped at the free throw area. I was so happy that Harry hadn't announced me first, as I wouldn't have known where to go.

"At forward, Joel Massie."

Massie ran directly at Red and he put his hand out and Red slapped it just like the high school players do.

"At the other forward, Billy Nyman."

Nyman sprinted to the free throw area and stood next to the taller Forslund.

"At guard, Jeffrey Pricco."

Each of my teammates bolted onto the court with a big smile. Cheers reverberated off the gymnasium walls.

I was the only one left. My heart was pounding so hard I expected it to break through my chest. It felt like all eyes were on me.

"At the other guard," Rizzie started. "Tom 'the Bomb' Pelissero."

The crowd cheered. I ran to my teammates, smiling about my new nickname. All four of the guys met me at the free throw line and we formed a circle. Instinctively, we all put our hands together in the middle and said, "Let's go!" Just like the Speedboys. Just like our heroes.

Forslund won the tip and the ball came to me. I dribbled it up court. It felt like a beachball under my hand, but I got it across the timeline. I passed it to Pricco. He made a nifty move around Borseth and delivered a beautiful bounce pass to Red. He then tossed it to Massie who was cutting through the lane and Joel laid it in off the glass for our first basket. All those nights of working hard on the fundamentals had paid off, and we had the lead.

We stole the ball quickly from the Lakers. Pricco passed it to me, and I dribbled toward the basket and was fouled hard by Borseth, knocking me to the floor. Just like we had been taught to foul. I would be forced to make my two free throws.

I stepped to the free throw line, and noticed how far it was from that line to the basket. It never seemed that far at the Washington gym. Could I get it to the basket? Nothing like hundreds of people watching. An airball was possible.

I dribbled once when I heard a voice from the crowd.

"Don't step over the line."

It was my mother. Her timing was always perfect.

I took another dribble and clutched the ball and shot it from my hip without stepping over the line.

Swish. It went in.

The crowd cheered.

The referee handed me the ball for my second shot.

"Just like the first one Tommy," my mother yelled. "Then get back on defense."

So many instructions. So little time.

I dribbled twice and put the shot up. My momentum took me over the free throw line, but the referee didn't call a fault.

The ball rolled around the rim and dropped in.

The 76ers were leading the Lakers 4-0.

No one associated with this grade school basketball program could have imagined how much this moment meant to me, and really to all of us boys. Not John Bonk. Not Jack White. Not Harry Rizzie. Not Superintendent Newman or the school board. We were as close as we could be to becoming Speedboys. Just like Barnaby. Just like Milakovich. Just like Barbacovi.

And just like the Speedboys, my team lost. Lakers 26-76ers 22.

We fought back tears in the locker room. We had never been in a game situation before, let alone experienced a loss. We didn't handle it well.

"Boys, you played well," Coach Milakovich said. "You don't win them all. I know first-hand."

We nodded as we wiped our eyes.

"When you lose," Milakovich said, "it isn't the end of the world. You just work harder. You listen to your coach. You study your opponent for the next time you play them. You're in this intramural program to learn the game. And one day, we want you to play for the Bessemer Speedboys."

That brought a big smile to our faces. We showered quickly and went back out to watch the Royals play the Celtics and cheer them on, like they'd done for us. That night the Royals beat the Celtics 14-10 and moved to the championship game to face the Lakers.

On Tuesday night my team lost again, this time to the Celtics 19-9. The Lakers, led by Kevin Borseth, won the championship game 26-11 over the Royals. There was no trophy awarded to the champs. No participation medals for all the players. Just bragging rights, which was more valuable on the playground than a hunk of metal.

CHAPTER 63

I t was 7 a.m. on a January morning when 50 miners on the 28th level of the Peterson Mine in Bessemer "put down their tools and were hoisted to the surface for the very last time." The iron ore mining era had ended near where it began.

Iron ore production began on the Gogebic Range in 1884 at the Colby Mine, just up the road from the Peterson Mine. Over 5 million tons of ore was mined at Peterson from its opening in 1953 to its quiet ending in 1966. As told to the *Ironwood Daily Globe* by Granite City Steel Co, the owner of the mine, "*it wasn't economically feasible to develop additional tonnage.*"

The mining equipment would be removed and sold off in pieces to other mines across the United States and foreign countries. Apparently, there was a great demand for mining equipment, but none for the Gogebic Range's iron ore.

Over 170 workers lost their jobs with the closing of the Peterson Mine. It came as no surprise. There had been layoffs, furloughs, strikes, and now the final nail in the coffin: closure of the last operating iron ore mine in the area. In April, mine superintendent Albert Johnson would transfer to the Erie Mining Company while Arthur Martini, the assistant superintendent at the Peterson Mine, would be transferred to the Scully Mine at Wabush, Labrador, Canada.

Chalk up another loss for Bessemer. The miners would take it in stride, hold their heads high, and never look back. That's how you survive; fighting for another day.

After basketball practice, Don Barbacovi stopped at Super Valu to bag groceries for customers and make a few dollars.

"Hey, Donny," customer Jingers Perotti said. "You gonna crush those Midgets Friday night?"

"Ah, I hope so Jingers," said Barbacovi. "Just don't want to get too confident. Things happen to us at the end of games, and I don't want to bring bad luck our way. Thanks for your support, though. I promise you, you'll see our best effort."

Ray Barbacovi walked down from his office and met his son at the front of the store.

"Don, I have some groceries I need you to deliver," his father said. "Here's the list. You can knock off after that if you like."

Don looked over the addresses.

"Dad, these folks didn't pay me last time I dropped off groceries," Don said. "Do I need to collect?"

"No, they'll pay when they can," his father replied. "Let me worry about that. You just drop these groceries off."

But Don had done the bookwork in his dad's office, and he found a long list of elderly Bessemer customers that received groceries and never paid or couldn't pay.

"But Dad, how can you run the business like this?"

"Son, building a community is just as important as building a business.

Art Stancher and Ray, the Super Valu store owners, were not concerned about getting paid by people who were down on their luck. It was more important that these customers were fed. If the folks had the means to pay on their accounts, that was just fine with the owners. But if the customer didn't have the money, well, Art and Ray were not going to ask for it.

Don loaded his car and dropped off the groceries. A tradition of giving had just been handed down from father to son.

CHAPTER 64

Fling High the Bessemer Banner

The town folks in Bessemer had a hop in their collective step. On Friday night the Bessemer Speedboys would have their best opportunity, maybe their only opportunity, to break the long, arduous 42-game losing streak.

Since losing in the District Championship game on March 9, 1963, the losing streak had spanned four seasons, four graduating classes, three head coaches, and over 30 different players. A team trapped in the past.

But today at Abelman's Clothing, at Ben Franklin, at Guglie's Barbershop, at the Tip Top, at the Drug Store, at St. Sebastian School, at A.D. Johnston High School, and at every other establishment in town, there was an unmistakable buzz that the losing streak could finally end.

The *Ironwood Daily Globe* wrote the following on Thursday's sports page:

"The Speedboys have high hopes of ending the streak on their home court on Friday night. Bessemer, with driving determination, that almost upended the Ashland squad last week, will be out to avenge a 70-64 loss handed them by Hurley in the first game of the season."

The paper offered a glimmer of hope but protected their journalistic integrity by not making a bold prediction that the Speedboys would in fact do the one thing they hadn't done in over 1,000 days: win a game.

The Speedboys currently had the longest losing streak in Michigan High School basketball at 42 games. It was well short of the Michigan record for losses in a row set by White Pigeon High at 61 games from 1961 to 1965. Prior to White Pigeon's streak, Three Rivers High School lost 54 games in row from 1930 to 1933. Now, the Speedboys were getting dangerously close to that dubious distinction.

A victory by Bessemer would be front page news. The *Globe* hedged their bet by scheduling one of their best photographers to be at A.D. Johnston gymnasium for the game and potentially capture history in the making.

"Hey, Bomber," Dad yelled to me. "You going to the game?"

Since Harry Rizzie introduced me as "Tom the Bomb" at the basketball tournament, my father has enjoyed calling me by that nickname.

"Of course!" I replied. "All my buddies are going, too."

"I'm planning to go, too," Dad said. "I got the night off and my old buddy Paul Pozega is in town."

"Okay, see you there."

"Bomber," Dad said. "You got one job tonight."

I looked at him waiting for my assignment.

"Bring one home!" he said.

I smiled.

It was Friday night, January 21, 1966, and the A.D. Johnston gymnasium was once again the place to be. The sweet smell of victory hung in the air. The fans were loud and animated even during the junior varsity game.

Playing in front of their largest crowd of the year, the Bessemer junior varsity thrashed the Hurley Midgets JV 45-27. First blood had been drawn, tempting the crowd with the forgotten taste of victory on their tongues, leaving them hungry for more.

Junior varsity coach Rance English pranced along the sideline after the game, the single button on his maroon sport coat about to burst from pride, or from the added 15 pounds since his Marine Corps days. He had just directed another win for the underclassman. He held his head high, listening to the shouts from the Speedboys' supporters who had not seen much of English's coaching this past year.

"That a boy, Rance," shouted one admirer. "You know how to win."

You can't blame English if he imagined that the Bessemer School Board would approach him at the end of the season about taking the varsity reins next year. After all, he was a winner and that's what the school and the town wanted. Of course, Rance would ponder any offer that came his way and strategize how to respond. One chess move at a time. But for tonight, "to the victors go the spoils," and he and his JV team had earned it.

The Bessemer vs. Hurley rivalry has been intense for many years, in all sports. In October 1946, when the two teams met on the football field, the *Ironwood Daily Globe* told the story of the rivalry this way:

"Fighting an uphill battle all the way, the Bessemer Speed Boys, rated pregame underdogs, came back from the verge of defeat with a fourth quarter touchdown and extra point to upset a spiritless Hurley Midget team 7-6 at Lincoln high school field Saturday.

Amidst the pandemonium that broke loose when a last-minute desperation pass by Hurley connected for a touchdown that was ruled invalid, the Bessemer fans celebrated the hard-earned victory by tearing down the goal posts at the north end of the field. Each Speedboys player getting a piece of the wood goal post as remembrance of the victory.

Meanwhile, police broke up a mob scene at midfield where rabid Hurley fans cornered the officials to protest the reversal of the last-minute Hurley touchdown as one official had called the touchdown good and then another official overruled him, saying Hurley's end Dominic Gentile had come down out of bounds in the end zone."

It would likely be no different Friday night.

In the Speedboys' locker room, the varsity players heard the thunderous crowd cheering the junior varsity team onto victory. Milo Barnaby, the senior captain, was reading the faces of his teammates. He saw both trepidation and determination. Barnaby, the boy who had never tasted victory in his three years on the varsity, grappled with what he might say before the game to settle them down.

Rick Syrjala was sitting on the bench, head down and holding a basketball. He bounced it between his legs every few seconds. He was quietly going through a checklist of things he must do to help his team win. How he would get in position to block out his opponent. How he would get the rebound and fire an outlet pass to a guard for a fast break.

Jim Milakovich was serious, as always. The game couldn't start soon enough. He palmed a basketball and chatted with Milo about strategy.

Don Barbacovi sat quietly near his locker, confident in winning but not daring to speak of it to his teammates. For the same reason a baseball player would avoid telling a pitcher he had a no-hitter going in the ninth inning, Barbacovi kept his thoughts to himself. He didn't want to jinx anything.

Denny Forslund was talking with his younger teammates about hunting, fishing, and incomplete homework, anything and everything except basketball. The game would start soon enough.

Dick Schwartz, the quiet player who had hitchhiked to the season opener and dropped 21 points on Hurley in a losing effort, was hoping his name would be called for the starting lineup. Either way, he knew he would get plenty of minutes.

Coach Carl Gregas came out of his office and headed to the locker room. "Men, how are you feeling?" he asked as he walked through the door.

"Great!" the team shouted in unison.

"Okay, bring it in, boys," Gregas said.

Jim Milakovich put his foot up on a bench and leaned in. Mark Borseth knelt and tied his high-top sneakers for the second time, getting the laces just right. Tiny Louie Menara tried to find a spot where he could see around his taller teammates. Paul Carpenedo threw his warm-up jacket over his shoulder and leaned in. Mike Betlewski stood beside team manager Tom Holappa, who was stuffing towels into a duffel bag. Jimmy "Odie" Rastello added scissors and medical tape to the first aid kit and closed it up tight.

"Boys, you have shown since the beginning of the season that you can compete," Gregas said. "You've shown each team that you belong in this league. Now, you need to show your opponents, your fans, and most importantly, yourselves, that you can win! Tonight is the night that we end this losing streak. Now go get 'em!"

With the force of a U.P. winter blizzard, the Bessemer Speedboys blew out of the locker room door, ran through the tunnel and onto the hardwoods of A.D. Johnston gymnasium, where no Bessemer varsity team had won a game since Kennedy was President.

The capacity crowd greeted the Speedboys with thunderous applause. The shouting and stomping of feet nearly drowned out the pep band, which was playing the Bessemer school song.

> *"Fling high the Bessemer banner,*
> *Don't let the standards fall.*
> *Three cheers for Bessemer, for good ole' Bessemer,*
> *The school we love the best of all. U, rah rah!*
> *Bring out the ball boys and blow the whistle,*
> *Fair play will win this game.*
> *For Bessemer's honor must be,*
> *Defend and hail the Gold and Blue."*

At the other end of the court, Hurley Midget star Gary Gotta stood with hands on hips as he stared down the Speedboys. Jim Milakovich stared back, like two gunslingers meeting at high noon. Gotta and Milakovich gave each other a respectful nod.

The teams ran through their respective pre-game warm-ups. The layup drill ended with a Milakovich left-handed dunk to the thrill of the hometown crowd. The fans wanted to stuff that losing streak just like that.

Just before tip-off, both teams ran back through the tunnel and into their respective locker rooms to go over the game plan. There was some jostling in the tunnel between the opposing teams, but nothing that the papers would write about.

"Have a seat, boys," coach Gregas shouted to his over-stimulated team.

The young guys sat on the bench while the upperclassmen paced.

"Settle down, settle down," Gregas yelled. "Tonight, we're going to start the game with Barbacovi, Milakovich, Syrjala, Barnaby and Schwartz."

Dick Schwartz clapped his hands, letting everyone know he was ready to drop bombs on the Midgets.

"Men, there isn't anything I can say that I haven't already said to you this season," Gregas said. "So, I would like to have your captain say a few things. Milo?"

Captain Milo Barnaby walked over and stood next to the head coach. He pulled off his warm-up jacket revealing his number 14 white jersey. His head was down as he searched for the right words to say. He rubbed his right hand back and forth across his crew cut, then rested his hand on the back of his neck. When he finally spoke, the seasoned veteran was articulate. He hoped his body wouldn't show his nerves.

"Guys, it's been a long haul," Barnaby said. "I'm a senior and I have never won a game. Never. But I don't feel bad about that because I got this opportunity to play basketball and represent my school and my town. Only a few of us get the opportunity to put on a Bessemer Speedboys jersey. It's a privilege really. It also comes with responsibility. To play as hard as we possibly can. As the losses piled up, I never saw one of you give up."

He grabbed a basketball from Odie, the manager, and held it with both hands.

"Now, for our parents, our fans, and our entire town. Let's end this streak now!"

They once again stormed out of the locker room like a strong north wind.

My friends and I were perched in the northeast upper bleachers as usual. Jay, Jeff, Jim, Joel, John and other boys with first names that started with a J, along with Kevin Borseth and Art Boline sat with great anticipation for tonights game. I figured three or four of them would one day wear the blue and gold of the Bessemer Speedboys.

Borseth was a shoe-in. I could only dream of joining these guys in that quest.

As I looked across the court into the south stands, I saw three longtime friends sitting side by side: Dave "Ramp" Rampanelli, Paul "Doc" Pozega, and my dad, Johnny Pel. Three champs from 1947 Upper Peninsula Class B Basketball Championship team. Three guys who remember what it felt like to have fans line up along the streets on a Sunday for a welcome-home parade to celebrate the glory they had brought back to their hometown. Now these men sat elbow to elbow, spots of gray in their hair, content to no longer be kings of the world, just three among many faithful Bessemer fans.

The hometown heroes were dressed in white, the villains from Hurley appropriately dressed in black. The tension in the building had been rising for the past hour, a reflection of the long and bitter rivalry between Bessemer and Hurley. By tipoff, it was about to blow.

The Bessemer faithful rained boos down on the Hurley players as their starting lineup was announced, and the Hurley fans returned the favor for the Speedboys. Opposing fans started pointing at each other and jeering from across the court like schoolboys challenging each other to an after-school fight.

The opening tip-off was controlled by the Speedboys, much to the delight of their hometown fans. Don Barbacovi dribbled the ball up and saw a wide-open Dick Schwartz. Schwartz received the pass and hit the basket from ten feet and the local boys were quickly ahead 2-0. But Hurley's Bert Canalia tied it up 10 seconds later with a layup. 2-2.

From that moment on, the first quarter was filled with the sound of the referee's whistles. There was a definite tilt in the floor in favor of the Speedboys. Time and again, the Midgets were called for a foul and were outraged. The Speedboys were delighted. The local lads went to the charity stripe often and made their free tosses.

If not for Hurley's Canalia, who scored his team's first five points, the Midgets might have been out of the game by the end of the first quarter. But they were not.

Through sheer determination, the Hurley Midgets tied the game 11-11 and looked to be taking it to the Speedboys. Hurley's star Gary Gotta clapped his hands when Bessemer took a time-out to regroup. He and his teammates were making the Speedboys doubt themselves yet again.

Gary Niemi, one of the long-suffering Speedboys under Coach John Bonk, was seated behind the players' bench. He yelled encouragement to his former teammates as they ran off the floor for the time-out. He, as much as anyone, wanted to see these guys win.

"Rick, you can take those guys underneath," Coach Gregas told Syrjala in the huddle. "Guys, Hurley is trying to stop Jimmy, so let's work it into Rick."

Bessemer's Syrjala knew how to follow orders. On the next possession, he drove to the basket hard, made a layup, and was fouled. He made his free throw, and the Speedboys quickly grabbed control of the game.

When the first quarter ended, the Bessemer Speedboys were leading the Hurley Midgets 18-13. One quarter down with three to go.

Jim Milakovich and his teammates had been here before. Leading after the first, second and even the third quarter, only to lose it in the fourth. As he broke out of the huddle to start the second quarter, he implored his teammates to keep scrambling and driving and making things happen.

Milakovich took an outlet pass from Dennis Forslund to open the second quarter, drove the length of the court for the easy basket, and was fouled by Hurley's Gary Gotta. It was Gotta's third personal foul. The Hurley ace was pulled out of the game by coach Bill Zell.

With Gotta on the bench, the Speedboys started to build a more comfortable lead. Schwartz replaced Forslund and they increased the tempo.

Milakovich found his range on the left side. He scored three field goals, all from 15 feet, in a matter of two minutes. He had been deadly from that distance all season long.

Again and again, Barbacovi and Barnaby got to the free throw line and made their tosses. The Speedboys were building a lead. But could they hold it?

Coach Zell didn't like what he was seeing from his Midgets. They were digging themselves a big hole. One that they would have trouble climbing out of.

Before the half was over, Zell reinserted Gotta even though #23 had three fouls. The junior star responded with two quick baskets and resuscitated his team to keep the game close at 30-24. Just what the doctor ordered.

Gotta had the Hurley fan base energized, and they knew victory went through his hot hand tonight. They beckoned their black and white to turn up the heat on both ends of the court.

Bessemer coach Gregas put Schwartz on the bench and asked 6'4" Forslund to check back into the game. With Syrjala, Milakovich, Barbacovi, Barnaby and now Forslund in the game, the Speedboy five were now the taller of the two teams on the court. They were also the more physical.

"Feed Eggy!" Coach Gregas pleaded. "Get it into Forslund."

Hurley's Gotta heard the opposing coach's plan and leaned inside to block out Forslund. Barnaby tossed the ball into Forslund. He caught it with his back to basket and turned to try a hook shot. Gotta went up for the block and tapped it away. A clean block.

Canalia got the rebound and the Hurley Midgets went the other way. Hurley's Perlberg took a shot that was off the mark; Speedboy Forslund went for the rebound but Hurley's Gotta was there and tipped the ball back into the basket. But the whistle blew and the referee waved off the basket. The man in the black and white striped shirt called a foul on Gotta for going over the back of a Bessemer's Forslund.

The Hurley star had picked up his fourth foul, and the first half was not yet over.

The anguish coming from the Hurley fans was immense. Red faces, arms waving, and words of outrage filled the gymnasium. Gotta shook his head in disgust.

"How could you make that call?" he shouted at the referee.

"Not another word, son," the referee said.

"Just let us play," Gotta said in frustration.

That was enough. The referee called a technical foul on Gotta.

Gotta bit his tongue and headed to the bench. Bill Zell sent Wayne Nasi in to replace him for the rest of the second quarter.

The teams walked to the other end of the floor where Forslund made his free throws. Barnaby then took the technical foul shot, and the Speedboys took command. When the second quarter ended, the Speedboys enjoyed a 35-26 lead.

Seldom in the last three years had the fans seen their beloved Speedboys going into halftime with a lead. But the scoreboard did not lie. The men in white were beating the men in black.

"More pop and popcorn for everyone!" John Stancher shouted as if he was buying a round for everyone. He led the fifth- and sixth-grade contingent to the refreshment stand at halftime.

The wait for popcorn and pop was long. I finally got to the front of the line and bought an orange pop and took a quick sip to quench my thirst. The pop was warm but still tasted good. I turned to head back to my seat, but a Hurley high school boy bumped into my arm, spilling my drink. I looked up at him in surprise, trying to hide my displeasure.

"Hey, kid, you just spilled your pop on your shoes," the boy said to me. "Ha! Ha!"

As he was about five years older and had a hundred pounds on me, I just shrugged and continued my walk to the stairs with a bag of popcorn but no pop. I would have to bum some off a buddy in the stands.

The cheerleaders in their blue skirts and white blouses went onto the court and did a routine. Their timing and rhythm were even better than the Speedboys' tonight.

"The Speedboys can't be beat.

It's winner take all from everyone we meet."

The cheer ended with Doris Mascotti held high in the air, her arms in the shape of a V for victory. She stood braced on the knees of Mary Jane Berwald and Barbara Ippolite. Dorinda Lund and Marcella

Boline did the splits in front of them with BHS proudly displayed on their hips.

When the third quarter got underway, Hurley's Gary Gotta was on the bench with four fouls. Needing a boost to change the trajectory of the game, Hurley's coach Zell put on the full court press.

The Bessemer ball handlers were unfazed. With head fakes, deft bounce passes, and the occasional overhead pass, they broke press after press. A far cry from the ineptitude on display the past two seasons.

Milakovich hit a jumper from the left side to stretch the Speedboys lead to 16. Barnaby got a steal and fed Dick Schwartz for a routine layup. The Speedboys were ahead by 18. Hurley called a timeout. Zell demanded his team be more aggressive. He put Gotta back in the game with four fouls, hoping the referees would swallow their whistles.

Gregas substituted Mark Borseth for Barnaby to give the senior a breather.

"Anyone want to say it now?" Kevin Borseth said as he turned around to us in the stands. "Are we gonna win?"

"Sit down, Kevin!" his buddies said in unison. "Don't be a jinx."

Kevin sat back down and cheered for his brother, who had the difficult assignment of guarding Hurley's Bert Canalia. Like Gotta, Canalia had starred for the Midgets all season, and they really needed him to step up now.

The teams traded baskets, and with 3:19 to go in the third quarter, Coach Zell took his Hurley star Gotta out of the game to prevent him from getting his fifth foul. Gotta's nine points were high for the team. Zell needed more from all his players.

The Midgets continued to press on defense even though they were getting into foul trouble. With each swish of the net, the Speedboy fans grew louder and louder. When the third quarter ended, Bessemer was leading 52-36.

Coach Gregas tried to look stoic in the player huddle in his tweed coat and his thin black tie still perfectly knotted. But his players could see his hands were shaking as he drew up a play on his clipboard to get the ball inbounds to open the fourth quarter.

A 16-point lead entering the final quarter would be a comfortable lead for most teams, but not the Speedboys. Throughout this 42-game losing streak, the Speedboys had found every possible way to blow a lead, and their coach knew that as well as anybody.

Gregas sent out Forslund, Milakovich, Barnaby, Barbacovi and Schwartz to start the most important quarter of their career. Not one of them had ever won a varsity basketball game.

Milakovich and Barnaby walked together as they stepped onto the court for the fourth quarter.

"We've been here before, Jim," said Barnaby over the noise of the crowd. "Against Hurley in the opener. Against Ontonagon and Maple. We didn't finish the game."

"I'm with you, Milo," Milakovich replied. "Coach said we can't let the young guys freeze up." Milakovich was just a junior, but everyone knew he was the guy who wanted the ball in his hands with the game on the line. Barnaby, the senior, would be happy to oblige.

The three champs from the 1947 team, Doc, Ramp and Johnny Pel, were now standing in the upper deck, their hands gripping the railing. Each of them would rather be playing in the game than watching it. It was excruciating.

The play Gregas drew up to start the fourth quarter didn't work at all. Hurley stole the inbound pass and Canalia scored. Then after a missed opportunity by the Speedboys on their end, Gotta got the rebound and drove the length of the court and scored. Now it was 52-40 and the momentum had shifted to Hurley's side.

Feeling that a comeback was possible, Hurley coach Zell put on the full court press again. They had nothing to lose, and this time their press was suffocating the frazzled Speedboys.

Bessemer's Barnaby frantically ran along the end line trying to get the ball in. He finally found his 6'4" center Forslund along the north sideline. He threw it high in the air to Forslund, who grabbed the ball and turned to look for a teammate to pass it to.

As he turned, Hurley's Wayne Nasi came full speed toward Forslund to knock the ball out of his hands. The Hurley player's momentum inadvertently took him through Bessemer's big man with such force that Forslund fell backwards, hitting his head on the hardwood floor. The referee blew his whistle and called a foul on Nasi.

The boos rained down on Hurley's offending player, but quickly the gymnasium went quiet. All eyes focused on the Bessemer player splayed out on the floor. Big Dennis Forslund was in obvious distress. He appeared to be convulsing.

The cheerleaders cuffed their mouths and tears began streaming down their faces.

Gregas ran to Forslund's side. Zell called his players back to the Hurley bench. Principal John Sartoris sprinted to the phone in the janitor's office and called for an ambulance. Staff Sergeant Adrian Anglim, leader of the ROTC program, sprang out of his office and onto the court, kneeling beside Forslund to offer aid.

"His jaw is locked," barked Anglim. "We've got to get his mouth open."

"Is there a doctor, a nurse?" Gregas yelled towards the crowd.

Forslund was now in a full convulsive state, arms twitching in rapid, involuntary movements. Choking sounds could be heard in the silent gym.

"He swallowed his tongue," Anglim yelled. "He can't breathe."

A woman emerged from the stands and rushed to Forslund's side. She knelt next to him as Anglim tried to get Forslund's jaw unclenched.

"I'm a nurse," the woman told Anglim. "I can help. We've got to get his mouth open or he'll choke to death."

"Back off, back off," Gregas implored his Speedboys players who had gathered around Forslund. "Let him breathe."

Anglim finally pried open Forslund's jaw just enough for the nurse to stuff a rolled-up game program between his teeth.

Fans on both sides stood and craned their necks to get a glimpse of the player as the situation unfolded. Others sat down and prayed silently that the sophomore center would be alright. Players walked about on the court unable to do anything but watch their teammate in distress. A feeling of helplessness filled the gym, and panic began to set in. One minute became five and five minutes became ten as they worked furiously on Forslund.

After an excruciating fifteen minutes, the paramedics arrived and brought in a stretcher. They hoisted Forslund onto the gurney and the emergency team quickly rolled him out of the gym. Staff Sergeant Anglim and the heroic nurse walked on each side of the stretcher reassuring Forslund he was going to be alright. But the player was not responding to verbal cues. The crowd applauded him, but Forslund could not hear them. He was in a fragile state.

It was as shocking a moment as anyone had ever witnessed in A.D. Johnston gymnasium. Ending the losing streak was the least of their concerns.

Rick Syrjala checked into the game to replace Forslund, who was now heading east toward Divine Infant Hospital in Wakefield with ambulance lights flashing.

Players and coaches on both teams looked stunned and subdued. The cheerleaders were comforting each other. The pits in the stomachs of all the fans had drained the passion from their cheers and sucked the energy out of the gym.

The Bessemer Speedboys were on the precipice of ending one of the longest losing streaks in Michigan high school basketball history, and then this? What was this black cloud that hung over this team?

When the game finally resumed, Bessemer led Hurley 52-40. Play quickly became chippy. An extra push here and an elbow there. Some Speedboys were gunning for the player that made the hit on Forslund. But Hurley players had each other's backs and quickly racked up multiple fouls as they defended one another. Things were heating up on both sides.

With three minutes left in the game, the pot finally boiled over. The Midgets took a shot but missed. Rick Syrjala went up for the defensive rebound, but Hurley's Gary Gotta went over Syrjala's back and tipped the ball into the basket. Hurley had scored, but the referee blew his whistle and again signaled NO BASKET. He again pointed to Gotta and called a fifth and final foul on the young man. Gotta had fouled out. He was incensed.

"How could you?!" Gotta yelled at the referee.

The referee blew his whistle again and teed up Gotta for his second technical foul and an automatic disqualification from the game.

The referee pointed to the east end of the floor and directed Gotta to the locker room. Gotta stood and stared. The referee pointed again. Gotta, hands on hips, just kept staring. Gotta's father, Marco, came out of the stands and onto the court and started to yell at the referee.

"Couldn't just let the boys settle it among themselves, could you?" Marco Gotta yelled.

The referee pointed at Marco Gotta, then pointed at the exit. He had thrown the senior Gotta out of the building.

The referee planted himself at midcourt with his arms folded across his chest, ignoring the onslaught of jeers from the Hurley supporters who felt the referees had gone too far.

A.D. Johnston High School Principal John Sartoris had seen enough. He walked onto the court in front of the Hurley bench, grabbed Marco Gotta by the arm, and firmly directed him to the exit. A chorus of boos followed the father and son as they both left the court; Marco Gotta up the south steps and out into the cold, his son Gary out through the tunnel toward the visiting locker room.

The crowd lining the tunnel allowed young Gotta to pass, but he didn't quite know where he was going. He pulled his jersey out of his shorts in disgust and then, in a huff, cut through the boiler room where some chain-smoking fans had taken refuge.

Gotta's head was down. His temper hotter than the boiler he walked by. He finally found his way into the hallway that led towards the visitor's locker room. There, in frustration, he punched a window. The smokers heard the crash. When they poked their heads into the hall, they saw the floor covered in shattered glass.

Back on the court, the Speedboys were trying hard to concentrate on the final three minutes of the game. They'd played three excellent quarters against the pressing Midgets' five, but the major stoppages of play in the fourth — first, Forslund's serious injury, and then the double Gotta ejection — was enough to throw off even the best team's rhythm.

As the crowd calmed down and the referees discussed the number of fouls called and who would shoot the free throws, Sergeant Anglim came out of the tunnel after helping to load injured Forslund into the ambulance. He headed straight to the Speedboys bench, put his hand on Coach Gregas's shoulder and told him that Forslund was conscious. The sophomore center "came to" in the ambulance. It was a good sign.

Fans sitting behind the bench heard the good news and shared the update with the people sitting around them. The news quickly spread up into the stands.

"Your attention please," the public address announcer said. "Dennis Forslund is awake and on his way to the hospital. He is speaking and says, "Go Speedboys!""

The crowd erupted. Whether he said it or not was irrelevant to the fans. Everyone in the gym felt they had permission to enjoy the game again.

In the Speedboys' huddle, Milo Barnaby tried to settle down the troops.

"Okay, you heard Denny is alright," Barnaby shouted above the cheering crowd. "Now, we're going to go out and win this game. Keep your heads. Concentrate on what you do well. Let's finish this."

As they broke the huddle, Milo caught the eye of his girlfriend Mary Lee. She had both hands cupping her cheeks and gritting her teeth as she looked at her guy. She looked stressed. Milo gave her a wink.

The only Bessemer player who clearly wasn't feeling lighter was forward Jim Milakovich. He had been sick with the flu right up until game time. Whether it was from the illness or seeing his teammate Forslund convulsing on the court, he was nauseous.

"I just want to see that clock hit zeros, Don," Jim whispered to teammate Barbacovi.

"It's gonna happen Jim," Barbacovi replied, "and it's gonna be glorious."

More than 50 fouls had been called in the game, 35 on the visiting team. Hurley coach Bill Zell's strategy to press the entire game had backfired as the referees kept calling fouls on his team's overly aggressive play. With two minutes to go in the game, Hurley's Canalia, Powell, and Gotta were all gone with five fouls each. George Rubatt, Herbert Perlberg, and Brian Nasi were each playing with four fouls.

Everyone in the building, including the Midgets players and their fans, could feel that history was about to be made.

With one minute remaining, the Speedboys led Hurley comfortably 72-50. Bessemer coach Carl Gregas called a timeout and pulled his starters. The crowd gave a standing ovation to Syrjala, Barnaby, Milakovich, Schwartz, and Barbacovi as they walked triumphantly to their bench. Many Hurley fans stood and applauded showing good sportsmanship and acknowledging the Bessemer players' three-year struggle and congratulating them on the imminent end to the streak.

The substitutes on each team traded baskets in that final minute. But it would be the Bessemer fans who would count down the final seconds of the game...*three!...two!...one!...*then the clock hit 0:00, just like Milakovich had wished, and the party was on.

The cheerleaders leaped in the air. The Bessemer fans poured onto the floor. The players embraced each other, then found their families and girlfriends and hugged them, too. Coach Gregas picked up his young daughter and held her on his hip to prevent her from being stepped on by the joyous throng that had come onto the floor.

Bob Olson, the WJMS sports broadcaster, was shouting into his microphone in the hopes of being heard over the commotion engulfing him.

"Bessemer has done it!" he shouted. *"The Bessemer Speedboys have broken their 42-game losing streak with a convincing 74-52 win over the visiting Hurley Midgets. It's pandemonium in the A.D. Johnston gymnasium. There are fans of all ages screaming and yelling on the court. What a night for basketball in the county seat."*

Students got behind Olson and screamed into the microphone an unintelligible chorus of joy. Olson, being the professional he was, just kept talking.

"Well, we'll be back in a few minutes, when I get my hearing back, with more on the dramatic end to one of the longest losing streaks in Michigan high school basketball history. The Bessemer Speedboys are winless no more."

Team manager, Tommy Holappa, reached into the team's first aid kit and pulled out a pair of scissors. He ran and gave it to team captain Milo Barnaby who was busy hugging his girlfriend Mary Lee.

"You've got to cut it down, Milo," Holappa said, pointing to the net. "It's a piece of history."

"I'll need a ladder." Barnaby said.

But no ladder would be needed. The team and its adoring fans gathered under the home basket and raised Milo Barnaby up onto the strong shoulders of center Rick Syrjala to cut down the net.

In that act, Syrjala lifted not just his teammate, but the entire town of Bessemer. The collective joy of the community now resting on his shoulders.

Barnaby reached up, grabbed each loop of the net, and cut. As he did so, a photographer for the *Ironwood Daily Globe* captured the moment, which most certainly would be featured on the next day's front page. Those fans below grabbed pieces of the net on the court, seeking a memento from this dramatic night.

With his last snip, Barnaby gripped the net with his hand, pulled it from the rim and thrust it in the air. The fans around him erupted in joyful cheers. No championship had been won, no trophies had been earned, but everyone in the gym knew exactly what the net stood for: a symbol of what a person, a team, and a town can accomplish when faced with adversity and refuses to give up.

In the locker room, photographers from the *Daily Globe* and the high school yearbook asked for a picture of the team holding the net. Rather than push to the front of the picture, Milakovich, Barbacovi, Barnaby, and Syrjala stood to the side and let the young guys stand in front holding the net. It was never about glory for this special four. It was always about the team. Even now when the streak was over, they took pride in what they'd accomplished, but little credit. They just stood proudly by their coach as the cameras snapped.

Barnaby asked the team managers Holappa and Rastello to cut the net into smaller pieces and give each player a piece of history. They gladly obliged. Barnaby told the team that the next day, if possible, they would visit Denny Forslund in the hospital and present him with his share of the net.

Athletic Director Jack White came into the locker room as the final photo was being taken.

"Carl, WJMS wants you for an interview," White said.

Gregas laughed. "What will I say?"

With that the team yelled and ran with their coach back onto the court where the crowd had refused to leave the gym. Former player Gary Niemi, who had suffered so much through all the losing, ran over to his cousin Don Barbacovi and gave him a big hug. Barbacovi tore off his sweaty jersey and squeezed into the crowd to hear sportscaster Bob Olson discuss the game on the radio.

Olson had set up near the scorer's table and was trying frantically to get Coach Gregas through the crowd for an interview. He reached towards the coach and finally pulled him to the microphone.

"I'm here with the winning coach, Carl Gregas," started Olson.

"Well, that's the first time I've ever heard that," responded Gregas with a laugh.

"Coach, what does this mean?" Olson asked.

"Well, in simple terms," Gregas said, "it means we finally won a game. But in the bigger picture, it sends a strong message to everyone who loves this school and loves this town, that in the end, teamwork will win the day."

Standing in the bleachers were the three former Speedboys, Ramp, Doc and Johnny Pel, beaming as they watched the joyous scene on the court. Nineteen years had passed since they themselves had been the center of Bessemer's adulation, here in this very gym. Now the pride was back.

It had been 1,051 days since Bessemer's last victory. Throughout the losing streak, the fans had wanted victory as badly as the players. Everyone felt that any night could be *the* night the streak would end. Finally, after four different seasons of losing, the Speedboys were rewarded for never giving up. For playing as a team. For giving credit to others when things went well, and for accepting responsibility when things did not. They had embodied not just Bessemer's hopes and dreams but the town's very essence, its fighting spirit, and in so doing had finally accomplished what they had always set out to do. They brought one home.

EPILOGUE

The victory against the Hurley Midgets would be the Speedboys only win in the 1965-66 season. They would lose their final eight contests and finish 1-16 in the season.

Yet, etched in every fan's mind as the defining moment of the season was the sight of Milo Barnaby perched on the shoulders of his teammate Rick Syrjala, cutting down the net in celebration. That picture would be clipped from the sports page of the *Ironwood Daily Globe* and pasted into scrapbooks by players, parents, grandparents, fans and young Bessemer boys, like me.

The Bessemer Herald wrote the following that summed up the battle to win:

"Bessemer basketball fans displayed genuine faith in the Speedboy team during their long 42 game losing streak. The Speedboys won the admiration of friend and foe alike by breaking through for a highly coveted win against Hurley last Friday. Coach Carl Gregas and his crew are to be complimented for the determination and spirit that enabled them to reward the patient fans. Bessemer's basketball prospects are on the upswing. The grade school program is a start in the right direction. It won't be long before the Speedboys will be back on top of the heap in basketball."

In January 2019, in the process of writing this book, I met with former Bessemer basketball coach John Bonk; the same coach that went 0-33 at the helm of the Speedboys. We met in a little café in Ashland, Wisconsin. I spoke with him for hours about his life in Bessemer and the losing streak.

After Bonk resigned as coach in Bessemer, he spent the next 30 years teaching and coaching at his alma mater Drummond High

School. He won plenty of games in multiple sports at Drummond, including basketball and baseball. He had long ago put losing behind him.

The 78-year-old Bonk said he had not followed the fortunes of the Bessemer Speedboys since he left after the 1964-65 season, but he never forgot that he didn't win a game while coaching there.

During our conversation, Bonk asked me one important question.

"So, did the Bessemer Speedboys ever get good?"

I was happy to answer.

"Well, Coach," I said. "Do you recall initiating the intramural basketball program in 1964 with Harry Rizzie to teach fundamental skills to grade-school boys?"

"Yes, of course," Bonk replied. "We needed it bad in Bessemer."

"Well, those same young boys in your program grew up and became Bessemer Speedboys. From 1970 to 1974, they won four conference championships, five district tournament titles, and one Upper Peninsula regional championship. In 1974, the Speedboys went to the state tournament for the first time since 1948."

Bonk smiled broadly and his eyes welled up with tears.

"And, Coach, two of the boys from your first intramural basketball program, Kevin Borseth and Dave Betlewski, were named M-W Conference "Player of the Year" and 1st Team All-Upper Peninsula Basketball in 1972 and 1973 respectively. So, yeah, Coach, they got good."

No longer able to hold back the tears he let them flow. Finally, Coach Bonk got a win for Bessemer.

In Memory of

Holly Sliva Tisdall

Holly epitomized the small-town girl. Fun, kind, and energetic, who had a joyful smile for everyone she met. She showed compassion and empathy, ensuring no friend felt excluded.

Holly was the one person who encouraged me to tell my stories, even when she had heard them many times before. As I would tell a story, she would smile, laugh, and ask,

"Is that story really true?"

She told me I should share my stories in a book someday.

So, I did.

In 2021, when her brother Dennis told me

Holly had passed away, I said,

"Tell me it's not true."

Holly, with each story I told, I thought of you.
Your courageous spirit inspired me to finish.
Your unwavering friendship is forever in my heart.
Tom

ACKNOWLEDGEMENTS

There are many people who gave me a few minutes or even hours of his or her time to make this book a reality.

I want to thank: My son Tom, for his encouragement and guidance on my original outline and first few pages. Jim Fiorelli, for his feedback after his beta read of my initial draft. Rick White for reading my manuscript and offering creative suggestions. Joe Maccani for being an excellent sounding board for my ideas. My good friend Susan Link for her copy editing. My granddaughters Tegan and Finley who encouraged their "Papa Tom" to tell them a Bessemer bedtime story. Thanks to my grandson Silas and my photographer friend Tom Dahlin for helping me with the concept for the book cover.

I want to thank my brothers John, Paul, Gerry, Peter and Patrick, my wife Joy, my daughters Angela and Maggie and my grandchildren who encouraged me to spend endless hours capturing my stories on paper about a most wonderful town and innocent time in my life.

Then there are those folks that answered questions over the phone, via e-mail, in-person at the local coffee shop or invited me into their homes to offer their remembrances. Their stories about Bessemer, specifically during 1963-1966 period, was of significant importance to the development and depth of my writings. This includes: Bob Abelman, Andy Abraham, Rose Aspinwall, Don Barbacovi, Milo Barnaby, Bessemer Area Historical Society, Bessemer Area School District, Bessemer Public Library, Art Boline, George Boline, Marcella Boline, Ginny Strelcheck Boline, John Bonk, Kevin Borseth, Mark Borseth, Jackie Burt Gunderson, Paul Busch, Dion DiMucci, Drummond Public Library, Ric English, Dennis Forslund, Sherri Forslund, Bunny Gheller, Gary Gotta, Carl Gregas, Janet Hellman, John Hellman,

Andy Hill, Ironwood Daily Globe, Joe Jurasin, Marge Leaf, Mitch LeClaire, Joe Maccani, Tom Maccani, Dee Dee Proft Maki, Mark Martini, Brian Mattson, Louis Menara, Bob Merlis, Jim Milakovich, Roy Mcdjewski, Jan Massie, Joel Massie, Gary Niemi, Paul Pozega Jr., Paul "Doc" Pozega, Connie Pricco, Jeff Pricco, Sue Pricco Sofio, Bruce Rampanelli, Bruce Richardson, Ed Rickard, Jim Rooni, Dennis Rolando, Bill Ryan, George Sabol Jr., Mary Corona Sandell, Ed Savitski, Mike Savitski, Richard Schwartz, Maripat LeClaire Schorr, Stan Servia, Joan Steiger, Joan Bria Strasser, Charles Supercynski, The Bessemer Herald, Lynne Wiercinski, and Joy Borseth Young.

Most of all, I want to thank my mother and father for being exemplary parents and sharing their stories with me so that one day I might write *Bring One Home*.

PHOTOS

All photos courtesy of Bessemer Area School District.
From "The Drift" yearbook unless otherwise noted.

1947 U.P. Class B High School Basketball Champions

*Back Row: Coach Helgi Pukema, Allan Syrjala, Dave Webber, Robert Baron,
Donald Skwor, Ray "Windy" Kangas, Robert Vogler*
*Front Row: John Pelissero, Eddy Balasz, Ray Fournier, Paul "Doc" Pozega,
Dave "Ramp" Rampanelli, John Backman. Missing: Royal Smith*

1947 Bessemer Cheerleaders

Front: Margy Gustafson, Prudy Melanson
Back: Joan Marleau, Mary Lou Shogren, Becky Gray, Dorothy Ruusula, Bernice Michelli

1947

#15 Dave Webber
#14 John Pelissero

1948 U.P. Class B High School Basketball Champions

*Front: Ray Fournier, Robert Barron, Dave Webber, Ray Kangas,
Donald Skwor, John Backman*
*Back: Ed Balasz, Ken Grenquist, Don Jasper, Don Niemi, LeRoy Holappa,
Allan Syrjala, Coach Pukema*

1948 Cheerleaders

Front: Dorothy Ruusula, Joan Marleau, LaVerne Jacobson, Betty Mikkola
Back: Marilyn Nobert, Theresa Witburn, Bernice Michelli, Mary Lou Shogren

1952-53 District Champions Bessemer Speedboys

Holding trophy–#14 Jim Beissel, #5 Norman Crockett, #8 Bob Harris, #12 Kurt Carlson, Bob Pozega, Kenneth Masse, Jim Strelcheck, Jay Bennetts, Coach Pete Fusi, William Perpich, Ray Panosso, Gerald Block, Jack White, Charles Supercynski

1955-56 M-W Conference and District Champions Bessemer Speedboys

Front: J. Maccani, M. DeStasio, E. Milewski, K. Van Holla, R. Anderson, Coach Pete Fusi. Back: H. Longhini, D. Sjoman, A. DaPra, M. Gustafson, D. Flaa, J. Corgiat, D. Voss, E. Hoffner, R. Gamache, C. Coxey

1956-57 District Champions Bessemer Speedboys

Jim Corgiat carried off the court after making the winning basket at the buzzer. Coach Pete Fusi's team includes: Edwin Smith, Mike Destasio, Jim Corgiat, Donald Voss, Jim Johnson, James Seeke, David Bulinski, David Carpenedo, Eugene Milewski, Dennis Sjoman, Ray Berg, Jerry Felix, Dennis Novascone.

1962-63 Bessemer Speedboys

Gerald Erickson, Gary Niemi, Mark Martini, Brian Mattson, Tom Manninen, Marshall Tillner, Coach Jim Peterson, Bill Nemacheck, Byron Johnson, Dick McDermott, Bill Ryan, Lou Marconeri, Rick Sofio

1963-64 Bessemer Speedboys

Milo Barnaby, Bill Ryan, Gary Niemi, Larry Pann, Bruce Richardson, Bill Nemacheck, Coach John Bonk, Andre Re, Don Johnson, Greg Hill, Mark Martini, George Sabol, Brian Lind. Managers Fran Strelcheck and Gerald Erickson. Missing Pat Bennetts

1963-64 Cheerleaders

*Jackie Burt, Marcella Boline, Patricia Perotti,
Connie Pricco, Joy Borseth*

1964-65 Bessemer Speedboys

Mike Betlewski, Don Barbacovi, Jim Milakovich, George Sabol, Donald Johnson,
Coach John Bonk, Rick Syrjala, Mark Martini, Milo Barnaby, Bob Abelman, Bill Joki

1964-65 Cheerleaders

Joy Borseth, Jackie Burt, Marcella Boline,
Bernadine Drazkowski, Sue Pricco and Florence Switzer

1965-66 Bessemer Speedboys

Front: *Managers Tom Holappa and Jim Rostello*
Mike Betlewski, Don Barbacovi, Jim Milakovich, Richard Syrjala, Milo Barnaby, Mark Borseth, Richard Schwartz, Paul Carpenedo, Lou Menera, Coach Carl Gregas. Absent: Dennis Forslund

1965-66 Cheerleaders

Doris Mascotti, Mary Jane Berwald, Barb Ippolite, Dorinda Lund, Marcella Boline

Jim Milakovich and Gary Gotta, Hurley, fight for a rebound

*Cutting down the net: Don Barbacovi, Jim Milakovich, Mark Borseth,
Louis Menera, Coach Carl Gregas, Richard Schwartz, Michael Betlewski,
Milo Barnaby, Rick Syrjala, Paul Carpenedo*

78

The streak is over. Jubilation in A.D. Johnston gymnasium

WJMS Bob Olson with winning Coach Carl Gregas

**1972-73 Bessemer Speedboys
M-W Conference Champions,
District Champions**

Mgr. Dennis Martell, Dave Trevarthen, Coach Irwin Demerse, Ric English, Dave Webber,
Dave Turula, Mike Burla, Dave Betlewski, Ralph Weimeri, George Boltne, Fran Re,
Dennis Silva, Gary Strelcheck, Jeff Haapoja, mgr., Charles Kellett

1971-72 Bessemer Speedboys
M-W Conference Champions District Champions

Kneeling: Clayton Kananen, Gary Strelcheck, Kevin Borseth, Bob Obradovich,
Mike Hoffner, Dave Betlewski
Standing: Dennis Martell (mgr.), James Boullion, Ric English, Fran Re,
Coach Irwin DeMerse, Dave Webber, Dennis Sliva, Don Gugliemotto (mgr.)

1973-74 Bessemer Speedboys
Great Western Conference Co-Champions, District Champions
Upper Peninsula Class C High School Basketball Champions

Kneeling: Steve Wiercinski, Co-Captains Mike Burla, Gary Strelcheck, Ron Fiori
Standing: Coach Joe Green, John Begalle, George Boline, Jeff Haapoja, Mark Mattson,
Mike Korpela, Roy Jones, Ralph Wiemeri, John Mattson, Dave Turula, Bruce Jacobs,
Jeff Gumm, Coach Irwin DeMerse

1961-62 St. Sebastian Knights

(Front): Bob Martin, Tony Proft (mgr.), Robert Re (holding Fr. Francis Krysty Trophy) Tom Mazari, Tom Kulik, George Carpenedo, Joe Bonovetz, Gerry Peterson, Joe Maccani, Dennis Vargovich, Dennis Gayan, Bob Maki, Mike DeMarte, Ron Carpenedo, Don Barbacovi, Jim Vargovich, Ass't coach Joe Modjewski, Coach Dennis Novascone. (Photo courtesy of Joe Maccani)

1960-61 St. Sebastian Cheerleaders

Front: Janis Kay, Florence Switzer, Sue Pricco
Back: Fr. Francis Krysty, Rene Johnson, Connie Pricco, Patty Perotti, Fr. Bretal

1964-65 St. Sebastian Knights B Team – Tournament Champions

Fr. Leslie Borman, Dave Begalle (14), Mike Massie (21) Jim Partanen, John Pelissero
Back row: Ben Graham, John Lesky, Jim Aspinwall, Dave Partanen (hidden)
(Photo courtesy of Ben Graham)

1968-69 St. Sebastian Knights

(Seated L-R): Jeff Corullo, Jeff Elias, Captain Tom Pelissero,
John Mattson, Paul Pelissero
(Back) Mike Novascone, Randy Gierl, Dennis Martell, Coach Harry Rizzie,
Mike Burla, John Begalle, Co-Captain John Stancher

Captain Tom Pelissero, Harry Rizzie
Outgoing captain Mike Hoffner
St. Sebastian Knights. (1968)
Photo: Courtesy Beth Mattson DeVerna

Paul #9 and me #10 as St. Sebastian Knights 1968

Pelissero Family

John and Mary Lou Pelissero with six sons
John, Paul, Patrick, Pete, Gerry and Tom (1968)

Learning to ski on Sellar Street

Our father John Pelissero with his five boys
Paul, Dad holding Peter, Tom, Gerry and John. (1961)

Pel Gardens — Shovel and Shoot

Grandson Silas Grieger on Bessemer Main Street, 2023
Photo: Tom Dahlin

My Bessemer

(Tom Pelissero-Bob Rupar) Written and produced 1978

Sipping drinks out at the harbor,
Passing time on the drug store corner.
Seeing friends and familiar faces,
In a setting of hometown places.
I remember My Bessemer.

High school days and the weekend dances,
Things we did in our school room classes.
Games we played, when that hometown spirit,
Rang so loud, that I still can hear it.
I remember My Bessemer.

(1ˢᵗ Chorus)	*(2ⁿᵈ Chorus)*
I remember,	*I remember,*
the red ore mines,	*the fields of corn*
the S curve drive,	*the styles we wore,*
4th of July.	*and so much more.*
I remember,	*I remember,*
Old Powderhorn,	*the small-town care,*
the winter storms,	*the clean fresh air,*
the place I was born	*I long to be there.*

Parked at Osiers, beneath the moonlight,
Twinkling stars through the trees at midnight.
Sky blue lakes and the leaves at autumn,
Snow that fell like the purest cotton.
I remember My Bessemer.

But you can't go back again, so they say,
To relive memories of yesterday.
But when I'm there it all feels the same.
Home in My Bessemer.
Bessemer, Michigan.
Yeah, I'm going home again, to Bessemer Michigan.

BIBLIOGRAPHY

Note: All newspapers cited were reviewed on various dates through Newspapers.com

Prologue
Sage, Carolyn W. (1947). Review of Pep Meeting for Team and Coach. *Ironwood Daily Globe*, Mar. 25, p. 5.
Sonnesyn, H.O. Sonny. (1947) Review of Sports Slants. *Ironwood Daily Globe*, Mar. 21, p. 10.
Sonnesyn, H.O. Sonny (1924) Column in *Ironwood Daily Globe*. Oct. 7, p.7.
Obituary for Peter (Pietro) Pelissero. (1946) *Ironwood Daily Globe*. May 5, p.2.
Review of Parade and Pep Meet Held for UP Title Holders. 1948. *The Bessemer Herald*, Mar. 25, p. 1.
Pelissero, John F. Review of Conversations with Dad 1960-1990
Rolando, Dennis. 1998. *Bessemer*. Edited and published by Dennis Rolando, p. 83-84
Savitski, Ed Jan. 16, 2021, e-mail Q&A with Thomas L. Pelissero
Rampanelli, Bruce. Mar. 2, 2021. Telephone interview with Thomas L. Pelissero
Pozega, Paul Jan. 4, 2021 & Jul. 13, 2021. Telephone and in person interviews with Thomas L. Pelissero
"Speed Boys Tip Whiz Kids 46-45" (1947) *Ironwood Daily Globe*. Mar. 24., p. 8.
"Alma Leads All The Way" (1947) *Detroit Free Press*. Mar. 23, p. 29.
"Bessemer Enters Semi-Finals at Lansing Friday Night" (1948) *The Bessemer Herald*. Mar. 18, p.1.
The Drift, A.D. Johnston High School, (1947)
School Songs. (1935). First Annual Honors Banquet Program. May 8, p 1-2
High School Basketball State Champions Class B 1947, MHSSA – Past Champions *https://www.mhsaa.com/sports/boys-basketball/past-champions*

Chapter 1
Review of Budget Adopted by Board on Temporary Basis. 1962. *Ironwood Daily Globe*, Mar. 28, p. 10.
Milakovich, James. Jan. 15, 2019. In person. Interview with Thomas L Pelissero.
"Name Walter Newman School Superintendent" (1962) *The Bessemer Herald* Feb. 15, p.1.

Chapter 2
Bonk, John. Jan. 11, 2019, and Feb. 8, 2023. In person. Interview with Thomas L Pelissero.
Hill, Andy. October 2023. Various in-person discussions and draft reviews with Thomas L. Pelissero
Sonnesyn, H.O. Sonny. 1929. "It's All in the Slant." *Ironwood Daily Globe*, Apr., page 7.
Sartoris, John. 1940. WW II D.D.S. Form 1-order number 1804. *Ancestry.com*
"A.D. Johnston Instructors." 1963, *Ironwood Daily Globe*, Aug. 20, p. 3.

"All Smiles." 1953. *Ironwood Daily Globe*, Mar. 12, page 4.
"Class C Championship Trophy." 1956. *Ironwood Daily Globe*, Mar. 12, p. 5.
"Speed Boys Romp to 78-66 Win." 1956. *Ironwood Daily Globe*, Mar. 17, p. 5.
"Speed Boys Trim L'Anse Hornets to Win Title." 1957. *The Bessemer Herald*, Mar. 14, p. 1.
"Prairie View Beat Superior" (1961) Janesville Daily Gazette. Mar. 11, p.8.
"Big Jim Beissel All U-P" (1953) *The Bessemer Herald*. Apr. 2, p.4.
"Beissel on U-M Basketball Team" (1954) *Ironwood Daily Globe*. Dec. 4, p.7.
"High School Note" (1930) *The Bessemer Herald*. Nov. 7, p.7.

Chapter 3
Bonk, John. Jan. 11, 2019 & Feb. 8, 2023. In person interviews with Thomas L Pelissero.
Gregas, Carl. Feb. 6, 2019. In person interview with Thomas L. Pelissero.
"Speed Boys to Play Ontonagon" (1962) *Ironwood Daily Globe*. Nov. 16, p.6.
"Speed Boys Rally For 60-59 Win Over Ironwood" 1963. *Ironwood Daily Globe*, Feb. 23, p. 5.
"Speed Boys Cop 67-63 Decision Over Cardinals." 1963. *Ironwood Daily Globe*, Mar. 7, p 14.
"Bears Withstand Bessemer Rally to Win 67-62" 1963. *Ironwood Daily Globe*, Mar. 11, p. 5
"Bessemer Instructors" 1959. *Ironwood Daily Globe*, Jun 30, p 2.
"Green Bessemer 5 Faces Strong Houghton Team", 1958. *Ironwood Daily Globe*, Nov. 21, p.8.
"Only 3 seniors are listed as letter winners" 1961. *Ironwood Daily Globe*. Mar 3, p. 5
"Indians Retain Lead in League" (1963) *Ironwood Daily Globe*. Jul. 9, p. 6.
"Giants, Tigers Are Victorious". (1963). *Ironwood Daily Globe*, Jun. 29, p. 5.
"Formidable Task Faces Bessemer's New Coach" (1963). *Ironwood Daily Globe*, Nov. 19, P.8.
Mattson, Brian, e-mail and telephone correspondence. Mar. 7-9 2022.
"Spears Play Here Tonight" (1965) Ironwood Daily Globe Jan. 23, p.6.
School Song (1960s) Lyrics provided via messenger by Maki, J. and Partanen, P. Jan. 31, 2025

Chapter 4
"247 Enroll at St. Sebastian", 1960. *Ironwood Daily Globe*, Sept. 8, p. 10
"20 Will Graduate From St. Sebastian" 1921. *The Bessemer Herald*, Jun. 17, p. 1.
"St. Sebastian School To Open Monday". 1959. *The Bessemer Herald*, Sept. 17, p. 1.
"New St. Sebastian School Architect's Sketch Drawing" (1958) *Ironwood Daily Globe*. Jul. 31, p. 2.
Rolando, Dennis. 1998. *Bessemer*. Edited and published with Dennis Rolando., p. 52.
Rolando, Dennis. Dec 11, 2018. "Puritan House Move" In person interview with Thomas Pelissero
"New St. Sebastian School Is Modern In Every Detail". 1959. *The Bessemer Herald*, Sept. 24, p.1.

Richardson, Bruce. Mar. 3, 2020. Telephone Interview with Thomas L. Pelissero.
Niemi, Gary. Oct. 23, 2018 & Jul. 5, 2019. Telephone and In Person Interview with Thomas L. Pelissero
Ryan, Bill. Aug. 6, 2019. Telephone interview with Thomas L. Pelissero
"Trophy Presentation". 1960. *Ironwood Daily Globe.* Apr. 1, p. 10.
"Two More Rooms for St. Sebastian School" (1921) *Ironwood Daily Globe.* Aug. 22, p 2.
"Kennedy Assassinated". 1963. *Ironwood Daily Globe*, Nov. 22, p.1.
"Parochial School Has Total of 190 Students". 1964. *Ironwood Daily Globe.* Sept 5, p. 2.
Bonk, John. Jan. 11, 2019, Feb. 2021* & Feb. 8, 2023. In person and phone* interviews with Thomas L Pelissero.
Martini, Mark. Aug. 27, 2019. In person interview with Thomas L. Pelissero
Pricco, Connie. Jan. 14, 2019. In person interview with Thomas L. Pelissero
"High School Note". 1930. *The Bessemer Herald.* Nov. 7, 1930, p. 7.

Chapter 5
Martini, Mark. Aug. 27, 2019. In person interview with Thomas L. Pelissero
Maccani. Joe. Mar. 1, 2021. Telephone interview with Thomas L Pelissero
Niemi, Gary. Oct. 23, 2018 & Jul. 5, 2019. Telephone and In Person Interview with Thomas L. Pelissero
Pricco, Connie. Jan. 14, 2019. In person interview with Thomas L. Pelissero
Richardson, Bruce. Mar. 3, 2020. Telephone Interview with Thomas L. Pelissero.
Ryan, Bill. Aug. 6, 2019. Telephone interview with Thomas L. Pelissero
Speedboys Game Day program-1963-64.
"Speed Boys Lose Opener 56-33". 1963. *The Bessemer Herald.* Nov. 28, p. 1.
"C. Gregas Hired As Teacher and Coach". 1963. *Ironwood Daily Globe*, p. 2
"4 M-W Quintets Open Campaigns". 1963. *Ironwood Daily Globe*, Nov. 21, p.8
A.D. Johnston High School Yearbook. "The Drift". 1964. Bessemer City Library.
School Song (1960s) Lyrics provided via messenger by Maki, J. and Partanen, P. Jan. 31, 2025

Chapter 6
"Street Widening Plan Proposed". 1959. *Ironwood Daily Globe*, Sept. 12, p.2.
"City Council Approves Christmas Tree Plan". 1959. *The Bessemer Herald*, Oct. 22, p.1.
Boline, Marcella. Mar. 3,5,6 2021. Telephone interview with Thomas L. Pelissero.
Borseth, Joy. Mar. 29-30, 2020. E-mail response to questions from Thomas L. Pelissero
Boline, Ginny. Oct. 18, 2019. In-person interview with Thomas L. Pelissero
Monopoly [Board game]. (2014). Hasbro.
Candyland [Board game]. (1949) Milton Bradley, Hasbro.
Mouse Trap [Board game]. (1963) Hasbro.
Richardson, Bruce. Mar. 3, 2020. Telephone Interview with Thomas L. Pelissero.
Ercoli, Marilyn. Jul. 14, 2021, Sept 1, 2023. In person conversation with Thomas L. Pelissero.

Chapter 7

"Speed Boys Lose Opener 56-33". 1963. *The Bessemer Herald.* Nov. 23, p. 6.

"Oredockers Post 74-40 Triumph Over Bessemer", *Ironwood Daily Globe*, Nov. 28 p. 14.

"Midget Chalk Up 67-34 Win over Bessemer", 1963. *Ironwood Daily Globe,* Dec. 4, p.8

"Midgets, Red Devils To ClashIn Wright Gym". 1963. *Ironwood Daily Globe*, Dec. 5, p. 8.

"Cardinals Romp to 81-37 Win Over Bessemer". 1963. *Ironwood Daily Globe*. Dec. 7, p. 6.

Bonk, John. Jan. 11, 2019, and Feb. 8, 2023. In person interview with Thomas L Pelissero.

Chapter 8

"Simulated Tree Is Constructed". 1959. *Ironwood Daily Globe*. Nov. 20, p.2.

"Santa Claus to Visit Bessemer". 1963. *Ironwood Daily Globe* Nov. 25, p.7.

Maccani. Tom. Oct. 25, 2018. E-mail response to questions from Thomas L. Pelissero.

Pricco, Jeff. Oct. 26, 2018. E-mail response to questions from Thomas L. Pelissero

Chapter 9

"Streets Closed For Children's Sledding", 1963. *Ironwood Daily Globe*. unmarked month and page.

"Wage Discussion Spices Council Meet" (sledding streets) 1968 *Ironwood Daily Globe*, Nov. 19, p. 21.

Chapter 10

Martini, Mark. Aug. 27, 2019. In person interview with Thomas L. Pelissero

Richardson, Bruce. Mar. 3, 2020. Telephone Interview with Thomas L. Pelissero.

"Maple Scores 50-40 Triumph Over Bessemer". 1963. *Ironwood Daily Globe*. Dec. 14, p. 4.

Sabol, George Jr., Apr. 19, 2020. Telephone interview with Thomas L. Pelissero

Chapter 11

Abelman, Bob. Jul. 25, 2019. In person interview with Thomas L. Pelissero

Pelissero, Paul. 2022. In person discussion with Thomas L. Pelissero

Chapter 12

Maccani. Joe. Mar. 1, 2021. Telephone interview with Thomas L Pelissero

Gheller, Bunny. Dec. 10, 2019. Conversation with Thomas L. Pelissero.

Proft, Dee Dee. Dec. 10, 2019. In person interview with Thomas L. Pelissero

"World War II Draft Registration Card." Ancestry. 1942. www.ancestry.com.

"Inside St. Sebastian Church" - Rolando, Dennis. 1998. *Bessemer*. Edited and Published with Dennis Rolando, p. 29

Chapter 13

"Banquet Given By Holy Name Honors Group." 1961. *Ironwood Daily Globe*.

May 26, p.10.
"Pricco, Sue. December 3, 2019. In person interview with Thomas L. Pelissero

Chapter 14
(No citations)

Chapter 15
"Skiers Invade Area". 1963. *The Bessemer Herald,* December 26, p.1.

Chapter 16
"Red Devils Romp To 82-44 Victory Over Bessemer". (1964) *Ironwood Daily Globe,* Jan. 11, P. 6.
"Red Devils Maul Speedboys 82-44". (1964) Jan. 11, p.1.
"3 M-W Contests Are Slated For Tomorrow Night" and "Slalom Star" (1964) *Ironwood Daily Globe.* Jan. 27, p.10.
"Midgets Hand Bessemer 9th Straight Loss". (1964) *Ironwood Daily Globe.* Jan. 29, p. 8.
"Cards Recapture Lead, Defeating Bessemer 79-47". (1964). *Ironwood Daily Globe,* Feb. 1, P. 8.
Barnaby, Milo. Aug. 2, 2019, and 2022. Telephone interviews with Thomas L. Pelissero
Bonk, John. Jan. 11, 2019, and Feb. 8, 2023. In person interview with Thomas L Pelissero.
Martini, Mark. Aug. 27, 2019. In person interview with Thomas L. Pelissero
Richardson, Bruce. Mar. 3, 2020. Telephone Interview with Thomas L. Pelissero.
Ryan, Bill. Aug. 6, 2019. Telephone interview with Thomas L. Pelissero
Sabol, George Jr. Apr. 19, 2020. Telephone interview with Thomas L Pelissero
Niemi, Gary. Oct. 23, 2018 & Jul. 5, 2019. Telephone and In Person Interview with Thomas L. Pelissero

Chapter 17
LeClaire, Mitch. Feb. 23, 2020. E-mail correspondence with Thomas L. Pelissero
Schorr, Maripat, Jan. 26, 2025 . Messenger discussion with Thomas L. Pelissero
Obituary, Robert M. LeClaire (1960) *Duluth News-Tribune.* Jul 23, p. 6.

Chapter 18
"A.D. Johnston High School Receives Thirteen Flags" (1964). *The Bessemer Herald,* Jan. 16, p.1
"Maple Chalks Up 64-50 Decision Over Bessemer" (1964) *Ironwood Daily Globe,* Feb. 8, P.5.
"Body of Peter Gedda Came This Morning" (1921) *Ironwood Daily Globe.* Sep. 10, P.8.
"27 Points Give Vronch M-W Title". (1940) *The Bessemer Hearld.* Nov 22, P. 1.
"Francis Cychosz War Casualty" (1941) *The Bessemer Herald* Dec. 26, P. 1.
"Bessemer Season Reported Missing". (1941*) Ironwood Daily Globe.* Dec. 22, 1941.

Francis A. Cychosz Awarded Purple Heart (1943) *Ironwood Daily Globe*. Aug. 17, P. 7.
"Camp At Ft. Brady Named For Soldier" (1933). *Ironwood Daily Globe*, Jul. 1, P. 10.
Oral History of Joseph C. Bria (1999) received Jan. 6, 2023, from J. Strasser

Chapter 19
"White Pine Mine's Expansion" 1965. *Ironwood Daily Globe* May 8, p.3.
"Geneva Mine On Five Days" 1964. *Ironwood Daily Globe* Apr. 29, p.1.
"White Pine Mine, Smelter Struck" 1964. *Ironwood Daily Globe* Sep. 1. P.1.
Pricco, Connie. Jan. 14, 2019. In person interview with Thomas L. Pelissero (1964). https://www.history.com/This-Day-In-History/America-Meets-The-Beatles-On-The-Ed-Sullivan-Show. History Channel. Feb. 9, 1964. https://www.history.com/this-day-in-history/america-meets-the-beatles-on-the-ed-sullivan-show.
KDAL Channel 3 TV Shows – Sunday Feb. 9. (1964) *Ironwood Daily Globe*, Feb. 7, P. 7
"Leap Year Sales-45's including the Beatles 78c. (1964) *Ironwood Daily Globe* Ad, Feb. 26, p.6.
"It's Here Meet The Beatles!" (1964). *Chicago Tribune* ad, Jan. 30, p. 38.

Chapter 20
Abelman, Bob. Jul. 25, 2019. In person interview with Thomas L. Pelissero
Busch, Paul. Sept. 24, 2019. Telephone interview with Thomas L. Pelissero
"Freshman League Ends Campaign" (1964) *Ironwood Daily Globe*. (Feb. 21, p, 10.
Niemi, Gary. Oct. 23, 2018 & Jul. 5, 2019. Telephone and In Person Interview with Thomas L. Pelissero

Chapter 21
Milakovich, James. Jan. 15, 2019. In person. Interview with Thomas L Pelissero.
Borseth, Kevin. (2020) Message about Boline Court to Thomas L Pelissero
Boline, George and Art. (2020 & 2025) Discussion about Boline Garage Basketball Court with Thomas L. Pelissero

Chapter 22
"Speed Boys Losing Skein Extended" (1964) *The Bessemer Herald*, Feb. 27, P. 1.
Richardson, Bruce. Mar. 3, 2020. Telephone interview with Thomas L. Pelissero.
Martini, Mark. Aug. 27, 2019. In person interview with Thomas L. Pelissero
"Orientals Hand Winless Speed Boys 15th Loss" (1964) *Ironwood Daily Globe*, Feb 29, p. 5.
Bonk, John. Jan. 11, 2019 & Feb. 8, 2023. In person interviews with Thomas L Pelissero
Rolando, Dennis. (1998). *Bessemer*. Edited and published by Dennis Rolando, p. 85

Chapter 23
"Bears Register 64-44 Decision Over Bessemer" (1964) *Ironwood Daily Globe*.
Mar. 6, p. 8.
Bonk, John. Jan. 11, 2019 & Feb. 8, 2023. In person interviews with Thomas L
Pelissero.
"Board Approves Suggestion by Super. Newman" (1964) *Ironwood Daily Globe*.
Apr. 17, p. 2.
Martini, Mark. Aug. 27, 2019. In person interview with Thomas L. Pelissero
Richardson, Bruce. Mar. 3, 2020. Telephone interview with Thomas L. Pelissero.
"Little Drummond In Land of Trees" (1962) *The Capital Times (Madison Wisconsin)* Mar. 13, p.13.
"Team, Coaches To Be Honored" (1964) *Ironwood Daily Globe*. Mar. 23, p, 2.
"Players, Others Feted with Lions" (1964*) Ironwood Daily Globe*, Nov. 12, p, 2.
"18 of Loop's Top Players Honored with Association" (1964) *Ironwood Daily Globe*. Apr. 9, p.8.
"PM Changes in Personnel Told" (1965). *Ironwood Daily Globe*. Mar. 12, p.1.

Chapter 24
"Auto Kills A.D. Johnston" (1923). *The Bessemer Herald*. Oct. 5, p.1.
"A. D. Johnston Dies Thursday" (1923) *Ironwood Daily Globe*, Oct. 5, p. 1.
Bonk, John. Jan. 11, 2019 & Feb. 8, 2023. In person interviews with Thomas L
Pelissero.
"John Backman To New Post" (1964) *Ironwood Daily Globe*, Jun. 19, p 2.
"Consolidation Discussed at School Meeting"- intramural progress (1964) *Ironwood Daily Globe*. Dec. 16, p. 2.
"Little Drummond In Land of Trees" (1962) *The Capital Times (Madison Wisconsin)* Mar. 13, p.13.
"Board Approves Suggestion by Supt. Newman" (1964) *Ironwood Daily Globe*.
Apr. 17, p.2.

Chapter 25
"Bessemer Defeats Hurley in Area's Last Game Of The Season" (1964) *Ironwood Daily Globe*. Oct. 31, p. 8.
Richardson, Bruce. Mar. 3, 2020. Telephone interview with Thomas L. Pelissero.

Chapter 26
"Johnson Celebrates Biggest Landslide" (1964) *Ironwood Daily Globe*. Nov. 4, p.1.
"Russian Tanker Intercepted" (1962) *Ironwood Daily Globe*. Oct. 25, 1962, p. 1.
"Soviet Retreat In Cuba Crisis Hailed in Europe as U.S. Victory" (1962) *Ironwood Daily Globe*. Oct. 29, p.1.
"Kennedy Names Three For Negotiation" (1962) *Ironwood Daily Globe*. Oct. 29, p.1.

Chapter 27
"Strike Ends At White Pine" (1964) *Ironwood Daily Globe*. Oct. 19, p.1.
"Gasoline, Coal Bids Approved with School Board" (1964) *Ironwood Daily Globe*. Sept. 17, p. 2.

Chapter 28
"1964 M-W All Conference Teams" (1964) *Ironwood Daily Globe*. Nov. 12, p.8.
"Bessemer's Basketball Team Has 6 Lettermen" (1964) *Ironwood Daily Globe*. Nov. 17, p 10.
"Dockers Rout Bessemer Quint 96-47 Game" (1964) *Ironwood Daily Globe*. Nov. 25, p.6.

Chapter 29
Clark, Petula. 1964. *Downtown*. Universal-MCA Music Publishing: Tony Hatch.
Sandell, Mary (2020-2023). Text discussion with Thomas L Pelissero.

Chapter 30
Martini, Mark. Aug. 27, 2019. In person interview with Thomas L. Pelissero
"P-M Assigning 5 From Iron River to Local Mines" (1961) *Ironwood Daily Globe*. Oct. 31, p. 6.
"Two Killed At Mine" (1963) *Ironwood Daily Globe*. Oct. 23, p.1.
"Employers, Workers Are Given Recognition on Livelihood Day"-Peterson Mine (1965) *Ironwood Daily Globe*. May 19, p.15.
"Operation of Peterson Mine To End Feb. 4" (1965) *Ironwood Daily Globe*. Nov. 12, p. 10.
"PM Changes in Personnel Told" (1965) *Ironwood Daily Globe*. Mar. 12, p. 1.
"Mine Inspector's Report Filed on Ore Production" (1962) *Ironwood Daily Globe*. Feb. 22. p. 7.
"Cary Mine Closing Jan. 28; Geneva Terminates Feb. 19 (1965) *Ironwood Daily Globe*. Jan. 5, p. 1.
"Ore Production in County Up in 1960, is Report" (1961). *Ironwood Daily Globe*. Mar. 25, p. 4.
"Election Held By Lions Club" (1965) *Ironwood Daily Globe*. Apr. 28, p. 8.
"PM Officials Transferred" (1966) *Ironwood Daily Globe*. Apr. 5, p. 3.
Chesterfield is a trademark brand owned by Philip Morris International. Registration number 5997710 (2020)

Chapter 31
Abraham, Andy. 2020, Mar. 29. *"The Galaxies"* Telephone interview with Thomas L. Pelissero
Boline, Ginny. Oct. 18, 2019. In-person interview with Thomas L. Pelissero
"Bus with Orchestra Gets Stalled" (1959) Iron County Miner. Feb. 6, p.2.
Bie, M. (2023) "Rock 'n' Roll Legends Survived Northwoods Cold". *Our Wisconsin* Feb./Mar. 2023. p. 31-33
Huey, P. (2009, Feb. 3) "Buddy Holly: The Tour From Hell". *StarTribune*. https://www.startribune.com/buddy-holly-the-tour-from-hell/38282249
DiMucci, Dion. Nov. 22-23, 2020. E-mail correspondence between agent Bob Merlis, DiMucci and Thomas L. Pelissero.
"The Galaxies, (a.k.a. Danny and the Galaxies)" (2017) *Michigan Rock and Roll Legends Hall of Fame website*. https://michiganrockandrolllegends.com/hall-of-fame/artists/333-galaxies-a-k-a-danny-and-the-galaxies

Chapter 32
"Midgets Defeat Speed Boys by 62-41 Margin" (1964) *Ironwood Daily Globe.*
Dec. 2, p. 8.
"Cardinals Drub Bessemer 86-56 For 4th Victory" (1964) *Ironwood Daily Globe.*
Dec. 5, p. 6.
Richardson, Bruce. Mar. 3, 2020. Telephone interview with Thomas L. Pelissero.
"600,000 Gallons Water Used Fighting Donich Block Fire" (1951*) Ironwood
Daily Globe.* Feb. 10, p. 1.
"Speed Boys Cop 67-63 Decision Over Cardinals" (1963) *Ironwood Daily Globe.*
Mar. 7, p. 14.
Rooni, Jim (2020-2025), Conversation about game programs storage and scoring.
Daniels, Mike (2022-202424) Various in-person and text discussions with
Thomas L. Pelissero
Borseth, Kevin, Jan. 16, 2019, e-mail correspondence with Thomas L. Pelissero

Chapter 33
"Freshman League Ends Campaign" (1964) *Ironwood Daily Globe.* Feb. 21, p.10.
"Cardinals Drub Bessemer 86-56 For 4th Victory" (1964) *Ironwood Daily Globe.*
Dec. 5, p. 6.
Bonk, John. Jan. 11, 2019 & Feb. 8, 2023. In person interviews with Thomas L
Pelissero.
Gunderson (Burt), Jackie. Feb. 2021. Telephone interview with Thomas L Pelis-
sero.
"Upper Peninsula Basketball Champions" (1966) *Ironwood Daily Globe.* Mar. 10,
p.8.
"M-W Champions" (1966) *Ironwood Daily Globe.* Nov. 18, p.8.
"District Basketball Champs of This Area" (1967) *Ironwood Daily Globe.* Mar. 2,
p.8.
"Consolidation Discussed at School Meeting"- intramural progress (1964) *Iron-
wood Daily Globe.* Dec. 16, p. 2.
Daniels, Mike (2022-202424) Various in-person and text discussions with
Thomas L. Pelissero
Hill, Andy. Oct. 2023. Various in-person discussions and draft reviews with
Thomas L. Pelissero

Chapter 34
"Skiing Activity Picks Up Here" (1964) *Ironwood Daily Globe.* Dec. 7, p. 10.
"Big Powderhorn Opening Friday" (1964*) Ironwood Daily Globe.* Dec. 10, p. 14.
"Big Powderhorn Opens New Major Ski Area" (1964) *The Bessemer Herald.* Dec.
24, p. 1.
"About 3,000 Skiers Stay In Bessemer In Past 13 Weekends" (1964) *Ironwood
Daily Globe.* Mar. 17, p 2.
"Action Is Taken To Close Barber School Next Year" (1960) *Ironwood Daily
Globe.* Apr. 12, p. 10.
"Skiing Activity Picks Up Here" (1964) *Ironwood Daily Globe.* Dec. 7, p. 10.
Boline, Art Oct. 22, 2019. E-mail correspondence on hostels.

Massie, Joel , email correspondence on housing December 27, 2023.
"Many Places in Bessemer Area Furnish Skier Accommodations" (1965) *Ironwood Daily Globe*. Jan. 8, p. 2.

Chapter 35
"Consolidation Discussed at School Meeting" (1964) *Ironwood Daily Globe*. Dec. 16, p. 2.
"Grade School Tourney Mar. 7-8" (1966) *The Bessemer Herald*. Mar. 3, p. 1.
"Tigers Register 68-61 Decision Over Bessemer" (1964) *Ironwood Daily Globe*. Dec. 12, p. 6.
Ryan, Bill. Aug. 6, 2019. Telephone interview with Thomas L. Pelissero
Sabol, George Jr. Apr. 19, 2020. Telephone interview with Thomas L Pelissero
TV Guide KDHL and WDSM Week of Dec. 5-11 (1964) *Ironwood Daily Globe*. Dec. 4, p. 7.

Chapter 36
(No citations)

Chapter 37
"Triumph Is 5th For Polar Bears" (1964) *Ironwood Daily Globe*. Dec. 21, p. 8.
"Bessemer Invades Ironwood, Wakefield Goes To Ashland" (1965) *Ironwood Daily Globe*. Jan. 7, p. 8.
"Red Devils Post 74-51 Decision over Bessemer" (1965) *Ironwood Daily Globe*. Jan.9, p. 6.
Ryan, Bill. Aug. 6, 2019. Telephone interview with Thomas L. Pelissero
Bonk, John. Jan. 11, 2019 & Feb. 8, 2023. In person interviews with Thomas L Pelissero.

Chapter 38
"Ramsay Motorist Ticketed Tuesday" (1965) *Ironwood Daily Globe*. Jan. 13, p. 2.
"Orientals Drub Bessemer 76-37 For 10th Win" (1965) *Ironwood Daily Globe*. Jan. 16, p. 6.
Ryan, Bill. Aug. 6, 2019. Telephone interview with Thomas L. Pelissero
Niemi, Gary. Oct. 23, 2018 & Jul. 5, 2019. Telephone and In Person Interview with Thomas L. Pelissero
"Speed Boys Cop 67-63 Decision Over Cardinals" (1963) *Ironwood Daily Globe*. Mar. 7, p. 14.
Martini, Mark. Aug. 27, 2019. In person interview with Thomas L. Pelissero
Milakovich, James. Jan. 15, 2019. In person interview with Thomas L Pelissero.
Barbacovi, Don. Jun. 20, 2019, Feb. 9, 2022, Mar. 24, 2023, and e-mail. In-person interviews with Thomas L. Pelissero

Chapter 39
Bonk, John. Jan. 11, 2019 & Feb. 8, 2023. In person interviews with Thomas L Pelissero.
Barbacovi, Don. Jun. 20, 2019, Feb. 9, 2022, Mar. 24, 2023. In-person interviews with Thomas L. Pelissero

Gregas, Carl. Feb. 6, 2019. In person interview with Thomas L. Pelissero.
Martini, Mark. Aug. 27, 2019. In person interview with Thomas L. Pelissero
Niemi, Gary. Oct. 23, 2018 & Jul. 5, 2019. Telephone and In Person Interview with Thomas L. Pelissero
Ryan, Bill. Aug. 6, 2019. Telephone interview with Thomas L. Pelissero
Sabol, George Jr. Apr. 19, 2020. Telephone interview with Thomas L Pelissero

Chapter 40
Barnaby, Milo. Aug. 2, 2019, and 2022. Telephone interviews with Thomas L. Pelissero
Jurasin, Joe. Apr. 16, 2020. Letter correspondence about mask to Thomas L. Pelissero.
"Oredockers Drub Bessemer, Climb Into 3rd Place" (1965). Ironwood Daily Globe. Jan. 23, p. 6.
"Michigan's Longest Losing Streak Ends" (1965) The Herald-Palladium. Jan. 20, p. 18.

Chapter 41
"Bessemer Wins M-W Championship" (1956). *Ironwood Daily Globe*. Feb. 17, p. 5.
Midgets Wallop Winless Speed Boys by 86-57 (1965) *Ironwood Daily Globe*. Jan. 27, p. 8.
"10 Years Ago," (1965) *Ironwood Daily Globe*. Jan. 29, p. 4.
"Cardinals Post Sixth Straight Win by 63-48" (1965) *Ironwood Daily Globe*. Jan. 30, p. 6.
"Bessemer Loses to Iron River" (1965) *Ironwood Daily Globe*. Feb. 4, p.9.
"Tigers Move U To 4th", Beating Bessemer 84-50. (1965) *Ironwood Daily Globe*. Feb. 6, p. 6.
"Ontonagon Defeats Bessemer 82-68 in Homecoming Game. (1965) *Ironwood Daily Globe*. Feb. 15, p. 6.
"Speed Boys Lose 56-41 Decision to Stambaugh" (1965) *Ironwood Daily Globe*. Feb. 20, p. 10.
Ryan, Bill. Aug. 6, 2019. Telephone interview with Thomas L. Pelissero.

Chapter 42
Leaf, Marge. Apr. 1, 2020. Interview about the interior of Tip Top with Thomas L. Pelissero.
Ryan, Bill. Aug. 6, 2019. Telephone interview with Thomas L. Pelissero.
Barnaby, Milo. Aug. 2, 2019, and 2022. Telephone interviews with Thomas L. Pelissero.
Pricco, Jeff (2019-2023) Various Q &A about end of streak game
Rooni, Jim. (2019-2023) Various Q &A about end of streak game.
"New Owner at Tip-Top Café" (1958) *Ironwood Daily Globe*. Apr. 11, p.2.

Chapter 43
"Victory is Fifth For Red Devils" (1965) Ironwood Daily Globe. Feb. 24, p. 8.

"Speed Boys Cop 67-63 Decision Over Cardinals." 1963. Ironwood Daily Globe, Mar. 7, p. 14.
"Orientals Whip Bessemer 104-46" (1965) *Ironwood Daily Globe*. Feb. 26, p. 8.
Bonk, John. Jan. 11, 2019 & Feb. 8, 2023. In person interviews with Thomas L Pelissero.
Barbacovi, Don. Jun. 20, 2019, Feb. 9, 2022, Mar. 24, 2023. In-person interviews with Thomas L. Pelissero
Gregas, Carl. Feb. 6, 2019. In person interview with Thomas L. Pelissero.
Maccani. Joe. Mar. 1, 2021. Telephone interview with Thomas L Pelissero
Martini, Mark. Aug. 27, 2019. In person interview with Thomas L. Pelissero
Milakovich, James. Jan. 15, 2019. In person interview with Thomas L Pelissero.

Chapter 44
"St. Mary, St. Sebastian Win Grade School Cage Tourneys" (1965) *Ironwood Daily Globe.* Mar. 1, p. 6.
"Parochial School Has Total of 190 Students". (1964) *Ironwood Daily Globe*. Sep. 5, p.2.
Pelissero, John (2022) Discussion topic St. Sebastian School and basketball in 1960s.

Chapter 45
"Cardinals Whip Bessemer 79-41; Ontonagon Loses" (1965) Mar. 5, p. 8.
"Class C Championship Trophy." (1956). *Ironwood Daily Globe*, Mar. 12, p. 5.
"Speed Boys Romp to 78-66 Win." (1956). *Ironwood Daily Globe*, Mar. 17, p. 5.
"Speed Boys Trim L'Anse Hornets to Win Title." (1957). *The Bessemer Herald*, Mar. 14, p. 1.
"Speed Boys Tip Whiz Kids 46-45" (1947) *Ironwood Daily Globe.* Mar. 24., p. 8.
"Alma Leads All The Way" (1947) *Detroit Free Press*. Mar. 23, p. 29.
"Bessemer Enters Semi-Finals at Lansing Friday Night" (1948) The *Bessemer Herald*. Mar. 18, p.1.
"All Smiles." 1953. *Ironwood Daily Globe*, Mar. 12, page 4.
"Speed Boys Cop 67-63 Decision Over Cardinals" (1963) *Ironwood Daily Globe*. Mar. 7, p. 14.
"Big Jim Beissel All U-P" (1953) *The Bessemer Herald*. Apr. 2, p.4.
"Beissel on U-M Basketball Team" (1954) *Ironwood Daily Globe*. Dec. 4, p.7.
Tareyton is a trademark brand of R.J. Reynolds Tobacco Company. Registration 5587936 (2018)

Chapter 46
Bonk, John. Jan. 11, 2019 & Feb. 8, 2023. In person interviews with Thomas L Pelissero
"The Open-Door Theory-Coach Howie Anderson" (1962) Article in *The Capital Times* (Madison Wisconsin) Mar. 13, p.13.
Milakovich, James. Jan. 15, 2019. In person interview with Thomas L Pelissero.
Arens, Addie. Librarian Drummond Public Library. Team info. Mar. 7, 2025

Chapter 47
"Revised Salary Schedule Set-Up for Teachers" (1965) *Ironwood Daily Globe.* Apr. 14, p 2.
"Education Board Makes Plans for Annual Election" (1965) *Ironwood Daily Globe.* May 12, p. 2.
"Vote Canvass Report Okayed by School Board" (1965) *Ironwood Daily Globe.* Jun. 16, p.2.
Gregas, Carl. Feb. 6, 2019. In person interview with Thomas L. Pelissero.
"Public Hearing on Budget Set Monday Night" (1965) *Ironwood Daily Globe.* Aug. 7, p. 2.
Martini, Mark. Aug. 27, 2019. In person interview with Thomas L. Pelissero
Niemi, Gary. Oct. 23, 2018 & Jul. 5, 2019. Telephone and In Person Interview with Thomas L. Pelissero
Pricco, Jeff (2019-2024) Various Q &A about Bessemer
Ryan, Bill. Aug. 6, 2019. Telephone interview with Thomas L. Pelissero.
Richardson, Bruce. Mar. 3, 2020. Telephone interview with Thomas L. Pelissero.
Sabol, George Jr. Apr. 19, 2020. Telephone interview with Thomas L Pelissero

Chapter 48
"License Plates Are Now On Sale" (1963) *Ironwood Daily Globe.* Jan. 26, p. 10.
"Feb. 29 Deadline for Buying License Plates" (1964) *Ironwood Daily Globe.* Feb 26, p. 2.
"Three Rivers High Finally Wins One" (1933) Lansing State Journal. December 16, p.13.

Chapter 49
"License Plates Are Now On Sale" (1963) *Ironwood Daily Globe.* Jan. 26, p. 10.
"Feb. 29 Deadline for Buying License Plates" (1964) *Ironwood Daily Globe.* Feb 26, p. 2.
Ad-Ski Big Powderhorn Mountain-Season Ticket Sale (1965) *Ironwood Daily Globe.* Aug. 27, p.15.

Chapter 50
"6 Letterman Carry Speed Boys' Hopes" (1965) The *Ironwood Daily Globe.* Nov. 23, p. 8.
Boline, Marcella. Mar. 3-6, 2021. Telephone interviews with Thomas L Pelissero.
Gunderson (Burt), Jackie. Feb. 2021. Telephone interview with Thomas L Pelissero.
Schwartz, Richard. Feb. 22, 2022. Telephone interview with Thomas L. Pelissero
Gregas, Carl. Feb. 6, 2019. In person interview with Thomas L. Pelissero.
Gotta, Gary. Feb 24 and Feb 26, 2021. In person and telephone interviews with Thomas L. Pelissero.
Barbacovi, Don. Jun. 20, 2019, Feb. 9, 2022, Mar. 24, 2023. In-person interviews with Thomas L. Pelissero
Milakovich, James. Jan. 15, 2019. In person interview with Thomas L Pelissero.
English, Ric. Feb. 23, 2023. E-mail Q&A interview

"Midgets Down Bessemer by 70-64 Margin". (1965) *Ironwood Daily Globe*. Nov. 24, p. 6.
"St. Sebastian Five Loses in Tourney" (1963) *The Bessemer Herald*. Mar. 7, p.3.

Chapter 51
"Church Announces Plans" (1966) *The Bessemer Herald*. Mar. 24, p.1.
"Reports Given On Skin Testing" (1962) *Ironwood Daily Globe*. Feb. 14, p. 7.
"Cards Defeat Bessemer by 55-33 Margin" (1965) *Ironwood Daily Globe*. Dec. 1, p. 12.
"St. Sebastian School Opens" (1965) *Ironwood Daily Globe*. Aug. 31, p.16.

Chapter 52
Gregas, Carl. Feb. 6, 2019. In person interview with Thomas L. Pelissero.
English, Ric (2024) e-mail discussion about father's coaching career.
Abelman, Bob, Jul. 25, 2019. In person interview with Thomas L. Pelissero

Chapter 53
(No citations)

Chapter 54
TV Guide in Globe (1965) *Ironwood Daily Globe*. Dec. 3, p. 7
"Tigers Deal Bessemer 37th Straight Loss" (1965) *Ironwood Daily Globe*, Dec. 4, p. 8.
"Bears Rack Up 71-63 Victory" (1965) *Ironwood Daily Globe*. Dec. 13, p.8.
Gregas, Carl. Feb. 6, 2019. In person interview with Thomas L. Pelissero.
(2019). "The Game of Life." Wikimedia Foundation. Oct. 11, 2019. https://en.wikipedia.org/wiki/The_Game_of_Life.

Chapter 55
TV Guide in Globe (1965) *Ironwood Daily Globe*. Dec. 3, p. 7
"Popeye." (2022). Wikipedia. May 4, 2022. https://en.wikipedia.org/wiki/Popeye.
Pelissero, Mary Lou (2019) In person interview with Thomas L. Pelissero

Chapter 56
Gregas, Carl. Feb. 6, 2019. In person interview with Thomas L. Pelissero.
English, Ric. Feb. 23, 2023, May 2024. E-mail correspondence with Thomas L. Pelissero

Chapter 57
"Unbeaten Red Devils Wallop Bessemer 5" (1965) *Ironwood Daily Globe*. Dec 18, p. 6.
Gregas, Carl. Feb. 6, 2019. In person interview with Thomas L. Pelissero.
English, Ric. Feb. 23, 2023, May 2024. E-mail correspondence with Thomas L. Pelissero
Maccani, Joe. Mar. 1, 2021. Telephone interview with Thomas L Pelissero

Chapter 58
"Panthers Post 7th Victory by 82-35 Margin" (1966) *Ironwood Daily Globe*. Jan. 8, p. 6

Barnaby, Milo. Aug. 2, 2019, and 2022. Telephone interviews with Thomas L. Pelissero

Chapter 59
"Redskins Beat Speed Boys by 71-50 Margin" (1966) *Ironwood Daily Globe.* Jan 12, p 10.
Gregas, Carl. Feb. 6, 2019. In person interview with Thomas L. Pelissero.
Barbacovi, Don. Jun. 20, 2019, Feb. 9, 2022, Mar. 24, 2023. In-person interviews with Thomas L. Pelissero
Pelissero, Mary Lou (2019) In person interview with Thomas L. Pelissero

Chapter 60
Barbacovi, Don. Jun. 20, 2019, Feb. 9, 2022, Mar. 24, 2023. In-person interviews with Thomas L. Pelissero
Milakovich, James. Jan. 15, 2019. In person interview with Thomas L Pelissero.
Associated Press, "Presidents Goes Before Congress Tonight" (1966) *Ironwood Daily Globe.* Jan 12, p. 12.
"Dockers Nip Speed Boys in 63-60 Thriller" (1966) *Ironwood Daily Globe.* Jan. 15, p. 8.

Chapter 61
"Grade School Tourney" (1966) *The Bessemer Herald.* Mar. 3, p. 1.
"Consolidation Discussed at School Meeting" (1964) *Ironwood Daily Globe.* Dec. 16, p. 2.

Chapter 62
"Grade School Tourney" (1966) *The Bessemer Herald.* Mar. 3, p. 1.
"Grade School Tourney Results. (1966) *The Bessemer Herald.* Mar. 10, p. 1.

Chapter 63
"Iron Ore Mining Era Ends" (1966) *Ironwood Daily Globe.* Jan. 29, p. 13.
Barbacovi, Don. Jun. 20, 2019, Feb. 9, 2022, Mar. 24, 2023. In-person interviews with Thomas L. Pelissero

Chapter 64
Barbacovi, Don. Jun. 20, 2019, Feb. 9, 2022, Mar. 24, 2023. In-person interviews with Thomas L. Pelissero
"Michigan's Longest Losing Streak Ends" (1965) *The Herald-Palladium.* Jan. 20, p. 18.
"Three Rivers High Finally Wins One" (1933) *Lansing State Journal.* December 16, p.13.
"Bessemer Still In Title Chase". (1949) *Ironwood Daily Globe.* Oct. 21, p.8.
Barnaby, Milo. Aug. 2, 2019, and 2022. Telephone interviews with Thomas L. Pelissero
Boline, Ginny. Oct. 18, 2019. In-person interview with Thomas L. Pelissero
Boline, Marcella. Mar. 3-6, 2021. Telephone interviews with Thomas L Pelissero.
Borseth, Mark. Feb. 23, 2022. Telephone interview with Thomas L Pelissero

English, Ric. Feb. 23, 2023. E-mail Q&A interview

Forslund, Dennis. Feb. 17, 2022. Telephone interview with Thomas L Pelissero

Gotta, Gary. Feb 24 and Feb 26, 2021. In person and telephone interviews with Thomas L. Pelissero.

Gregas, Carl. Feb. 6, 2019. In person interview with Thomas L. Pelissero.

Gunderson (Burt), Jackie. Feb. 2021. Telephone interview with Thomas L Pelissero.

Maccani, Joe (2019-2020) Various Q&A about end of streak game

Martini, Mark. Aug. 27, 2019. In person interview with Thomas L. Pelissero

Massie, Joel (2019-2023) Various Q&A about end of streak game

Milakovich, James. Jan. 15, 2019. In person interview with Thomas L Pelissero.

Nasi, Wayne (2019) Discussion at Sharon's about injury to Forslund.

Niemi, Gary. Oct. 23, 2018 & Jul. 5, 2019. Telephone and In Person Interview with Thomas L. Pelissero

Pricco, Jeff (2019-2023) Various Q&A about end of streak game

Rooni, Jim. (2019-2023) Various Q&A about end of streak game.

Ryan, Bill. Aug. 6, 2019. Telephone interview with Thomas L. Pelissero

Schwartz, Richard. Feb. 22, 2022. Telephone interview with Thomas L. Pelissero

"3 M-W Contests Highlight Fridays Basketball Slate" (1966) *Ironwood Daily Globe*, Jan. 20, p. 8.

"10 Speedboys Receive Varsity Letters for 65-66 Campaign" (1966) *Ironwood Daily Globe* Apr. 7, p. 10.

"Fighting Speedboys Win" (1966) *The Bessemer Herald.* Jan. 27, p. 1.

"Speed Boys End 42-Game Skein on 74-52 Win" (1966) *Ironwood Daily Globe.* Jan. 22. P. 8.

Photo: "Net Comes Down" (1966) *Ironwood Daily Globe.* Jan. 22, p. 8.

"Bessemer's Tough Losing Streak became history 50 years ago" (2016) *Wakefield News/Bessemer Pick & Axe.*

"Player Is Not Seriously Hurt" (1966) *Ironwood Daily Globe.* Jan. 22, p. 14.

"Fans Salute Speed Boys Cagers" (1966) *The Bessemer Herald.* Jan. 27. P 2.

"Michigan's Longest Losing Streak Ends" (1965) The Herald-Palladium. Jan. 20, p. 18.

Epilogue

Bonk, John. Jan. 11, 2019, and Feb. 8, 2023. In person interview with Thomas L Pelissero.

Photo: "Net Comes Down" (1966) *Ironwood Daily Globe.* Jan. 22, p. 8.

"Fans Salute Speed Boy Cagers" (1966) *The Bessemer Herald.* Jan. 27, p. 2.

"13 Area Players Awarded All-UP Basketball Honors" (1972) *Ironwood Daily Globe.* Mar. 27, p.14.

"M-W All Conference Teams Named" (1972) *Ironwood Daily Globe.* Mar. 21, p.12.

"Betlewski Player of Year in M-W" Ironwood Daily Globe. Mar. 28, p.18.

"Dave Betlewski" (1973) *Ironwood Daily Globe.* Apr. 16, p.6.

ABOUT THE AUTHOR

Thomas L. Pelissero is a gifted storyteller who was born and raised in Bessemer, Michigan. He graduated from A.D. Johnston High School in 1973, where he was a multi-sport athlete for the Bessemer Speedboys. In 1978 he paid tribute to his hometown by penning the lyrics to the song "My Bessemer." He earned a B.A. from University of St. Thomas and an MBA from Concordia University, both in St. Paul, Minnesota. In 2019, he was named a Distinguished Alumni of his high school alma mater. Tom is known for his sense of humor and regaling friends and family with colorful stories. When he retired, he and his wife, Joy, moved back to the Upper Peninsula of Michigan, where they enjoy skiing, hiking, fishing, hunting, family gatherings and preserving local history through the Erwin Township Historical Society.